The Economics
of Modern Britain

GW00472001

The Economics of Modern Britain

AN INTRODUCTION TO MACROECONOMICS

SECOND EDITION

John Black
Department of Economics, University of Exeter

MARTIN ROBERTSON · OXFORD

First published in 1979 by Martin Robertson, Oxford
Second edition published in 1980

British Library Cataloguing in Publication Data

Black, John, *b. 1931*
　　The economics of modern Britain.
　　2nd ed.
　　1. Great Britain—Economic conditions—1945–
　　I. Title
　　330.9′41′0857　　　　HC256.6

　　ISBN 0-85520-372-2
　　ISBN 0-85520-371-4 Pbk

Filmset by Santype International Ltd., Salisbury, Wilts
Printed and bound in Great Britain by Billing & Sons, Ltd., Guildford, London, Oxford, Worcester

Contents

Acknowledgements

I would like to thank all those who have made writing this book possible: first my teachers, colleagues and pupils, whose brains I have picked over the past thirty years; second, the hard-working statisticians, particularly those of the Central Statistical Office, without whose monumental efforts in producing the Blue Book on *National Income and Expenditure*, and the *United Kingdom Balance of Payments*, the factual aspects of this book could never even have been contemplated; third, the patient efforts of those who have kindly read drafts of the text and have helped to free it from some, though it is too much to hope all, of the errors with which it started. I alone an responsible for any that remain.

Thanks are due especially to Miss Sally Black, Mrs Rachel Douglas, Mrs Susan Hughes, Dr J. Podolski, Mr D. C. Stafford and Dr P. Stoneman. I must, finally, thank my family for putting up with the process of writing at all hours for several months.

Preface

There are already so many books on macroeconomics in print that anybody who writes yet another ought to offer some justification for it. The reason why I embarked on this book was that, when I came to lecture on macroeconomics to first-year students at my own university, I found it impossible to suggest any one book, or even any pair of books, that would provide an adequate background for the first-year macroeconomics course I had set myself to teach.

There are several different aspects of macroeconomics which it is essential that a first-year university economics course should cover. One of the problems facing the teacher is that many aspects of the subject are incomprehensible until one knows sufficient about other aspects to follow their meaning, or to appreciate that they are important enough to justify some degree of hard slog in tackling them. It cannot be claimed that this problem is entirely solved in what follows. For many readers who already know some economics, particularly for those who have already taken economics at A level, this may not present too much of a problem. For those who have done no economics before, it is quite seriously suggested that they should read the book at least twice, since the point of many sections is difficult to appreciate in full without at least some elementary knowledge of bits that follow.

ASPECTS OF MACROECONOMICS

The following appear to me to be the main components that a first-year course in macroeconomics ought to contain.

(1) A description of some elementary theories about how the economy works. Some aspects of this are very well covered in existing texts; unfortunately they are often treated so much in isolation

from the remaining components of the course that many students find it hard to take it seriously as an account of the real world. Other aspects are less well treated; for example, the relation between effective demand and output is rarely given much attention in elementary texts, though it is vital in understanding modern criticisms of 'Keynesian' macroeconomics.

The theories are stated in a mathematical form, and some help is given with the manipulative skills involved. The mathematics is only a tool, however; economics is not just a branch of mathematics.

(2) An account of some recent economic history, and a brief description of some of the institutional arrangements of a modern economy; the British economy is in fact taken as the real-world economy used here.

(3) Some statistical facts about the recent development and present (well, nearly present) state of the economy. To follow these, it is necessary to examine some of the basic national income accounting concepts used in the sources. It is my belief that national income accounting, considered in isolation from the purpose for which the figures are to be used, is an extremely dull subject. For this reason the necessary element of national income accounting is distributed among the chapters dealing with various uses of national income accounting data, rather than being concentrated into one indigestible section. I have deliberately tried to stick to sources that are relatively readily available, so that the reader who so desires can check and extend the data as easily as possible. Particularly intensive use has been made of the annual Blue Book on *National Income and Expenditure*, which readers are urged to buy for themselves.

Where necessary a brief description of purely statistical concepts has been included, but a detailed treatment of statistical topics is not possible here.

(4) A survey of some of the outstanding policy problems in macroeconomics, such as unemployment, inflation and balance of payments problems. It must be emphasized that the stress is on presenting the problems, rather than trying to present simple solutions to problems that have baffled governments (if not their critics) for generations.

This book tries to present the facts necessary to see that the problems are real and important, and that the theoretical models presented are relevant to real-world problems. It does not claim to prove the theories (or for that matter to disprove them). This would demand a level of understanding of the theories, and of the statistical methods employed to test them, that can be obtained only after years of experience. By the end of a three-year university economics course a student should be getting to the stage where he can seriously contemplate testing theories. What it is hoped that this book can do is to show that the theories are *prima facie* sufficiently relevant to the facts and problems of the real world for it to be worth-while embarking on the hard grind of such a course.

As an aid to this, each chapter includes, where appropriate, a checklist of important factual questions, and of important policy questions connected with the theme of the chapter. The answers to these questions will necessarily be fragmentary, owing to limitations both of space, and of the amount of economic knowledge that the student can at present be expected to absorb. In many cases the correct answer is not in fact fully agreed, even among professional economists.

POSITIVE AND NORMATIVE ECONOMICS

It is my belief that neither the positive nor the normative aspects of economics are of much interest without the other. Beliefs about what the real policy problems are, and about their solutions, must be conditioned by what one knows about economic facts and institutions. The view that one takes of facts, however, is liable to be influenced by one's opinions on matters of policy. It is possible, and indeed proper, to try to take as balanced a view as possible on policy questions, and not to present a one-sided case without referring to the objections that can be made to any policy. It is impossible, however, for any author to check for himself how nearly he has attained complete objectivity.

As a check on the danger that my opinions may be influencing the view I take of the facts to a greater extent than I myself can realize, in one of the concluding chapters I have let myself go on questions of opinion. The reader is frankly warned that the views in Chapter 28, while they are of course put forward in good faith, include points that I doubt my ability to prove conclusively even with unlimited time for research and space for argument. I certainly cannot claim to have proved them within the confines of this book, though it is hoped that many of the raw materials of proofs have been included in the more factual chapters.

It is up to the reader to assess for himself how far my opinions and preconceptions about the nature of economic processes in modern British society have been allowed to influence the factual statements made in other chapters.

Finally, the reader is strongly urged to read some other books as well as this one; a short list of suggestions is included at the end. I have not provided a reading list for each chapter, for two reasons. First, I do not believe that it is realistic to expect readers to follow up each chapter; and second, I believe that their time would be better spent in going systematically through a limited number of other books to gain an alternative systematic view of macroeconomics, rather than dipping selectively on each topic. For a connected view of any subject it is better to follow through somebody's thought-out view of how it fits together. I have provided such a systematic statement of my own views in this book; but it is not healthy to learn any subject by relying on the knowledge and opinions of one person only.

THE SECOND EDITION

This has been prepared during the academic year 1979–80. The tables have been up-dated to cover 1978, and the last two chapters take account as far as possible of events during 1979.

JOHN BLACK
Department of Economics,
University of Exeter

List of Tables and Figures

TABLES

FIGURES

The Economics
of Modern Britain

1. Introduction

The basic problems of macroeconomics are of concern to everybody. Macroeconomics is so called because it studies the behaviour of economic aggregates. These include the size of the national income, which affects the amounts of goods and services, both public and private, that people can afford; the levels of employment and unemployment; the rate of growth of the economy over long periods; the degree of fluctuation in the level of national income; and the rate of inflation of prices and wages.

This is in contrast to the concern of microeconomics, which studies questions such as what causes the activities of some firms or sectors of the economy to grow and others to contract; what causes people with some particular specialisms to be more or less liable to unemployment than other people; or what causes the prices of some goods and services to increase relative to those of others. Microeconomics is concerned with the fate of particular people or firms; macroeconomics with the aggregate, or average, for the whole economy, or for large sectors of it.

The economy employs people with tens of thousands of different skills to make millions of sorts of goods and services. To present any account of the aggregate of what they produce, since we cannot add up physical units of electricity, haircuts and sausages, we must value them all in money terms. If we want to measure the growth or fluctuations over time of aggregates such as the national income or its major components, we have to face the problem created by general inflation. We would not all become twice as well off in real terms if all prices doubled, so measuring goods and services at current prices is no use. To get over this type of problem, the goods and services produced at different times are valued at a common set of prices, usually those prevailing at some particular time. Chapter 2 considers these problems in detail when describing the national income.

Another major concern of individuals, firms and governments is how many people are employed, and how many are unemployed. The relation between production, employment and unemployment is discussed in Chapter 3.

Chapter 4 considers effective demand; this means efforts to buy real goods and services. What is the connection between changes in effective demand and changes in the real output of goods and services? If effective demand in Britain increases, this may have one of several different effects. It may cause increases in output and consequently in employment in Britain; it may cause increases in imports or declines in exports, causing increases in output and employment abroad but not at home; or it may cause no real change, but an increase in symptoms of excess demand, like queues and shortages, that are widely believed to promote inflation in prices and wages. How will the effects of an increase in effective demand be divided between these three directions? This question lies at the heart of doubts about the realism of some of the models of national income determination of the type originated by J. M. Keynes, and described below.

The other question examined in Chapter 4 is the source of changes in effective demand. What are the main components of effective demand? How much do they vary? Which components have been relatively stable, and which relatively prone to fluctuations?

The next group of chapters examines these questions in more detail. Chapter 5 considers how consumption is related to personal incomes. Chapter 6 considers how national income will behave if other elements of effective demand vary while consumption is a stable function of incomes. This is the model of the multiplier. The chapters following consider the behaviour of some of the other main components of effective demand. Chapter 7 considers investment. Chapter 8 considers the shares in the national income of wages and profits, and some of their implications for the level of employment and the determination of investment. Chapters 9 and 10 consider government expenditure, taxation and the national debt. Chapter 11 considers fiscal policy, i.e. the deliberate use by the government of changes in its budget to bring about changes in the national income, or to counteract undesired changes owing to alterations in other components of effective demand.

The next section of the book examines the role of money and

credit in the economy. Chapter 12 considers the nature of money, and what makes people want to hold it. Chapter 13 considers the effects of changes in the quantity of money. Chapter 14 considers banks, the principal monetary institution in modern Britain. In Chapter 15 we consider a simple general equilibrium model of the economy, in which the monetary and non-monetary aspects of the economy interact. Chapter 16 looks at some of the more important non-bank financial institutions in Britain. Chapter 17 then examines monetary policy, i.e. the deliberate use of the monetary and credit system by the government to try to influence macroeconomic objectives such as employment and inflation.

The next section of the book considers inflation. Chapter 18 discusses the definition, history and problems of measuring inflation, and analyses the harm it causes. Chapter 19 discusses the relation between the pressure of effective demand and inflation. Chapter 20 discusses various types of cost inflation, this being the name given to the process by which increases in one set of prices and wages start off a process of further increases in other wages or prices. Chapter 21 discusses some aspects of anti-inflationary policies such as price and wage controls.

The next section deals with the foreign trade and payments of the British economy. Chapter 22 discusses imports, Chapter 23 deals with exports and Chapter 24 considers the British balance of payments. Chapter 25 develops a model of the interaction between the domestic level of activity and the state of the balance of payments.

The final section of the book contains two chapters in which the author gives a more personal view of the recent history of the British economy, and the policies that are required for it in the future. Chapter 26 compares the recent experience of the UK with that of other developed economies, Chapter 27 provides a short historical account of the UK economy in recent years, and Chapter 28 contains a few of the author's own preferred answers to some of the policy questions facing the U.K. The last chapter does not claim to be objective; it is hoped that it helps the reader to assess how far the more factual chapters do in fact provide objective statements about the way the economy really works, and how far they reflect the author's own preconceptions, opinions or prejudices.

The reader will notice that many chapters contain quite substantial tables. These form an integral part of their chapters, and should be read carefully. It is of course neither necessary nor possible to learn them all by heart; they are however intended to drive home certain points.

First, they try to show wherever possible the relative importance of the facts they refer to; for example, many of the parts of national expenditure or of foreign trade are expressed as percentages of the national income. Second, they give detailed figures for several years, as well as summary figures such as the growth rates over periods of years, or indicators of the amount of variation between the years.

One of the outstanding characteristics of the real-world economy is the fact that many sectors of the economy persistently fluctuate in the short run, in ways that are hard either to predict or to control. If space and the sources used allowed examination of variations within years, this pattern of short-run variation would be seen to continue within years.

The tendency of the economy to short-run oscillations has important consequences for macroeconomics. In particular, it helps to explain why economic policies have failed to stabilize the economy in the way that many simple but static theories of the economy suggest that it ought to be quite simple to manage. Some of these theories are explained here in the chapters on multipliers, fiscal policy and monetary policy. The failure of these policies to do all that has been expected of them is due at least in part to the fact that short-run variations in the economy make it hard to be sure where it is at any one time.

Another motive for the inclusion of a fair amount of detail in the tables is to emphasize the fact that economic aggregates consist of various components, which do not usually all behave alike.

Remembering all the detailed figures is not necessary, but in following historical accounts of the various aspects of the economy it is very helpful to develop a sense for which were the relatively good, and which the bad, years for the UK economy.

2. The National Income

The national income is a measure of the total production of the economy in any period, whatever it is used for. It has a central place in macroeconomics. Human welfare is not of course related solely to economic goods, but many aspects of welfare are determined mainly by economic factors.

We may be concerned with resources to provide private goods for consumption now, public goods like education or defence, or investment to enable us to produce more in the future. The national income measures the resources available for all these purposes. A change in national income is not an infallible indicator of changes in human welfare; a large rise in the inequality of income distribution or in the level of environmental pollution could mean that a rise in national income still left us feeling worse off. However, the structure of income distribution and the degree of environmental damage do not usually change at all suddenly, so normally a higher national income means more welfare, and a lower national income means somebody going without something they want.

We are therefore interested in the answers to a number of questions about the national income. These include the following:
(1) What determines the size of the national income at any one time?
(2) Is it as large as it might have been, given the resources available to produce it?
(3) How fast has it been growing?
(4) What determines its rate of growth?
(5) How stable has it been?
(6) How could it be made larger, and fluctuations reduced or avoided?
(7) Have problems over growth and fluctuations been becoming worse?

5

NATIONAL INCOME STATISTICS

To try and answer some of these questions we have to make use of national income statistics. In order to understand what we are doing in using these statistics, it is necessary to follow some basic national income accounting concepts, and to examine some of the statistical problems that arise in collecting the figures. The chief source that will be used for these is the annual government publication, the 'Blue Book' on national income and expenditure. The volume produced in September 1979 and entitled *National Income and Expenditure, 1979 Edition* provides information for the years 1968 to 1978 in considerable detail, with less detailed information for the earlier period of 1957–67. We will refer to this source below as the 1979 Blue Book.

It is intended to keep the amount of technical detail on national income accounting down to a minimum, and to introduce complexities only when they are needed. Some degree of complexity is however inevitable if we are to understand the figures at all.

Table 2.1 shows figures for the UK national income in 1978, all the figures being derived from the 1979 Blue Book (Table 1.1). It starts off by looking at the main groups of expenditures that generate national income. Since there are hundreds of thousands of different types of goods and services that people buy, they all have to be measured in common units if they are to be added up at all, and the units used are the actual 1978 prices paid by the purchasers, including any indirect taxes on the goods, such as VAT. Table 2.1 gives the figures in three forms: as £m, as £b (1 billion = 1 thousand million), and as percentages of the total of domestic expenditures. All subsequent tables will give monetary figures in the form of £b, rounded to the nearest £0.1b. They have all been derived from sources giving more detail, and any percentages quoted have been based on the more detailed figures. In following the facts, however, very few people can cope with more than a very few decimal places, and it is far more important to grasp the orders of magnitude and the relative importance of different components of national income than to have more precise figures.

TABLE 2.1   *UK National Income at Current Prices in 1978*

	£m*	£b**	%DEMP†
Private consumption	96,086	96.1	60.2
Government real current expenditure	32,693	32.7	20.5
Gross domestic fixed capital formation	29,218	29.2	18.3
Value of physical increase in stocks and work in progress	1,528	1.5	1.0
Domestic expenditure at market prices	159,525	159.5	100.0
+ Exports of goods and services	47,636	47.6	
Total final expenditure	207,161	207.2	
− Imports of goods and services	−45,522	−45.5	
Gross domestic product at market prices	161,639	161.6	
− Taxes on expenditure	−23,238	−23.2	
+ Subsidies	+3,598	+3.6	
Gross domestic product at factor cost	141,999	142.0	
+ Net property income from a abroad	+836	+0.8	
Gross national product at factor cost	142,835	142.8	
− Capital consumption	−18,310	−18.3	
National income	124,525	124.5	

* £m = £ million at current (i.e. 1978) prices
** £b = £ billion (i.e. thousand million)
† %DEMP = % of domestic expenditure at market prices
Note The items below each horizontal line are totals of those above it; e.g., domestic expenditure at market prices = consumption + government real current expenditure + gross fixed investment + value of real changes in stocks.
Source: Blue Book on *National Income and Expenditure 1979*, Table 1.1.

Consumption

The largest single category of expenditure is consumption; in 1978 this totalled £96.1b. This is money spent by individuals or families; it includes spending on consumer durables, such as television sets, but excludes spending on the acquisition of owner-occupied houses. Consumption is examined in more detail in Chapter 5.

Government Expenditure

The next largest, though much smaller, category of final expenditures is real government expenditure. This covers things like education and defence, but excludes grants to persons, e.g. pensions or student grants. It includes spending by local authorities as well as the central government, but excludes spending on the nationalized industries. Real government current expenditures in 1978 were £32.7b; the government sector will be examined in more detail in Chapters 9 and 10.

Investment

The next component of expenditure is gross fixed investment. This covers spending on building long-lived assets such as factories, machines, houses, goods vehicles and roads. These expenditures may be carried out by firms, by nationalized industries, by the government or by individuals running unincorporated businesses or building houses for themselves. The full title of this item is 'Gross domestic fixed capital formation'; to grasp the full implications of this definition, we consider it word by word. It is called 'gross' since it includes not only additional machines or vehicles, but also new ones being made to replace others that have worn out or become obsolete. It is 'domestic' since it includes only operations within the UK; building factories or mines abroad is excluded. It is called 'fixed' to distinguish if from changes in stocks of materials or of unsold finished products. Gross domestic fixed capital formation in 1978 was £29.2b. Investment is considered in more detail in Chapter 7.

The final component of expenditure is investment in net additions to stocks, called 'Value of physical increase in stocks and work in progress' in Table 2.1. This is the value of the changes in the real quantities of stocks of materials, fuels or unsold products, and of work in progress, such as partly completed machines, ships or buildings, which firms are holding. The total of this item is quite small, only £1.5b in 1978, but it is listed separately because it fluctuates from year to year much more severely than any other component of expenditure.

Considering the main types of expenditure as percentages of total domestic expenditure, in 1978 consumption was 60 per cent, real government expenditure was 20.5 per cent, fixed investment was 18 per cent and investment in stocks was 1 per cent.

Final Uses v. Intermediate Products

It should be noted that all these categories are purchases for 'final uses'. There are lots of other transactions going on in the economy, where firms buy from one another many 'intermediate products', such as fuels like coal, oil or electricity, materials like steel or nylon, and professional services like surveying, accounting or insurance, all of which are used up in the course of production of other things. These intermediate goods are not included in the concept of 'expenditure', which covers only 'final products', i.e. those used for present enjoyment in the case of consumption goods, or to add to our ability to produce in the future in the case of investment goods.

Foreign Trade

The total of these items gives domestic expenditure at market prices. This was £159.5b in 1978. Many of the expenditures that generate incomes in the UK take place abroad; in 1978 £47.6b of exports of goods and services were sold to non-residents. This is added to gross domestic expenditure to get total final expenditure, of £207.2b in 1978.

Not all of the total final expenditure corresponds to output in the UK, however; in 1978 £45.5b was spent on imports of goods and services to the UK. This is subtracted from total final expenditure to get gross domestic product at market prices. The actual determination of exports and imports will be discussed in Chapters 22 and 23.

Market Prices and Factor Cost

All the calculations so far have worked in terms of market prices, i.e. what the purchaser actually paid in cases where the good was sold in a market. In the case of non-marketed goods and services provided by the government, such as defence, the cost of providing them is treated as if it were a market price. In other cases, where no actual market transaction ever took place, such as in valuing the services rendered to their owners by owner-occupied houses, an estimate is made of what a market price would have been. If one is concerned with measuring the purchaser's welfare, or predicting the purchaser's behaviour, market prices seem the natural ones to use. Market prices do not however correspond exactly to what the producers get for themselves, since the government taxes expenditure on some goods, e.g. by VAT, and subsidizes purchases of others. In 1978 taxes on expenditure were £23.2b, and subsidies were £3.6b. Starting from market prices, subtracting taxes on expenditure and adding subsidies, the amount actually received by those who produced the gross domestic product was £142.0b in 1978. This amount is referred to as gross domestic product at factor cost; this was available to be divided between wages, profits and other factor incomes. Domestic product at factor cost can be regarded as 'value added' by the factors of production; in the case of capital it includes depreciation on existing assets. Details of this approach to national income can be found in Table 1.2 of the Blue Book.

Gross National Product and National Income

There are two further adjustments to be made in arriving at national income figures. Some of the property incomes generated in the UK are paid to residents abroad, and some residents of the UK are in receipt of property incomes from abroad. The net amount of these property incomes, i.e. receipts from abroad minus payments made to non-residents, was £0.8b in 1978. This has to be added to gross domestic product to get a gross national product of £142.8b in 1978.

Finally, not all of the gross investment included in gross national product represents net additions to the amount of captical. Old capital goods are wearing out through use or are becoming technically obsolete all the time. Because this deterioration in the value of existing capital goods does not correspond to a set of market transactions, the depreciation of capital is very hard to measure reliably. It was estimated by the Central Statistical Office however that in 1978 there was £18.3b of loss of value of existing capital, and this 'capital consumption' can be subtracted from the gross national product to get national income, net of depreciation, of £124.5b in 1978. The problems involved in measuring depreciation are discussed in Chapter 7.

There are thus a number of different aggregate measures of the level of income in the economy: domestic expenditure, total final expenditure and gross domestic product, all at market prices; and gross domestic product, gross national product and national income, all at factor cost. Which of these aggregates we use will depend on the particular purpose for which the figures are required.

GROWTH AND FLUCTUATIONS

The first use to which the national income statistics will be put is to
consider the recent history of domestic activity in the UK. For this
purpose we use Table 2.2. We want to know how fast output has
grown; how steadily growth has taken place; how far output has at
any time fallen short of what could have been produced; and how
much potential output has been lost through irregular growth.

We first have to decide which of the various possible national
income aggregates to use. The choice made is gross domestic product at factor cost. It is possible to explain the reasons for preferring
this measure word by word. A gross rather than a net concept was
chosen partly because the difficulties of estimating depreciation
make gross figures more reliable than net ones, and partly because,
in so far as we are concerned with the effects on employment of
variations in output, it is gross investment and not net investment
that creates jobs.

A domestic rather than a national measure was chosen because in
the short run there are variations in property incomes from abroad
which it would not have been possible to avoid by any set of national economic policies.

A factor cost series was chosen because the interest is in what we
were able to produce, rather than in how much benefit was gained
from using the products, assuming this can be measured by what
people were willing to pay for them.

A second decision was what time period to study. The 1979 Blue
Book provides figures of gross domestic product at factor cost
(GDP) for the twenty-two years from 1957 to 1978 inclusive. The
argument for looking at the whole of this quite long period is that it
is interesting to see how far the special problems of very recent
years, when production has grown slowly and fluctuated severely,
are something new and different, and how far they represent a con-
tinuation in an accentuated form of problems that have existed for
some time.

Inflation

Column (1) of Table 2.2 gives the actual GDP at factor cost for each
year, at current prices. This means that the 1957 product is given in
terms of 1957 prices, the 1958 product in 1958 prices, and so on.

TABLE 2.2   *Growth of Gross Domestic Product at Factor Cost, 1957–78*

Year	Actual GDP (£b at current prices)	Infla- tion* (%)	Actual GDP (£b at 1975 prices)	Real growth** (%)	Trend GDP† (£b at 1975 prices)	Gap‡ (£b at 1975 prices)	Gap§ (%)
	(1)	(2)	(3)	(4)	(5)	(6)	(7)
1957	19.4	—	59.0	—	59.6	0.6	1.1
1958	20.2	4.3	58.7	−0.4	61.4	2.6	4.3
1959	21.2	1.6	60.7	3.4	63.2	2.5	3.9
1960	22.6	1.8	63.5	4.6	65.1	1.6	2.4
1961	24.2	3.3	65.8	3.6	67.1	1.4	2.0
1962	25.3	3.4	66.4	0.9	69.1	2.7	3.9
1963	26.9	2.5	69.0	4.0	71.2	2.1	3.0
1964	29.2	3.3	72.6	5.1	73.3	0.7	1.0
1965	31.2	4.0	74.5	2.7	75.5	0.9	1.2
1966	33.1	3.8	76.2	2.2	77.8	1.6	2.0
1967	34.9	2.8	78.1	2.6	80.1	2.0	2.4
1968	37.6	3.0	81.7	4.5	82.5	0.8	1.0
1969	39.6	3.7	83.1	1.7	85.0	1.9	2.2
1970	43.5	7.5	84.8	2.1	87.5	2.7	3.1
1971	49.4	10.9	87.1	2.6	90.1	3.1	3.4
1972	55.1	9.8	88.4	1.5	92.8	4.5	4.8
1973	64.2	7.5	95.6	8.2	95.6	0.0	0.0
1974	74.1	17.1	94.3	−1.4	98.5	4.2	4.2
1975	93.5	27.3	93.5	−0.9	101.5	8.0	7.8
1976	110.3	13.7	97.0	3.7	104.5	7.5	7.2
1977	125.2	11.9	98.4	1.5	107.6	9.2	8.6
1978	142.0	10.7	100.8	2.4	110.9	10.0	9.1

* The percentage increase over the previous year in the prices index, or 'deflator', used to reconcile the Central Statistical Office's figures for GDP at current prices in Table 1.1 with their GDP at 1975 prices in Table 2.1.

** Percentage increase over previous year for GDP at 1975 prices.

† Fitted to grow at 3 per cent per year through 1973 actual GDP at 1975 prices.

‡ Trend (5) minus actual (3).

§ Gap (6) divided by trend (5).

Note Years are grouped with spaces after peak years, for clarity. All figures are rounded to nearest £0.1 b or 0.1 per cent; they were calculated using more decimal places.

—indicates figure not available.

Source: Blue Book on *National Income and Expenditure, 1979*, Tables 1.1 and 2.1.

These current price figures show a very rapid rate of increase; however, nobody believes that the UK was seven times as well off in 1978 as twenty years before merely because the value of GDP at current prices was seven times higher. The problem is that the current price figures have been grossly swollen by inflation, i.e. the persistent price increases that have taken place over the period.

Column (2) shows a measure of inflation. There are quite a few possible measures of inflation, which are discussed in detail in Chapter 18. The one used here is the measure actually used by the Central Statistical Office in converting GDP at current prices, as shown in Table 1.1 of the Blue Book, to GDP at 1975 prices, as shown in Table 2.1 of the Blue Book. It will be seen that there has been some inflation every year, at rates ranging from a minimum of 1.6 per cent in 1959 to a maximum of 27.3 per cent in 1975.

Column (3) then gives the GDP for each year in £b at 1975 prices; this means that the goods produced in each year have been revalued at the factor cost prices it is estimated that they would have fetched in 1975. GDP at 1975 prices rose much more slowly than GDP at current prices, and in some years actually fell. Column (4) shows the percentage real growth for each year, i.e. the percentage change in GDP at 1975 prices over that in the previous year. Growth was irregular; as high as 8.2 per cent in 1973 and 5.1 per cent in 1964, while in three years GDP actually fell, by 0.4 per cent in 1958, by 1.4 per cent in 1974 and again by 0.9 per cent in 1975.

The Full Employment Growth Path

If we are to make any estimate of the possible production that has been forgone by failing to get the economy to grow steadily, it is necessary to estimate what would have happened had it been possible for the economy to remain on a 'full employment path'. There are various possible measures of the trend rate of growth of the economy. One method is simply to take an average of the actual annual growth rates. Over the whole period from 1957 to 1978 this gives an average growth rate of 2.6 per cent per annum. As a method this is open to the criticism that the value one gets for the growth rate depends quite strongly on the particular years included, if growth has in fact been irregular. Because of the two very bad years after 1973, which have not been made up for since, the British economy in 1978 was relatively depressed, and the average growth rate for a period ending in 1973 would have been rather higher.

A second method of estimating a possible growth path for output is to look at the 'peaks' in the economy, i.e. the relatively good years. One can argue that we did in fact succeed in producing 1973's domestic product (apart from any errors in the actual figures, which are believed to be under 1 per cent). Increases in productive capacity take place through various causes. These include changes in the size of the labour force, a growth in investment, which increases the amount of capital goods that firms have to use, technical inventions, and improvements in the quality of the labour force through higher educational standards. All of these changes happen gradually, and it seems unlikely that the rate of change of the upper limit, or 'ceiling', to possible production will change at all suddenly. If one takes a steady growth path increasing at 3 per cent per annum passing through the 1973 actual GDP at 1975 prices (see Figure 2.1), it passes within about 1 per cent of the GDP figures for 1957, 1964, 1965 and 1968. The 3 per cent growth path as an estimate of the maximum possible steady rate of growth may not be precisely right, but it is hard to believe that it can be very wrong as an estimate of how GDP could have grown up to 1973, and how it could have grown since 1973 if the economy could have been run so as to make full use of available resources.

The Output Gap

Column (5) in Table 2.2 gives the GDP at 1975 prices implied by a 3 per cent growth path, passing through the 1973 actual figure. Column (6) shows the 'gap' between this trend path of potential output and the actual GDP shown in column (3). Column (7) shows the output gap as a percentage of trend output. This shows that the percentage gap was 1 per cent in 1964 and (by assumption) zero in 1973. Having touched 4.3 per cent in 1958 it did not reach this level again until 1974, since when there has been a slump in the economy, with an 'output gap' of 9.1 per cent in 1978. Figure 2.1 shows the actual GDP, the 3 per cent trend GDP and the output gap.

It is believed by many people that in boom years like 1964 and 1973 the UK economy has been subjected to excessive aggregate demand, and that the economy could not in fact be run permanently at quite such a high level of output. To the extent that this is true,

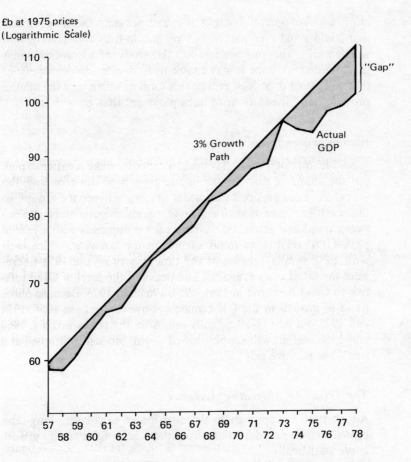

£b at 1975 prices
(Logarithmic Scale)

FIGURE 2.1   Actual GDP at 1975 factor cost and the 3 per cent growth path,
1957–78.

the 'gap' figures in Table 2.2 exaggerate the loss of potential output
in bad years. It also seems rather unlikely, given the present extent
of economists' knowledge about how the economy actually works,
that any possible set of policies could entirely remove unevenness in
the rate of growth of output, which has existed for as long as we
have any records. However, the figures show that real GDP in 1978
was only 5.5 per cent above its level five years earlier, in an economy that for the previous two decades had managed to grow at
about 3 per cent per annum. It is hard to believe that this does not

imply a loss of potential output of several per cent. Devising policies that could avoid even part of this loss would thus appear to be well worth-while. The justification for the study of macroeconomics must be that we hope it may enable us to devise economic policies that will avoid or at least reduce this form of waste, and the human problems and frustrations of unemployment that go with it.

Fluctuations

A final feature of Table 2.2 is that, in order to make it easier to pick out the shape of fluctuations in the growth of the economy, the years have been grouped with wider spacing between the groups, so that each group ends with a year of minimum percentage gap between trend and actual GDP. Thus each group ends with a year of peak GDP relative to trend, except for the last year, which ends with 1978 simply because at the time of writing the 1978 figures were the latest ones available. The peaks in the level of GDP relative to trend occurred in 1961, 1964, 1968 and 1973. Because of the trend of growth in the UK economy, however, only in 1958, 1974 and 1975 did real GDP actually fall. After the peaks in 1961, 1964 and 1968 real growth simply slowed down, but still continued at a small but positive rate.

The Trend–An Alternative Approach

An alternative approach to the question of calculating long-term growth trends and deviations from them is to 'fit' a steady growth curve statistically.

The method used for doing this is first to take the logarithms of actual GDP for each year. If growth had been completely steady, these would be a linear function of time. As growth has in fact varied, a linear function of time is chosen so as to minimize the sum of squares of deviations between actual log GDP and the log GDP predicted by the function. It is not possible here to explain the reasons why this method of fitting is adopted; readers not already familiar with the technique must take it on trust, or consult a statistics text or tutor.

If this technique is applied to GDP for the twenty-two years from 1957 to 1978 it gives a long-term growth rate of 2.75 per cent a year. GDP for 1978 was 3.2 per cent below the fitted trend path, while

GDP for 1973 was 5.2 per cent above it.

This approach to the relation of trends and oscillations in the economy is more difficult to understand than the method of finding a steady growth line passing approximately through the peaks in activity. It confirms the result that a long-term growth rate of something between 2.5 and 3.0 per cent a year appears realistic. It also confirms that, compared with the trend, 1973 was our last really good year, and 1978 an unprecedentedly bad one.

We can now use the information in Table 2.2 to answer a number of questions about the behaviour of inflation, real growth and the loss of potential output as measured by the output gap in the UK economy over the past twenty years. How fast did output grow, how regular was this growth, and how much potential output was lost owing to its irregularity?

Changes in Growth Rates

For this purpose we make use of two statistical concepts, the mean and the standard deviation. If R_i is the rate of inflation in year i, the average over the n years from 1 to n (e.g. from 1957 to 1978) is given by summing the R_i and dividing by n, so that

$$\mu = \frac{1}{n} \sum_{i=1}^{n} R_i .$$

μ, the Greek letter mu, is frequently used to refer to a mean or average, in this case the average rate of inflation over the period. Σ, the Greek letter capital sigma, is used to indicate that the items following it should be summed. The $i = 1$ below the sigma, and the n above it, indicate the range of values of i over which the summation is to be performed.

Table 2.3 shows the mean rates of inflation, real growth and percentage output gap for the period 1957–78 as a whole, and for three parts of it. The parts distinguished are 1957–68, lumping the earlier cycles together since they were not dissimilar, and now seem a long time ago, 1969–73, and 1974–78. Table 2.3 shows that inflation has been getting worse; it averaged 3.1 per cent a year in 1957–68, 7.9 per cent in 1969–73 and 16.1 per cent in 1974–78. Over the whole period inflation averaged 7.3 per cent a year.

Real growth has slowed down; it averaged 3.0 per cent a year in 1957–68, 3.2 per cent in 1969–73 and only 1.1 per cent in 1974–78.

TABLE 2.3   *Average Growth Rates and Variability, 1957–78*

| Period | Inflation | | Real growth | | Output gap | |
	Mean* %	Standard deviation* %	Mean* %	Standard deviation* %	Mean** %	Standard deviation** %
1957–68	3.1	0.8	3.0	1.6	2.4	1.4
1969–73	7.9	2.5	3.2	2.5	2.7	1.6
1974–78	16.1	6.0	1.1	1.9	7.4	1.7
1957–78	7.3	6.2	2.6	2.1	3.6	2.5

* Units: per cent per year.
** Units: per cent of 'trend'.
Source: as Table 2.2.

Over the whole period it averaged 2.6 per cent. A real growth rate of around 3 per cent per annum, which was achieved up to 1973, is slower than those achieved in many other advanced economies, whether market economies like West Germany and Japan or planned economies like the USSR. However, given that the UK population has grown at only about 0.5 per cent a year, a 2.5 per cent growth rate of per capita income, i.e. income per head or per person, would double living standards in twenty-eight years.

The output gap has been increasing, from an average of 2.4 per cent in 1957–68 to 2.7 per cent in 1969–73 and 7.4 per cent in 1974–78. Given that the objectives of government economic policy have included stable growth with low inflation, the performance of the UK economy has been increasingly disappointing.

Have Fluctuations Become Worse?

We are also interested in the question of how much variation there has been in inflation, real growth and the output gap. The amount of variability in the economy is important because the more it varies, the harder it is to forecast how it will behave, and the harder it therefore is to devise policies that will succeed in controlling it. To measure variability we make use of the standard deviation. The theoretical reasons for choosing this particular measure of variability are beyond the scope of an elementary book on economics; readers wishing to examine them in detail should consult a statistical text. It can be seen however that the standard deviation of R_i is constructed so that any change in a particular R_i taking it further from the mean value μ will increase the standard deviation σ, where σ is defined by

$$\sigma = \sqrt{\left[\frac{1}{n} \sum_{i=1}^{n} (R_i - \mu)^2 \right]}$$

$$= \sqrt{\left[\left(\frac{1}{n} \sum_{i=1}^{n} R_i^2 \right) - \mu^2 \right]}.$$

σ is the Greek lower case letter sigma, and is normally used to indicate a standard deviation.

Table 2.3 shows the standard deviation of inflation, real growth and the output gap for the three periods 1957–68, 1969–73 and 1974–78, as well as for the period as a whole. The variability of all three has increased, though the rate of inflation has increased its variability more than the others. This increase in the variability of the behaviour of the economy is one of the problems facing the government in trying to devise economic policies to control it.

POLICY QUESTIONS

This brings us to some policy questions, which will be examined in later chapters:
(1) Could the UK grow faster?
(2) Could more stable growth be achieved?
(3) Are these objectives consistent?
(4) What would be the costs of achieving them, and would these costs be worth incurring?
(5) How are the objectives of more rapid and more stable growth related to the problem of inflation?

3. Employment, Unemployment and Output

One of the main macroeconomic problems is unemployment. People need to work, both for the income it gives and for self-respect and psychological satisfaction. If they are unemployed this appears to be both an obvious waste of resources from the point of view of society, and a source of frustration for the unemployed themselves. Economists are therefore interested in the answers to the following questions:

(1) What determines whether people are employed or unemployed?
(2) How is output related to employment?
(3) Has unemployment become more severe, and if so by how much?
(4) How far do the unemployment and the vacancies figures tell the whole story about the state of the labour market?

Table 3.1 contains some of the salient facts about the labour market in the UK since 1968. Column (1) gives figures for the total working population; this was 25.4m in 1968, fell to 25.2m by 1971 and rose again to 26.4m in 1978. This excludes members of the population who were infants, in full-time education, retired, disabled or housewives. The figures are available only as mid-year estimates.

Of the total working population, some were classified neither as employed nor as unemployed; from 2.2m to 2.3m were employers, self-employed (like many farmers, shopkeepers or professionals), or members of HM armed services. The remainder, i.e. those who can be regarded as being in the employment market, are shown in column (2). These were 23.2m in 1968, fell to 22.9m in 1971 and rose again to 24.2m in 1978.

20

TABLE 3.1   *Employment, Unemployment, Vacancies and Output, 1968-78*

Year	Working population* (m)	Employed + unemployed** (m)	Employed (m)	Unemployed** (000)	School leavers unemployed† (000)	Unemployed‡ %	Vacancies§ %	Output gap %
	(1)	(2)	(3)	(4)	(5)	(6)	(7)	(8)
1968	25.4	23.2	22.6	583	9	2.5	0·8	0.7
1969	25.4	23.2	22.6	576	10	2.5	0.9	1.8
1970	25.3	23.1	22.5	612	10	2.6	0.8	2.6
1971	25.2	22.9	22.1	792	16	3.5	0.6	3.2
1972	25.2	23.0	22.1	876	21	3.8	0.6	4.7
1973	25.6	23.3	22.7	619	8	2.7	1.3	0.0
1974	25.7	23.4	22.8	615	15	2.6	1.3	4.5
1975	25.8	23.7	22.7	978	48	4.1	0.6	8.9
1976	26.1	23.7	22.5	1,359	89	5.7	0.5	8.3
1977	26.4	24.1	22.7	1,484	105	6.1	0.6	9.8
1978	26.4	24.2	22.7	1,475	98	6.1	0.9	9.1
					Mean	3.8	0.8	4.7
					Standard deviation	1.4	0.28	3.0

* 'Working population' means all economically active. This includes three groups: (a) employers, self-employed and HM services; (b) employed; (c) unemployed. The figures are mid-year estimates.
** Unemployed means registered unemployed, including school-leavers. The figures are monthly averages.
† School-leavers unemployed are included in the total.
‡ Unemployment % gives (c) as a percentage of (b) + (c).
§ Vacancies means vacancies registered with employment exchanges, given as a percentage of (b) + (c), (monthly averages).
Source: Output gap, as Table 2.2; remainder, Central Statistical Office, *Economic Trends* (August 1979, Table 36).

EMPLOYMENT

Employment is shown in column (3): 22.6m people were employed in 1968; the number fell to 22.1m in 1971, rose to 22.8m in 1974, fell to 22.5m in 1976 and rose again to 22.7m in 1978.

UNEMPLOYMENT

Unemployment, including school-leavers, is shown in column (4): 583,000 people were unemployed in 1968; this rose to 612,000 in 1970, and to 876,000 in 1972. It then fell to 619,000 in 1973, and to 615,000 in 1974, then rose to reach 1,484,000 in 1977 and fell to 1,475,000 in 1978. These figures are monthly averages.

Unemployment among school-leavers, shown in column (5) and included in the total unemployment figures, increased in an even more spectacular manner. It was 9,000 in 1968, rose to 21,000 in 1972, fell to 8,000 in 1973, rose to 105,000 in 1977 and fell to 98,000 in 1978.

Over the decade as a whole, the working population rose by about 1m, employment rose by about 100,000 and unemployment rose by about 900,000.

The percentage unemployed is shown in column (6). Unemployment is traditionally calculated as a percentage of those employed plus those registered as unemployed (if it were calculated as a percentage of the total working population it would look slightly lower). As a percentage, it was 2.9 per cent on average from 1968 to 1973, 4.9 per cent on the average of 1974–78, and 6.1 per cent in 1978. It clearly has to be regarded as a major economic problem.

Looking at some data about the demand side of the labour market, vacancies registered with employment exchanges are shown in column (7). They averaged 0.7 per cent of the employed-plus-unemployed total from 1968 to 1972, rose to 1.3 per cent in 1973 and 1974, and fell to 0.7 per cent on the average of 1975–78.

All of these figures need to be interpreted with considerable caution, for several reasons.

(1) The actual figures for those employed, and for the working population, are subject to considerable error.

(2) Whether people are self-employed or employed is affected by changes in tax and national insurance rules. Whether people are self-employed or are not really economically active at all is often open to some doubt.

(3) Vacancies registered with employment exchanges are only an indicator of the total demand for labour. Only a minority of jobs are actually obtained through official employment exchanges; many people find jobs through private agencies, press advertisements or personal contacts. Even for occupations where recruitment typically

is via employment exchanges, the number of vacancies registered need bear little relation to the numbers firms actually want to recruit, and there is no compulsion to notify the exchanges promptly when vacancies are filled. In 1973, which was almost certainly a year of net excess demand for labour, the vacancies figure was less than half the figure for unemployment.

(4) The unemployment figure includes many people who are not easily employable, through physical or mental disability or through immobility. The figures also include an unknown number of those who actually are working but are fraudulently concealing this fact from the social security authorities. Some of the unemployed do not want to work, or at least not immediately; this includes people who are taking extra family holidays, and students without grants. The figures also include some people who are difficult to employ because their own assessment of their abilities exceeds that of prospective employers.

On the other hand, the unemployment figures exclude many people who are in fact both able and willing to work, such as those over retirement age and people seeking second jobs. The unemployment figures also should thus be regarded as an indicator rather than a measure of the extent of real unemployment.

UNEMPLOYMENT AND OUTPUT

This brings us to the question of the relation between unemployment and variations in output (see Figure 3.1). As an indicator of output variations, the output gap from Table 2.2 is shown as column (8) in Table 3.1. If we ask why people are employed, the answer is normally that somebody wants to buy the goods or services they help produce. This is obviously true for profit-making firms, and for individuals who employ others. It is also very likely to be true for government and other non-profit-seeking bodies, since they are usually short of money and are therefore reluctant to spend it on anything they do not need. We would thus expect that increases in production would be associated with increases in employment, and slumps in production with reductions in employment. This is in fact the case, though the correlation is not very close.

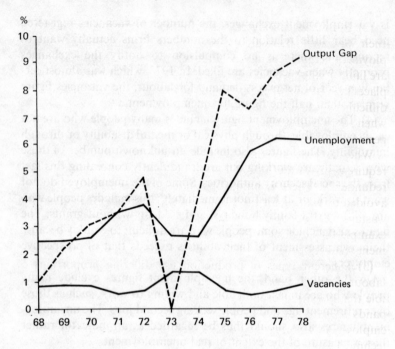

FIGURE 3.1   Unemployment, vacancies and the output gap, 1968–78.
Source: As Table 3.1.

There are several reasons why employment and output changes fail to correlate better.

(1) There are other ways of getting more output than hiring more workers. Existing workers can be asked to work harder, or be paid to work longer hours. Holidays and training courses can be deferred; output can be subcontracted to small firms whose proprietors do not get included in either the employment or the unemployment figures.

If output falls, there are alternatives to sacking people. They can be put on short time, or sent on holiday or for further training, or simply allowed to take things easy. A desire for goodwill induces employers to adopt some of these courses even if there is no trade union pressure, and there usually is union opposition to redundancies.

(2) Even after employers decide that they want to alter the size of their workforce, there are usually time lags before the level of employment actually changes. It takes time to recruit people, and there are limits to the speed at which new workers can be trained to take a place in a team when expansion is desired. Also, because it is difficult to sack people, firms are cautious about taking them on when demand expands until they feel sure the expansion is permanent.

When it comes to contraction of the labour force, there are legal requirements on periods of notice, and costs of compensation for redundancy. There is union opposition to sacking, which can be avoided by waiting for the labour force to decrease through natural wastage, i.e. as people retire or leave for personal reasons. The best example of the effects of these lags is seen in 1974, when employment went up by 0.6 per cent while real output fell by 1.4 per cent.

(3) Different types of production use differing proportions of labour inputs. If demand shifts between industries, it is quite possible that, if output declines in a labour-intensive industry and expands in an industry that is less labour-intensive, output and employment changes may differ. Because of the continual flow of technical innovations, changes in consumer tastes and changes in the intensity of foreign competition, the composition of production is continually changing. Maintaining total employment requires a continuous flow of new jobs to make up for losses of employment owing to products becoming obsolete or to competition from imports.

(4) The labour force varies greatly in its skills and rates of pay. If output shifts from industries using a lot of lower-paid workers, e.g. women, juveniles or unskilled immigrants, to one using mainly highly skilled men, then total output, measured in money value, can go up while employment, measured in numbers employed, goes down.

For all these reasons, the relation between output changes and employment changes over the past ten years has not been very precise. There is no real doubt, however, that if unemployment is to be reduced then total output must be increased.

How Little Unemployment Do We Want?

We next ask how far it is desirable that unemployment should be reduced. Clearly, in many cases unemployment involves costs both for the individuals concerned and for society as a whole; does it perform any economic functions that could make some of these costs worth-while incurring? There do appear to be some functions of unemployment.

(1) *Flexibility*: the goods and services that people want keep changing, sometimes at random and sometimes seasonally (e.g. the holiday industry), so output must be varied accordingly. Some of the need for flexibility can be met within firms, by shifting workers between departments. In other cases changes of job are required, and some unemployment results because the expansion by some firms does not match up exactly with reductions in labour require- ments by others.

(2) *Job search*: in some occupations it is hard to look for a better job while one is employed, so that some time can usefully be spent being unemployed while looking for a better job. If this helps get people into jobs that fit them better, then it can be an indirectly productive use of their time. In many occupations, however, it is actually easier to get a better job if you have some job already, so this argument does not apply.

(3) *Information*: the fact that jobs of a particular type are hard to find serves to warn people that in the short run it would be prudent to go easy on pay claims, for fear of making unemployment still worse, and that in the long run it would be prudent to train to do something else. Differences in the number of unfilled vacancies can give the same type of information; if job vacancies of a given type are hard to fill, this informs people that in the short run it would be probably be safe to demand a pay increase, and that in the long run this would be a good sort of job to train for.

In the case of unfilled vacancies, the social costs fall on people who cannot get the things they need because the jobs are unfilled; e.g. seats on buses or beds in hospitals. Excess supply and excess demand both cause loss and inconvenience to somebody; in choos- ing whether to run the economy with excess demand and a lot of unfilled vacancies, or excess supply and a lot of unemployment, we have to balance up which is worse.

If decent provision for maintainance of income during unemployment is provided by the social security system, and if the same people do not stay unemployed too long, it would seem that some unemployment can be justified by the economic functions just described. It is however very difficult to provide adequate unemployment insurance without setting up a situation where some people are better off not working. Also, if people do stay unemployed for long periods this reduces their employability in the future, as they lose specific skills through lack of practice, and their morale suffers generally through prolonged inactivity. Because of these factors the amount of 'functional unemployment' one would wish to see must be rather limited, and certainly below the 1978 level.

KEYNESIAN AND FRICTIONAL UNEMPLOYMENT

For the most part, therefore, unemployment has to be regarded as a cost to society that would be better avoided if we knew how. Unemployment can occur for two reasons: an inadequate level of aggregate demand, and a lack of correspondence between the particular sorts of goods and services that are demanded and the types of work that people are capable of performing.

Unemployment owing to overall lack of demand is called Keynesian unemployment, after J. M. (later Lord) Keynes, who in 1936 published *The General Theory of Employment, Interest and Money*, discussing problems of unemployment equilibrium. Unemployment owing to a mismatch between demand for labour of different types and the work that people are equipped to do is called frictional unemployment if it is short-lived, and structural unemployment if it persists for a long time.

If most parts of the economy are depressed, then increases in aggregate demand can increase employment. There are however usually some parts of the economy that have excess demand, owing to shortages of workers with particular skills or workers available to work in particular places, or to shortages of specialized machines or transport facilities, even when most parts of the economy are depressed. If aggregate demand rises, it is very likely that these particular shortages will get worse. It is the fear that particular shortages will lead to rises in prices and wages in the sectors concerned, which in turn will start off a general round of increased inflation, that has inhibited governments from trying to increase aggregate demand even at times when the level of unemployment was regarded as unacceptably high. We will come back to this aspect of unemployment in Chapters 18 and 19.

ALTERNATIVE REMEDIES FOR UNEMPLOYMENT

There are various possible ways of trying to reduce unemployment without any general rise in effective demand.

(1) It is possible to improve flows of information between workers seeking jobs and employers seeking people, so as to match them up sooner, e.g. by 'computer-dating' in employment agencies.

(2) It is possible to encourage mobility between places and/or occupations, by providing retraining facilities and financial assistance in moving, or by relieving the housing shortage so that people are less discouraged from moving by rehousing problems.

(3) The retiring age could be lowered. This however would involve an increased bill for pensions, and would harm elderly people who would rather have gone on working.

(4) Hours of work could be reduced. If this reduced the amount that people produced, however, it would make employing them less profitable, so that there is no guarantee that employment would rise in consequence.

All these measures are dubious in their results, or would take time to become effective. None of them can really be relied on to provide a quick cure for unemployment.

POLICY QUESTIONS

This leaves us with a number of policy questions about employment and unemployment:

(1) How could unemployment be reduced?
(2) How low should we aim to get it?
(3) What is the relation between unemployment and inflation?
(4) Would the economic costs of measures to reduce unemployment be worth incurring?

4. Effective Demand, Expenditure and Output

We have seen that the level of gross domestic product rises by varying amounts each year. This has given rise to variable levels of unemployment, and of activity, relative to a smooth trend. To understand why growth has happened in this irregular manner, we would need to be able to answer the following questions:
(1) What determines the total level of output?
(2) How far is output determined by demand, and how far by limits on possible supplies?
(3) How far do changes in demand lead to changes in actual output and employment, and how far to changes in imports, or to frustrated demand when goods and services are simply not available to satisfy the demand for them?
(4) How have the main components of demand varied over time, so far as we can tell from the expenditure figures?
(5) What happens as the result of changes in demand that do not get reflected in changes in actual expenditure and output?

EFFECTIVE DEMAND

When economists talk of demand, they mean 'effective demand'. This term was originated to distinguish between 'need' and 'demand'; everybody needs adequate food and shelter, but only those with a sufficient income can afford to buy them. 'Effective demand' has also been used to distinguish between what people

29

actually try to buy, and what they would like to buy in happier circumstances. If a worker is unemployed, his effective demand for goods and services will be less than what he would buy if he could get a job. The effective demand for investment goods means what firms actually try to spend, as opposed to schemes they would like to carry out when times are better and finance can be obtained. 'Effective demand' means what people actually do try to spend, not what they would do if only things were different.

DEMAND AND SUPPLY LIMITS TO OUTPUT

In a decentralized economy, goods and services get produced only when there is both a customer who is willing and able to pay for them, and a supplier who is willing and able to provide them. If there is a willing supplier but no customer, there will be no sale. On the supply side this will result in the accumulation of stocks of unsold goods, in the very short run; and as soon as production plans can be adjusted there will be unemployed workers or under-utilized machines. If there is a willing customer but no supplier, the result will be depleted stocks, then queues, delays in delivery and shortages of goods, and unfilled vacancies for workers.

If the market is not perfectly organized, there may be both unsatisfied customers and sellers who cannot find a market; this actually happens to some extent, but there is an obvious incentive for both parties to try to ensure that such a situation does not persist. In any but the very short run, we can assume that markets are sufficiently well organized that, where there is both a willing buyer and a willing seller, output will in fact take place. If output is limited, either a buyer or a seller is normally lacking.

BOOMS

When we consider what is limiting output in any particular situation, this will depend on the state of the economy at the time. In periods of very high demand, or booms, shortages of labour, capacity or materials will be widespread, so that output levels will be determined mainly by the ability of suppliers to provide goods and services. Output can be increased only by growth of the workforce, investment in more machines or improvements in techniques of production. In a boom output is said to be supply-determined.

Increases in demand during a boom will lead to very little increase in real output, but mainly to worse shortages, longer queues, greater delays, more imports and more rapid inflation.

SLUMPS

In times of very low demand, or slumps, excess supply conditions will be so widespread that output is determined mainly by effective demand, i.e. by what people are willing and able to buy. In a slump output is said to be demand-determined. Increases in the labour force during a slump will only lead to increased unemployment, and increases in the capital stock will lead to under-utilized equipment, unless demand is also increased.

INTERMEDIATE CASES

The normal state of the economy is neither extreme boom nor complete slump. In this intermediate state both sides of the market will have an effect on the total level of output. Thus part but not all of any increase in the labour force will result in more employment and more output, while part of the increase will in the very short run result in increased unemployment. Part but not all of any increases in demand will result in higher levels of output and employment; the rest of the increased demand will result in higher imports, or in increased delivery lags, queues and shortages in the more prosperous sectors of the economy.

It is believed that the proportion of any addition to demand that results in increased output will depend on how low a level of activity the economy started from, and on the speed with which demand is increased. The lower the initial level of output, the more sectors of the economy are likely to have spare labour and spare capacity, so that output can be increased promptly. The slower the increase in demand, the easier it will be to organize transfers of resources from sectors where they are plentiful to those where they are scarce. The higher the initial level of activity, on the other hand, the more sectors of the economy will be unable to expand output, owing to 'bottlenecks' imposed by scarcities of skilled labour or specialized machines or materials; and the faster demand rises the harder it will be to shift resources between sectors even when there are still parts of the economy with unemployed inputs.

DEMAND AND EXPENDITURE

There are no national income statistics that will tell us directly about changes in effective demand. The nearest we can get to such a measure is the series for total final expenditure at 1975 prices and its main components, which are shown in Table 4.1. At times of high overall activity it is very probable that actual expenditures will be restricted by the inability of the economy to supply more. Even if activity as a whole is not high, sudden large increases in any component, e.g. in gross fixed investment, will tend to create supply shortages in the types of goods mainly concerned. Thus there is a presumption that demand moves in the same direction as expenditures, but probably changes by larger amounts than are reflected in the actual expenditure figures. Information is available for some sectors of the economy on orders, order books and delivery lags; such information has its own problems of reliability, and is very partial in coverage, but it supports the general position described here.

Not all of total final expenditure is met by domestic output; around a quarter of it is met by imports of goods and services. At times of world-wide boom imports are in turn restricted by supply scarcities; at other times the extent to which final demands can be satisfied by imports depends on how easy it is to substitute between home-produced goods and imports. Because of the importance of imports, the final expenditure figures are a better indicator of demand movements for the UK economy than they would be for a closed economy, in which all final expenditures required matching domestic production. The actual determinants of imports will be discussed more fully in Chapter 22.

Let us then see what happened to total final expenditure between 1957 and 1978, bearing in mind that in booms the final expenditure figures understate the actual levels of effective demand. The facts are set out statistically in Table 4.1, and visually in Figure 4.1.

TABLE 4.1   *Growth of the Components of Total Final Expenditure at 1975 Prices, 1957–1978**

Year	Total final expenditure £b	%	Consumption £b	%	Government £b	%	Fixed investment £b	%	Stocks £b	Exports £b	%
	(1)		(2)		(3)		(4)		(5)	(6)	
1957	79.1		41.0		15.4		10.0		0.6	12.2	
1958	79.3	0.3	42.1	2.5	15.0	−2.7	10.1	0.8	0.2	12.0	−1.7
1959	82.8	4.4	43.9	4.3	15.3	1.8	10.9	7.7	0.5	12.4	2.9
1960	87.6	5.8	45.6	3.9	15.6	1.9	11.9	9.0	1.4	13.1	5.7
1961	90.0	2.7	46.6	2.3	16.1	3.5	13.1	9.8	0.7	13.5	3.2
1962	90.9	1.0	47.6	2.1	16.6	3.1	13.1	0.2	0.0	13.7	1.5
1963	94.5	4.0	49.7	4.3	16.9	1.6	13.3	1.3	0.4	14.4	4.9
1964	100.1	5.9	51.2	3.1	17.1	1.6	15.5	16.8	1.5	14.9	3.5
1965	102.2	2.1	52.0	1.6	17.6	2.6	16.2	4.8	1.0	15.6	4.8
1966	104.5	2.2	53.1	2.0	18.1	2.7	16.6	2.5	0.6	16.3	4.4
1967	107.9	3.3	54.3	2.2	19.1	5.7	18.0	8.4	0.5	16.4	0.8
1968	113.0	4.7	55.9	3.0	19.2	0.3	18.9	4.6	0.9	18.5	12.4
1969	115.0	1.7	56.2	0.5	18.8	−1.9	18.9	0.4	0.9	20.4	9.8
1970	118.3	2.9	56.7	0.9	19.1	1.4	19.4	2.6	0.8	21.5	5.4
1971	122.0	3.2	59.6	5.1	19.6	3.0	19.7	1.6	0.2	23.0	7.2
1972	126.6	3.8	63.0	5.8	20.5	4.1	19.8	0.2	0.2	23.3	1.2
1973	137.6	8.7	65.9	4.6	21.4	4.8	21.1	6.8	3.0	26.1	12.1
1974	136.3	−1.0	64.4	−2.3	21.7	1.4	20.6	−2.2	1.7	27.8	6.6
1975	133.0	−2.4	63.7	−1.1	23.0	6.1	20.5	−0.4	−1.5	27.1	−2.4
1976	138.0	3.8	63.9	0.2	23.5	1.8	20.6	0.4	0.4	29.6	9.1
1977	139.7	1.2	63.3	−0.8	23.3	−0.9	20.2	−2.1	1.2	31.7	7.0
1978	144.3	3.3	66.7	5.4	23.6	1.5	20.5	1.5	1.1	32.3	2.1
Average		2.9		2.4		2.1		3.5			4.8
Standard deviation		2.4		2.2		2.1		4.6			3.9

* Units: £b and percentage changes over previous year.

Source: Blue Book on *National Income and Expenditure, 1979*, Table 2.1.

£b at 1975 prices
(Logarithmic Scale)

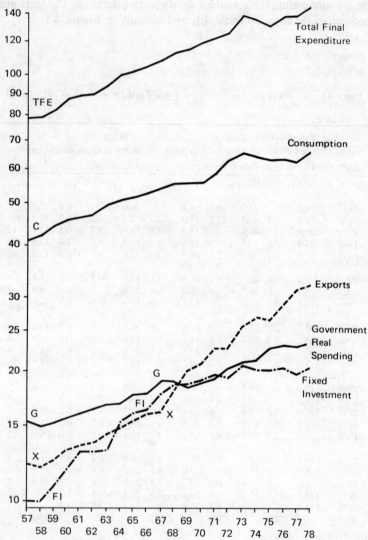

FIGURE 4.1   Growth of the components of total final expenditure at 1975 prices, 1957–78.

TOTAL FINAL EXPENDITURE

Column (1) of Table 4.1 shows total final expenditure at 1975 prices for each year from 1957 to 1978, in £b, and its percentage change each year. Up to 1973 total final expenditure grew each year, by percentages varying from 0.3 per cent in 1958 and 1.0 per cent in 1962 to 5.9 per cent in 1964. 1973 saw a growth of 8.7 per cent. After 1973 total final expenditure actually fell for two years, and while it has recovered a bit in 1978 it was still only 4.9 per cent above its 1973 level. As the 1973 peak was very high relative to trend, and was attained through an abnormally high annual increase, it is almost certain that 1973 had excess demand. 1978 by contrast was a slump year; thus effective demand, as distinct from final expenditure, was quite possibly still below its 1973 peak in 1978.

CONSUMPTION

Column (2) shows consumption, much the largest single component of total final expenditure throughout the period. Consumption rose fairly steadily up to 1973; its greatest annual increase, in 1972, was 5.8 per cent, and its lowest rise was 0.5 per cent in 1969. Since 1973 consumption has fallen, by 2.3 per cent in 1974; in 1978 it was only 1.2 per cent above its 1973 peak. Over the period as a whole the standard deviation of the percentage changes in consumption was 2.2 per cent, compared with 2.4 per cent for total final expenditure.

REAL GOVERNMENT EXPENDITURE

Column (3) shows real government expenditures, in £b, and their percentage changes. Real government expenditure was cut slightly in 1958, 1969 and 1977, but between these cuts it rose fairly steadily. Its most rapid growth was by 5.7 per cent in 1967 and by 6.1 per cent in 1975. The standard deviation of rates of change of real government expenditure was only 2.1 per cent.

FIXED INVESTMENT

Column (4) shows gross fixed investment, in £b, and its rates of change. Investment rose rapidly but jerkily up to 1973. In its good years fixed investment rose more rapidly than consumption or real government expenditure; by 16.8 per cent in 1964 and by 9.8 per cent in 1961, well above consumption's maximum increase of 5.8 per cent in 1972 or real government expenditure's maximum of 6.1 per cent in 1975. Fixed investment never fell before 1973, but in 1972 it rose by only 0.2 per cent. Since 1973 it has fallen, and in 1978 fixed investment was 3 per cent below its 1973 level. The standard deviation of rates of change of gross fixed investment over the whole period was 4.6 per cent.

STOCKS

Column (5) shows investment in stocks, in £b. As it was actually negative in 1975, i.e. stocks were reduced by £1.5b, calculations of percentage rates of change cannot be carried out. Stock-building was however easily the most irregular component of total final expenditure. While on the average of 1957 to 1978 only 0.7 per cent of total final expenditure consisted of stock-building, stocks contributed more to the overall variation of final expenditure than any other component.

EXPORTS

Column (6) shows exports of goods and services, in £b and their percentage changes. Exports grew rapidly and irregularly throughout, with falls in 1958 and 1975. Exports grew by 12.4 per cent in 1968 and 12.1 per cent in 1973; over the whole period, the standard deviation of changes in exports was 3.9 per cent. Over the whole period exports rose faster on average than any other component of total final demand: by 4.8 per cent per year, against 3.5 per cent for gross fixed investment and only 2.9 per cent for total final expenditure. In eight out of the last eleven years, 1972, 1975 and 1978 being the exceptions, exports have been the most rapidly growing component of total final demand. In a real sense the British economy has had 'export-led growth'.

Thus investment in stocks has been the most unstable component of total final demand; gross fixed investment and exports have been less stable than the average, while consumption and real government expenditures have behaved most steadily.

POLICIES FOR STABILIZATION

If economic policies are to lead to greater stability in effective demand, this must happen in one of two ways. Either the various components must be made to grow more steadily, or, if some are beyond control, the others must be induced to vary so as to offset the fluctuations in those that cannot be stabilized. In order to get anywhere towards either of these objectives, it is necessary to understand what determines the size of the various components of final demand; this we go on to do in the following chapters, which will discuss them in turn. The questions we will ask are:

(1) What determines consumption?
(2) Can government expenditure (which is clearly under the immediate control of the government) be used to offset fluctuations in the other components of expenditure?
(3) What determines investment? Can it be stabilized by monetary or fiscal policies?
(4) What determines exports? How can policy influence them?
(5) Can total output be boosted by policies to increase expenditure, or will these merely lead to excessive imports, inflation or both?

5. Consumption

We have seen that consumption is the largest component of expenditure, and that it is relatively stable. We will now try to see how far its variations can be explained. The questions we would like to be able to answer include:

(1) What determines consumption?
(2) Does consumption have a stable relation to income?
(3) How has the division of incomes between consumption and savings been changing?
(4) What has caused the share of savings in incomes to increase?

The main variable used to explain changes in consumption is changes in income. The common sense behind this is that consumption expenditures are financed mainly out of the incomes people receive. Everybody buys goods and services for current consumption; many people spend every pound they can get on them. On average the people of the UK consume about seven-eighths of the net-of-tax income that they receive.

OUTLETS FOR INCOME

There is however no rigid connection between income and consumption. Each income-receiving unit, i.e. each person or family, has four logically possible outlets for its income: (1) it can be paid away in taxes to the government; (2) it can be consumed; (3) it can be donated to others, either charities or individuals; or (4) it can be saved. On the average of 1968–78 about 21 per cent of personal incomes was paid in direct taxes and compulsory national insurance contributions; the remainder is called disposable income. On average over the same period, between 1.3 and 1.8 per cent of disposable

38

income was given away; about 10 per cent was saved, and the remaining 88 per cent was spent on consumption. This is using a definition of consumption that excludes the acquisition of houses for owner-occupation, but includes all other purchases of consumer durable goods such as cars or boats.

The actual proportion of income consumed varies widely between individuals or families, who can choose for themselves what gifts they will make, and whether to spend or to save the rest. If they already hold stocks of assets, as the result of past savings or inheritance, they can spend by running these down. If they have good income prospects so that they look good risks to lenders, they can buy on credit. In these cases it is possible to spend more than one's income, possibly for quite long periods, e.g. to finance professional training on credit, or to live on past savings during retirement.

In the years between 1968 and 1978 savings varied between 8 and 14 per cent of after-tax incomes. If such a change was liable to occur between any year and the next, consumption would be a very unstable part of expenditure. The reasons why the saving ratio does not vary suddenly must be sought in human motivation, not in any logical necessity.

Donations to charities or individuals arise from needs that do not vary much from year to year; the amounts concerned are small and stable, and we will take no further note of them.

CONSUMPTION *v.* SAVINGS

The division of income between consumption and savings is affected by various motives. Consumption makes people happy at once, and for some time to come if the goods bought are at all durable, as many are. Consumption expenditures are to some extent forced on people by the physical necessity for minimum levels of food, clothing and shelter in order to survive. Many people however eat, dress and house themselves at levels well above any physical necessity, not to mention consuming alcohol and tobacco to an extent that is known to be positively harmful. There are also however a great many social conventions about consumption which make it difficult to vary it, and there are some parts of consumption, such as electricity, fuel and rates, that depend largely on where you live, and cannot be changed immediately.

Saving too gives people benefits. Saving gives rise to assets, which will yield future income, and can be sold off if necessary, or used as collateral to obtain loans. This gives security in the face of possible fluctuations in one's future income, owing to unemployment, sickness or a slump in one's business. Having a stock of assets allows people to acquire houses for owner-occupation or to run small businesses on a self-employment basis if they want to. Assets also make it possible to retire on a better income than the state provides for pensioners.

It is because of the relative stability of both these sets of motives, to spend and to save, that the proportion of income spent on consumption, while it does change over time, does not change violently from year to year.

THE CONSUMPTION FUNCTION

This has given rise to the theory of economists that there is a 'consumption function', relating planned consumption expenditure to disposable income. For an individual the simplest, linear, form of the consumption function takes the form

$$C = A + bY$$

Where C is consumption, Y is disposable income and A and b are constants. Because of physical and social necessities, which force people with low incomes to consume but permit those with higher incomes more choice, it is generally assumed that the consumption function will have $A > 0$ (i.e., A is greater than zero), and $0 < b < 1$ (i.e. b is positive but less than unity). Each unit increase in Y gives a rise in C of b units, and b is called the 'marginal propensity to consume'. C/Y is the 'average propensity to consume', and will fall as Y increases.

Figure 5.1 gives a diagrammatic illustration of such a consumption function, where $OC_0 = A$, and if disposable income is Y_1, planned consumption is $Y_1 C_1$.

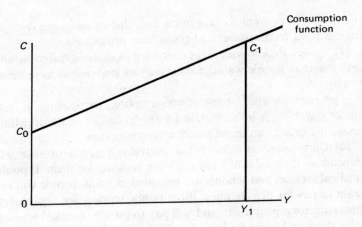

FIGURE 5.1   A linear consumption function.

OTHER FACTORS AFFECTING CONSUMPTION

The simple function given above will not be the whole story about what determines consumption. At the level of the individual, economists have suggested several other factors that can be expected to affect consumption, and a lot of research has been done on seeing exactly how much improvement in our understanding of consumption each of these can give. These complications include the following.

(1) *Family circumstances.* A family with several children will have to consume more from any given income than one with few or no dependants.

(2) *Past income and consumption.* People cannot change their consumption habits immediately when their income changes, even if they expect the change to be permanent. They may need to move house to give room for the extra durable goods they will want to buy if they have become better off; if they become poorer, they may wish their children to complete courses they have begun at schools even though they no longer feel able to afford the fees.

(3) *Future prospects.* If people expect rising incomes they are willing to spend more than would normally be spent at their current income level. If people are worried about future unemployment in a

slump they may want to save more than they would have done at their current income level had times been prosperous.

(4) *Assets.* People with large assets are likely to spend more and save less than people with the same current income but large debts to pay off.

(5) *Credit facilities.* A lot of consumption, particularly of consumer durables, is initially paid for on credit. The ease of getting consumer credit can therefore affect consumption.

(6) *Government services.* What individuals spend or save will depend on their view of what the state provides for them. If public medical services and schools are regarded as good, people will not want to pay for private ones; if the public services are regarded as unsatisfactory, people can and will pay to provide medical services, education or leisure facilities for themselves. If state pensions are regarded as generous, and if unemployment and sickness benefits are adequate, people will not need to save so much for their retirement or to cope with unemployment or sickness; if the state provision is regarded as only minimal, people will feel the need to save to supplement it.

A further complication of the relation between income and consumption deserved mention. The usual statistical tests of the connection imply that, at the individual level, income causes consumption but not vice versa. The view that people take the incomes as given and decide how much to consume may be correct for some groups, e.g. pensioners or the disabled. In many cases however people's incomes result at least partly from their own choices. They decide what careers to take up, whether to work overtime or take days off, whether to seek second jobs or extra casual work, and whether they can afford to retire, in the light of their desire for income, to be able to afford present consumption or savings. This does not mean that there is no connection between income and consumption, in fact quite the reverse; but it does greatly complicate the job of testing the connection statistically.

THE AGGREGATE CONSUMPTION FUNCTION

When we come to consider the causes of consumption at the macroeconomic level we are not dealing with individuals, but with

the question of what determines consumption for the whole economy. Can we expect to find an aggregate consumption function,
such as

$$C = A + bY$$

where C is now aggregate planned consumption, and Y the disposable income of all consumers?

When we look at the figures we find that there is a statistical fit,
though not a very good one, between actual aggregate consumption
and aggregate disposable income. In dealing with aggregates some
causes of individual variation become less important; e.g., family
size changes by whole persons for individuals, but the average
family size for the UK changes only by a tiny fraction of a person
each year. On the other hand there are some new worries about
the relation between income and consumption.

(1) What people will save depends on how incomes are distributed between them, unless everyone happens to have the same b
in their individual consumption function, which seems very unlikely;
and we know that income distribution does change over time.

(2) What people spend from a given income will depend on how
many of them there are. If national income grows we would expect
to see a bigger rise in consumption if the growth is due to there
being more people with the same income per head than if the
growth of income is due to the same number of people with larger
incomes per head.

SOURCES OF PERSONAL INCOME

To see what has actually happened to consumption we need to look
at the facts. First we need to know how disposable income is arrived
at; for this purpose we use Table 5.1. Its first section shows the
sources of personal income for the whole 'personal sector' as defined
in the National Income Blue Book. 'Persons' here includes not only
all families, but also some legal 'persons', notably private non-
profit-making bodies, including charities, universities and various
pension funds.

Personal incomes came from various sources. Income from employment provided £98.2b in 1978, or 68.5 per cent of total personal

TABLE 5.1   *Personal Income and Expenditure in 1978*

Source of personal income	£m		£b	% of total personal income
Employment*		98,156	98.2	68.5
Self-employment**		13,245	13.2	9.2
Rent, dividends and net interest		13,671	13.7	9.6
National insurance benefits and other grants from general government		17,853	17.9	12.5
Other		288	0.3	0.2
Total personal income†		143,213	143.2	100.0
Tax payments	19,672		19.7	
Additions to tax reserves	− 17		0.0	
National insurance and other contributions	10,023		10.0	
Total taxes and contributions		29,678	29.7	20.7
Disposable personal income		113,535	113.5	79.3

Use of disposable income				% of disposable income
Consumption		96,086	96.1	84.6
Net transfers abroad		218	0.2	0.2
Personal savings		17,231	17.2	15.2

* Income from employment was made up of: £b

Wages and salaries	84.4
HM Forces	1.6
National insurance and other (mainly pension) contributions by employers in respect of employees	12.1

** Income from self-employment includes £0.8b of 'stock appreciation' and £1.3b of depreciation in unincorporated businesses.

† Total personal incomes include £3.6b of income of private non-profit-making institutions, including universities and charities (some genuine like Oxfam, others tax devices for wealthy families).

Source: Blue Book on *National Income and Expenditure, 1979,* Table 1.3; notes use Tables 4.1, 4.3 and 4.4.

incomes. This included not only wages and salaries, and pay of HM forces, but also employers' contributions to national insurance and other (mainly pension) funds in respect of their employees.

Income from self-employment provided £13.2b, or 9.2 per cent of personal incomes. This figure included £2.1b of provision for depreciation and 'stock appreciation', i.e. of inflationary increases in the prices of stocks held by unincorporated businesses.

The next category was £13.7b of rent, dividends and net interest, i.e. property incomes. This provided 9.6 per cent of total personal incomes, a lot of it accruing to pension funds.

All the items so far were derived from some form of productive activity. Individuals also received 'transfer incomes', i.e. payments like unemployment and sickness benefits, pensions and student maintenance grants; all of these may be well deserved, but they are not provided as recompense for services rendered. In 1978 there were £17.9b of these, or 12.5 per cent of personal incomes. There was also an 'other' category, of vast complexity and minute size, which we will ignore. These all added up to a total personal income of £143.2b.

TAXES AND DISPOSABLE INCOME

This total personal income was not however all available to individuals to spend or save. Taxes on income, mainly income taxes, took £19.7b; national insurance and other (mainly pension) contributions took £10.0b, and −£17m is allowed for 'additions to tax reserves', i.e. an estimate of the money people would need to set aside to meet tax liabilities when the demand finally arrives. (For some property incomes, and for people with complicated tax appeals, the actual payment could be delayed for years.)

These deductions of £29.7b, or 20.7 per cent of the total, have to be subtracted from total personal income to get disposable income, of £113.5b in 1978. The figure for disposable income is larger than the everyday concept of 'take-home pay', since it includes incomes from property, an estimate of receipts in kind and the value of owner-occupied houses, but for a tenant with negligible property income disposable income and take-home pay will be almost identical.

It is thought by economists that consumption is related to disposable income rather than to any other income aggregate. We ignore here some slight problems arising from the fact that, since there are some forms of savings, such as life insurance and pensions contributions, that attract tax concessions, the size of an individual's disposable income may be dependent on his own decisions on how to divide it between consumption and savings.

In 1978 £96.1b of disposable income was spent on consumption, £17.2b was saved, and £0.2b was used to make transfers abroad.

CONSUMPTION AND DISPOSABLE INCOME

When we come to see how consumption has behaved over time, it seems helpful to use a slightly different set of figures from those in Table 5.1. Again the alternatives are derived from the Blue Book on *National Income and Expenditure*. First, the definition of the personal sector is narrowed by removing the private non-profit-making bodies, with £3.6b of income in 1978. The figures however still include pension funds. Whether people act in their consumption and savings decisions as though the pension funds on which they have claims belonged to them directly is open to question. Taking pension funds out of the figures we use to fit a consumption function would imply that people's consumption is not affected at all by the fact that they know they are entitled to pensions from these funds. Probably neither position is entirely correct; in any case no attempt to exclude the pension funds has been made here.

Second, the income figures have been adjusted by deducting the Central Statistical Office's estimates of the stock appreciation of unincorporated businesses. Because of the great speeding up of inflation since 1973, these have recently expanded very fast, and there is no reason to assume that the owners of small businesses regard them as income, or regard themselves as saving because they do not spend these amounts.

Third, the income and consumption figures all rise rapidly throughout the period in money terms because of inflation. To get them on a 'real' basis they have all been deflated by the price index of consumer goods used by the Central Statistical Office. The results are shown in Table 5.2 and Figure 5.1. Column (1) of Table 5.2 shows the income of the 'rest of the personal sector', excluding charities, etc., but still including pension funds, and adjusted by deducting the stock appreciation of unincorporated businesses. Column (2) shows the consumer price index, and column (3) shows incomes at 1975 prices. These rose rapidly up to 1975, fell slightly in 1977 and rose again in 1978.

Column (4) shows the percentage of incomes taken in income tax and contributions. This has risen from 19.5 per cent in 1968–70 to 22.5 per cent in 1974–78. Column (5) shows disposable income, at 1975 prices. This rose rapidly till 1973, then stagnated until 1977 but rose in 1978.

Column (6) shows consumption at 1975 prices. This rose rapidly

TABLE 5.2   *Personal Income, Disposable Income and Consumption, 1968–78.*

Year	Personal incomes at current prices* £b	Consumer price index**	Personal incomes at 1975 prices† £b	Tax and contri- butions‡ %	Dispos- able incomes at 1975 prices§ £b	Consump- tion at 1975 prices§§ £b	Consump- tion¶ %
	(1)	(2)	(3)	(4)	(5)	(6)	(7)
1968	36.0	49.2	73.2	19.1	59.3	54.3	91.5
1969	38.6	52.0	74.3	19.5	59.8	54.5	91.2
1970	42.6	55.0	77.5	20.0	62.1	55.9	90.1
1971	47.1	59.6	78.9	20.0	63.2	57.7	91.4
1972	53.3	63.5	84.0	19.2	67.8	61.1	90.0
1973	61.6	69.0	89.3	20.0	71.5	63.9	89.4
1974	74.2	80.9	91.7	21.5	72.0	62.4	86.6
1975	94.7	100.0	94.7	23.4	72.5	61.7	85.0
1976	109.8	115.5	95.0	23.7	72.5	61.8	84.8
1977	123.1	132.9	92.6	22.6	71.7	61.3	85.6
1978	140.6	144.0	97.7	21.1	77.0	64.7	84.0
Average 1968–70				19.5			90.9
Average 1971–73				19.7			90.3
Average 1974–78				22.5			85.2
Average 1968–78				20.9			88.1

* Refers to 'rest of personal sector', Blue Book Table 4.5, adjusted for stock appreciation using Table 4.3.
** Used by Central Statistical Office to get from Blue Book Table 4.9 to 4.10. Tabulated in Blue Book 2.5.
† From cols (1) and (2).
‡ Gives taxes and contributions from Blue Book Table 4.5 as percentage of col. (1).
§ From cols (3) and (4).
§§ From Blue Book Table 4.5, converted to 1975 prices using col. (2).
¶ Col. (6) as percentage of col. (5).
Source: Blue Book on *National Income and Expenditure 1979.*

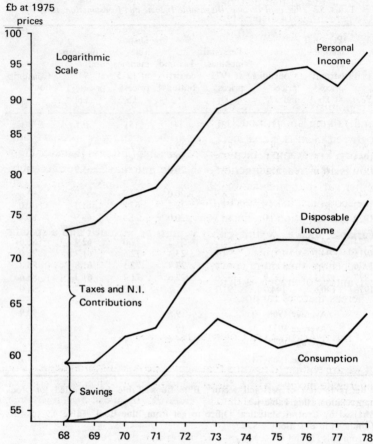

FIGURE 5.2   Personal income, disposable income and consumption at 1975 prices, 1968–78. (Logarithmic scale).

up to 1973 and then fell, but recovered in 1978. Column (7) shows the percentage of disposable income consumed; this has fallen from 90.9 per cent in 1968–70 to 85.2 per cent in 1974–78.

THEORIES AND MODELS

Economists often switch very freely between talking about theories and talking about models of the economy. The basic distinction between them is that a model has to be much more specific than a theory. For example, the theory of consumption says that consumption is an increasing function of income, and may also be affected by other variables such as wealth, and the rate of interest. In a model the economist has to specify the form of the relation, e.g. to assume that consumption is a linear function of income; and for each other variable, such as wealth, either it must be included and a specific form assumed for its effects, or it must be excluded completely. Models are thus more concrete and mechanical than theories; the advantage of models is that they can be compared with the facts, whereas theories cannot.

A FITTED AGGREGATE CONSUMPTION FUNCTION

If we are willing to assume that aggregate consumption depends on aggregate income, with a linear relation, and to fit a 'least squares' regression to the annual data for 1968–78, the line of best fit for C, in £b, is:

$$C = 19.7 + 0.59Y$$

where Y is the value of disposable incomes at 1975 prices. This does not mean that anybody believes that if disposable income were zero people would really consume £19.7b; it is merely the line that gives the best fit over the range of actual observations, which all lie between $Y = £59b$ and $Y = £77b$. The marginal propensity to consume, b, is estimated as 0.59. The relation has a fairly good fit (technically, $R^2 = 0.93$; this means that 93 per cent of the observed variance in C is explained by variations in Y).

A better 'explanation' of consumption can be found by including more explanatory variables and using a less highly aggregated model. Considering all the things that could have gone wrong, however, a connection between disposable incomes and consumption seems to be reasonably well established.

It is not possible to prove here, but it is sensible to explain that it is the author's belief, which will be reflected in the figures used in the next chapter, that the true marginal propensity to consume for the UK economy is a bit higher than 0.59, and that some of the rise in the proportion of incomes saved that we have seen has been due to factors other than the mere rise in incomes. Principal causes for this fall in the average propensity to consume are:

(1) *the slump in real output since 1973*: this has been deeper, and more prolonged, than any other recession since the Second World War. It has made people more worried about the dangers of unemployment in the short run, and less optimistic about continued economic growth in the longer run. Both of these changes would tend to make people save more;

(2) *inflation*: this has greatly increased since 1973. It reduces the real purchasing power of people's cash balances, and of many forms of security denominated in fixed cash terms, e.g. National Savings Certificates. If people want to restore the real purchasing power of these assets, which they need to hold to cope with emergencies, they have to save in order to do so. Part of the rise in savings during the most inflationary years could be due to this;

(3) *the increase in occupational and wage-related pension schemes*: this has compelled people to pay premiums that are not available to be spent. For people who would have been saving anyway, this increase in contractual savings could have been offset by a reduction in other forms of savings; but for those who would not otherwise have saved much this is impossible, so that some rise in their total savings was unavoidable.

It is consistent with this view, though it does not prove that it is right, that a regression of annual changes in consumption on annual changes in disposable income gives an estimate for *b* of 0.74.

THE MULTIPLIER

If there is indeed a relatively stable relation between income and consumption, this allows us to construct a model of how an economy will behave in which consumption is a function of income, while other elements of expenditure fluctuate in ways we cannot yet explain. This model, known as that of the multiplier, will be discussed in the next chapter.

6. The Multiplier

In this chapter we will consider models of how the national income would behave if there were a known and stable consumption function giving the level of consumption for each level of income, while other components of expenditure, such as government expenditure, investment and exports, were liable to change for reasons we will not here attempt to determine. It is however assumed that the other components of expenditure can be forecast reliably.

It is also assumed that the economy is sufficiently depressed that a high proportion of any additional demand gets reflected in actual expenditures. This is not usually completely true, but in a slump it may be sufficiently reliable for the resulting models to be of some use in forecasting the results of external disturbances or policy changes.

The multiplier tells us what size the national income must be in equilibrium, given the behaviour of investment and other expenditures not dependent on Y. If income is not already at the level indicated, we will need to investigate the process by which equilibrium will be approached.

EQUILIBRIUM

An economic system is said to be in equilibrium only if it is not tending to change. This will in general be true only if what is actually happening is consistent with what people expected. The equilibrium level of national income is the level at which it does not tend to rise or fall. If in any period spending plans and output plans are not consistent, then at least one of these sets of plans is bound to be frustrated, and both may be. For example if planned, or '*ex ante*',

51

spending exceeds planned, or '*ex ante*', production, then either some purchasers will be frustrated; i.e., consumers or investors will find that in the event, or '*ex post*', they have bought less than they wanted; or producers will find that they have produced more output than they forecast; or, most likely, a bit of each will occur. In any case plans for the next period will be revised in the light of experience. Only if on average spending and production plans are fulfilled will the level of national income not be liable to alter.

THE BASIC MULTIPLIER MODEL

We first consider a very simple economy, in which the only components of expenditure are consumption and investment. Thus

$$Y = C + I$$

where Y is income, C is consumption and I is investment. We assume a linear consumption function,

$$C = A + bY$$

and we also assume that investment is autonomous (i.e., we do not attempt to explain what determines it in this chapter). Thus

$$Y = A + bY + I.$$

We can tidy up this equation by grouping together on the left-hand side (LHS) all the terms including Y, and grouping the others together on the right-hand side (RHS); thus

$$(1 - b)Y = A + I. \tag{6.1}$$

We number the equation so that we can conveniently refer back to it. We thus have

$$Y = \frac{A + I}{1 - b}.$$

We can now see what will happen if I changes, while the other parameters including A remain constant. This is shown by using the sign ∂ for partial differentiation, where this indicates how Y will change when I changes, but other parameters that could be changed are not altered on this occasion. Thus

$$\frac{\partial Y}{\partial I} = \frac{1}{1 - b}.$$

Equally, if A changed while I remained constant, the partial derivative of Y with respect to A would be shown by

$$\frac{\partial Y}{\partial A} = \frac{1}{1 - b}.$$

$\partial Y/\partial I = 1/(1 - b)$ is 'the multiplier', Mark I. It tells us that for every unit increase in I, Y will rise by $1/(1 - b)$ units; i.e., each unit of change in investment has to be multiplied by $1/(1 - b)$ to find the total change in incomes that will result from it. If $b = 0.8$, the multiplier will be

$$\frac{1}{1 - b} = \frac{1}{1 - 0.8} = \frac{1}{0.2} = 5.$$

The multiplier comes about because each unit of investment gives rise to extra incomes, which allow the recipients to consume more, which raises incomes further, and so on.

The multiplier can also work in reverse; if I falls by a unit, then Y will fall by $1/(1 - b)$ units.

A DIAGRAMMATIC ILLUSTRATION OF THE MULTIPLIER

The multiplier is illustrated diagrammatically in Figure 6.1. Y appears on the horizontal axis and C and I on the vertical axis. The aggregate consumption function is shown by $C_0 C$. If investment is I_0 then total expenditure is shown by $C + I_0$, which is found by adding I_0 to C. For equilibrium $C + I$ must equal Y; the line of equality is drawn as OK (because of its slope OK is often referred to as 'the 45 degree line'). Thus for equilibrium Y must be such that $C + I_0$ intersects OK; this occurs at J_0, so equilibrium income is Y_0 and total expenditure is $Y_0 J_0$.

If investment rises to I_1 then total expenditure is shown by $C + I_1$; the equilibrium level of income is now Y_1, at which $C + I_1$ intersects OK at J_1, and total expenditure is $Y_1 J_1$.

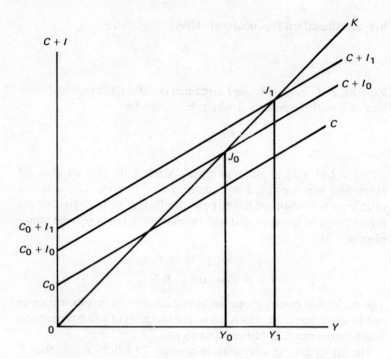

FIGURE 6.1   Determination of the equilibrium level of income.

INJECTIONS AND LEAKAGES

An alternative way of considering this model is to argue that, in equilibrium, 'injections' of purchasing power into the economy, i.e. components of expenditure that do not depend on incomes, must equal 'leakages', i.e. uses for incomes that do not give rise to any further incomes. If injections exceed leakages Y will rise, and if leakages exceed injections Y will fall. Only when leakages and injections are equal can Y stay at the same level, when it is said to be in equilibrium.

In this simple model the only injection is I, and the only leakage is savings, S, where savings is defined as the part of incomes not used for consumption; so that

$$S = Y - C = Y - (A + bY) = (1 - b)Y - A.$$

For equilibrium, i.e. for there to be no tendency for incomes to rise or fall,

$$S = I$$

so

$$(1 - b)Y - A = I$$

and

$$(1 - b)Y = A + I$$

as before.

If we are given all but one of the variables A, b, I and Y that appear in equation (6.1), we can always calculate the remaining one; e.g., if I is unknown,

$$I = (1 - b)Y - A.$$

THE GOVERNMENT SECTOR

In the previous model there was no government; this is clearly quite implausible for any modern economy. In this section we introduce a government sector, though we still retain the highly implausible assumption of a closed economy with no foreign trade. We now have

$$Y = C + I + G$$

where G is government expenditure.

The consumption function now relates consumption to disposable income, $(Y - T)$, where T is taxation.

$$C = A + b(Y - T).$$

We assume a uniform tax rate on all income, so that $T = tY$ where t is the tax rate. Thus

$$Y - T = (1 - t)Y$$

and

$$C = A + b(1 - t)Y.$$

I and *G* are autononous, and

$$Y = A + b(1 - t)Y + I + G.$$

Again we group terms in *Y* in the LHS and the others on the RHS:

$$[1 - b(1 - t)]Y = A + I + G. \qquad (6.2)$$

Thus

$$Y = \frac{A + I + G}{1 - b(1 - t)}.$$

Taking the partial derivative of *Y* with respect to *G*, i.e. holding *A* and *I* constant,

$$\frac{\partial Y}{\partial G} = \frac{1}{1 - b(1 - t)}$$

This is 'the multiplier', Mark II. If *I* varies, holding *A* and *G* constant, we get the partial derivative of *Y* with respect to *I*,

$$\frac{\partial Y}{\partial I} = \frac{1}{1 - b(1 - t)}.$$

Again, we can get the same results by applying the leakages = injections approach. In this model there are two leakages, savings and tax payments, and two injections, investment and government spending. Thus, for equilibrium,

$$S + T = I + G$$

$$S = (Y - T) - C$$

$$= (1 - t)Y - [A + b(1 - t)Y]$$

$$= (1 - t)(1 - b)Y - A$$

and

$$T = tY;$$

so

$$(1 - t)(1 - b)Y - A + tY = I + G;$$

thus

$$[1 - b(1 - t)]Y = A + I + G$$

as before.

Note that S = private savings; the government also saves an amount equal to its budget surplus, $B = T - G$, and these savings are not included in S.

From equation (6.2), if we know all but one of the variables A, b, G, I, t and Y we can calculate the remaining one; e.g., if t is the one we need to find, from (6.2),

$$b(1 - t)Y = Y - A - I - G$$

so

$$1 - t = \frac{Y - A - I - G}{bY}$$

and

$$t = 1 - \frac{Y - A - I - G}{bY}.$$

Example

Suppose we know that $Y = 1,000$, $b = 0.7$, $A = 110$, $I = 200$, $G = 200$ and t is unknown;

$$t = 1 - \frac{1,000 - 110 - 200 - 200}{(0.7)(1,000)}$$

$$= 1 - \frac{490}{700} = 1 - 0.7 = 0.3$$

so a tax rate of 30 per cent is required.

THE OPEN ECONOMY

The previous economies had no foreign trade; we now introduce it.

$$Y = C + I + G + X - M$$

where X = exports and M = imports.

As before, $C = A + b(1 - t)Y$ and I, G and X are autonomous. $M = mY$ where m is the propensity to import, and $T = tY$.

$$Y = A + b(1 - t)Y + I + G + X - mY.$$

Again grouping the terms in Y on the LHS,

$$[1 - b(1 - t) + m]Y = A + I + G + X \qquad (6.3)$$

so

$$Y = \frac{A + I + G + X}{1 - b(1 - t) + m}$$

and

$$\frac{\partial Y}{\partial X} = \frac{1}{1 - b(1 - t) + m}.$$

This is 'the multiplier', Mark III. It will be clear by now that 'the multiplier' is not any single formula, but a name given to a class of formulas, which are found by distinguishing between components of expenditure that depend on Y and components that do not.

Again we can use the leakages = injections approach. There are now three leakages from the economy – savings, taxation and imports – and three injections – investment, government spending and exports. For equilibrium,

$$S + T + M = I + G + X$$
$$S = (Y - T) - C$$
$$= (1 - t)Y - [A + B(1 - t)Y]$$
$$= (1 - b)(1 - t)Y - A.$$

$T = tY$ and $M = mY$; so

$$(1 - b)(1 - t)Y - A + tY + mY = I + G + X.$$

Thus

$$[1 - b(1 - t) + m]Y = A + I + G + X$$

as before. In this case total savings, i.e. private savings plus govern-ment savings $(T - G)$, must equal the outlets for them, which are investment and the foreign trade surplus, $F(= X - M)$, which is used on acquiring foreign assets.

Further examples of the multiplier model follow in Chapter 11 when we discuss fiscal policy.

LIMITATIONS OF THE MULTIPLIER MODEL

The multiplier model is a useful device, but it needs to be treated with some caution.

First of all, it cannot produce predictions of income better than the predictions of the various items of autonomous expenditure that are fed into it, i.e. of A, I, G and X. If these are predicted wrongly, the national income will be wrongly predicted also, even if the arithmetic of the model is right.

Second, the applicability of the model is strictly conditional on the real resources to produce the predicted output being available. If they are not, Y will not rise as predicted, in real terms; there will merely be a rise in imports, or in excess demand in various markets, leading to a tendency to more inflation.

The third limitation deserves a section to itself.

The Multiplier as a Process

The multiplier as described above is an equilibrium model, and tells us nothing about the process of getting to a new equilibrium. The model will only tell us where the economy will actually go if the process leading to the equilibrium is stable. What this means is best seen by the use of a simple example.

Suppose that

$$Y_i = C_i + I_i$$

where the subscript i shows which time period the variables refer to. Suppose that I_i is autonomous, but that C_i is a linear function of the income of the previous period:

$$C_i = A + bY_{i-1}$$

then

$$Y_i = A + bY_{i-1} + I_i.$$

Suppose that at time 1, I_i increases by one unit and stays at its new level in subsequent periods. Suppose that at time 0 the economy was in equilibrium, and let y_i denote the divergence of Y_i for periods $i \geq 1$ from its old equilibrium level. Thus

$$y_0 = 0,$$

and for $i \geq 1$,

$$y_i = 1 + b y_{i-1}.$$

Then

$$y_1 = 1 + b y_0 = 1 + b(0) = 1$$
$$y_2 = 1 + b y_1 = 1 + b(1) = 1 + b$$
$$y_3 = 1 + b y_2 = 1 + b(1 + b) = 1 + b + b^2$$

and so on; the general term is given by

$$y_n = 1 + b y_{n-1} = 1 + b + b^2 + \cdots + b^{n-1}.$$

Multiplying each side by b,

$$b y_n = b + b^2 + b^3 + \cdots + b^{n-1} + b^n$$

so subtracting $b y_n$ from y_n, all the terms on the RHS cancel except for the first term in y_n and the last in $b y_n$; thus

$$(1 - b) y_n = 1 - b^n$$

and

$$y_n = \frac{1 - b^n}{1 - b}.$$

If $0 < b < 1$, b^n becomes smaller and smaller as n increases; b^n is said to 'tend to zero' as n 'tends to infinity'. Thus, as n increases, y_n approaches the limiting value of $1/(1 - b)$.

This is the multiplier found above; it describes what will eventually happen if $b < 1$. The system is then said to be 'dynamically stable', or just stable. As b is the marginal propensity to consume, and $(1 - b)$ is the marginal propensity to save, which is assumed to be positive, the condition that $b < 1$ seems very likely to be satisfied.

b is the proportion of each unit of income that results in further expenditure, and $(1 - b)$ is the leakage between successive rounds of the multiplier process.

In more complicated multiplier models further leakages are added. Thus the proportion of income at each round of the multiplier process that gives rise to further domestic expenditures is decreased. In the multiplier Mark II above, the introduction of a leakage into taxation meant that b was replaced by $b(1 - t)$, which is certain to be less than b, so that the leakage increased. The multiplier Mark III above added leakages into imports, so that at each round of the multiplier process b is replaced by $b(1 - t) - m$, and leakage is further increased. In these more realistic multiplier models the conditions for stability seem pretty certain to be satisfied.

A more serious worry about the practical relevance of the multiplier model concerns the time period it refers to; 'eventually' seems an unduly long time off. Indeed, the multiplier process as described above is never actually complete in finite time; we are however interested in seeing how fast it approaches completion.

If b is near to unity, not only will the multiplier be large, but it will take a lot of stages of the multiplier process to achieve any given proportion of the eventual result. For example, with $b = 0.8$, the multiplier is $1/(1 - 0.8) = 5$, and after four stages of the multiplier process

$$y_4 = 1 + 0.8 + 0.8^2 + 0.8^3 = 2.95$$

i.e., the process is only 59 per cent complete.

In a model of the form of multiplier Mark III above, where leakages into taxation and imports are also allowed for, the leakage at each round is given by

$$1 - b(1 - t) + m.$$

If we have $b = 0.8$, $t = 0.25$ and $m = 0.2$,

$$1 - (0.8)(1 - 0.25) + 0.2 = 0.6.$$

The multiplier is thus $1/0.6 = 1.667$, and the part of this reached after four periods is given by

$$y_4 = 1 + 0.4 + 0.4^4 + 0.4^3 = 1.624$$

which is over 97 per cent of the ultimate level.

The multiplier has here been treated as a historical process, in which each 'round' of expenditures follows the previous one. It could however be interpreted as a logical sequence, in which people need not wait for the previous round to occur, but can predict it. If consumers predict the future rise in their incomes when deciding what to spend, and producers predict the increases in demand when deciding how many people to employ, the whole process of convergence could be speeded up. There is a danger however that if people made mistakes in making these predictions, this could lead to instability.

PROBLEMS

(Worked answers to these are provided below, but the reader is strongly urged to try and do them before referring to these.)

(1) Assume the simple model of equation (6.1), in which

$$(1 - b)Y = A + I.$$

Initially $Y = 800$, $A = 100$, $b = 0.6$ and $I = 220$. The government would like to raise Y to 900; how much extra I does it need to induce by monetary or fiscal policies to bring about this increase? (Assume that $Y = 900$ is feasible.)

(2) Assume the model of equation (6.2), in which

$$[1 - b(1 - t)]Y = A + I + G.$$

Initially $A = 100$, $b = 0.7$, $t = 0.25$, $Y = 800$, $I = 150$ and $G = 130$.
(a) What increase in G is needed to make Y rise to 900 (assuming this to be possible)?
(b) What effect will this have on the budget surplus, defined as $B = tY - G$?
(c) Suppose that *instead* of the method adopted in part (a) the government wants to raise Y to 900 by cutting t; what tax cut is needed?
(d) What effect will (c) have on the budget surplus, defined as in (b)?

WORKED ANSWERS TO PROBLEMS

(1) The model of equation (6.1) has

$$Y = C + I$$
$$C = A + bY$$
$$Y = A + bY + I.$$

Initially $Y = 800$, $A = 100$, $b = 0.6$ and $I = 220$. Check that these are consistent:

$$I = (1 - b)Y - A = (1 - 0.6)(800) - 100$$
$$= (0.4)(800) - 100$$
$$= 320 - 100 = 220.$$

This is what we are told for I. To increase Y to 900 by changing I, holding A and b constant, means

$$I = (0.4)(900) - 100 = 360 - 100 = 260.$$

Thus I needs to rise by 40.

This can be found by the alternative method, that

$$\frac{\partial Y}{\partial I} = \frac{1}{1 - b} = \frac{1}{1 - 0.6} = \frac{1}{0.4} = 2.5$$

so where ΔI indicates a discrete change in I, and ΔY indicates a discrete change in Y (the Δ notation is used when we do not wish to have to stipulate that the change is infinitesimally small),

$$\Delta I = 0.4(\Delta Y) = (0.4)(100) = 40.$$

This uses the multiplier approach to get the same answer.

(2) The model of equation (6.2) has

$$Y = C + I + G$$
$$C = A + b(1 - t)Y$$
$$Y = A + b(1 - t)Y + I + G.$$

Initially $A = 100$, $b = 0.7$, $t = 0.25$, $Y = 800$, $I = 150$ and $G = 130$.

Check that these are consistent:

$$C = 100 + (0.7)(1 - 0.25)(800)$$
$$= 100 + (0.7)(600) = 100 + 420 = 520$$
$$Y = 520 + 150 + 130 = 800$$

which shows the figures are consistent.

(a) What increase in G is required to raise Y to 900?

$$G = [1 - b(1 - t)]Y - A - I$$

$$= [1 - (0.7)(0.75)](900) - 100 - 150$$

$$= (1 - 0.525)(900) - 250$$

$$= 427.5 - 250 = 177.5$$

Originally G was 130, so G needs to increase by 47.5.
Alternatively, using the multiplier formula,

$$\frac{\partial Y}{\partial G} = \frac{1}{1 - b(1 - t)} = \frac{1}{1 - (0.7)(0.75)} = \frac{1}{0.475}$$

So $\Delta G = 0.475(\Delta Y) = 0.475(100) = 47.5$.

(b) What effect will this have on the budget surplus,

$$B = tY - G?$$

Originally, with $t = 0.25$, $Y = 800$ and $G = 130$,

$$B = (0.25)(800) - 130 = 200 - 130 = 70.$$

With $Y = 900$ and $G = 177.5$,

$$B = (0.25)(900) - 177.5 = 225 - 177.5 = 47.5.$$

Thus B falls by 22.5; this is less than the rise in G because the increase in Y increases tax receipts.

(c) The government now seeks to raise Y to 900 by cutting the tax rate t, holding G constant at its original level of 130 (NB: this policy is adopted *instead* of that in part (a)).

From equation (6.2),

$$t = 1 - \frac{Y - A - I - G}{bY}.$$

We can check that this is consistent with the original data:

$$t = 1 - \frac{800 - 100 - 150 - 130}{(0.7)(800)}$$

$$= 1 - \frac{420}{560} = 1 - 0.75 = 0.25$$

If Y rises to 900,

$$t = 1 - \frac{900 - 100 - 150 - 130}{(0.7)(900)}$$

$$= 1 - \frac{520}{630} = 1 - 0.8254 = 0.1746.$$

Thus a tax rate cut to 17.46 per cent is required.

As a check on this answer,

$$Y = C + I + G = A + b(1 - t)Y + I + G$$

$$= 100 + (0.7)(0.8254)(900) + 150 + 130$$

$$= 380 + 520 = 900$$

as required.

(d) The effect of (c) on the budget surplus is given by

$$B = tY - G = (0.1746)(900) - 130$$

$$= 157.14 - 130 = 27.14.$$

Thus the tax cut reduces the budget surplus from 70 to 27.14, i.e. by 42.86.

7. Investment

Investment is the class of expenditures that are designed to give rise not to immediate enjoyment, but to an increased ability to produce in the future. For this chapter we will confine ourselves to expenditures that produce physical man-made means of production. Expenditures on increasing 'human capital', via research and development or education, can be analysed in a similar way, but this is beyond the scope of this book.

Investment, as defined here, has been considerably less stable than other components of total expenditure; can we tell why this is so? We would like to be able to answer a number of questions about investment:

(1) Who invests?
(2) What type of goods do they buy?
(3) How far does investment produce new productive capacity, and how far does it merely replace existing capital goods as they wear out?
(4) What determines the level of investment?
(5) How could investment be stabilized?

WHO INVESTS?

Investment may be carried out by households, by firms, by nationalized industries or by the government. Table 7.1 shows some salient facts about investment in the UK over the eleven years from 1968 to 1978 inclusive.

Over this period 58 per cent of total gross fixed investment has been done by the private sector. Some of this was done by households buying dwellings for owner-occupation, but most of it was

TABLE 7.1   *Gross Fixed Investment at 1975 Prices, 1968–78*

Type of investment	Annual average at 1975 prices £b	Share of total %	Average annual increase %	Standard deviation of annual increase %
Total fixed investment	20.0	100	0.9	2.5
Analysis by sector				
Private	11.6	58	3.4	3.6
Government	5.2	25	4.3	8.3
Public corporations	3.6	17	−0.8	9.2
Analysis by type of asset*				
Vehicles	2.0	10	2.2	7.6
Plant and machinery	6.6	33	2.5	4.5
Other new buildings and works	6.8	34	−0.9	3.4
Dwellings	4.1	20	−0.8	5.9

* Total includes transfer costs of land and buildings, so items add to less than the total.

Source: Blue Book on *National Income and Expenditure, 1979,* Tables 10.2 and 10.5.

done by firms. Twenty-five per cent of gross fixed investment was done by the government, and 17 per cent by nationalized industries, particularly the electricity industry which is very capital-intensive.

WHAT TYPES OF GOODS DID INVESTORS BUY?

We next look at the types of assets that investors purchased, which can be classified as follows.

Vehicles, for use on roads, railways, at sea and in the air, absorbed 10 per cent of gross fixed investment.

Plant and machinery, or 'machines' in a broad sense, including things like computers, assembly lines or cranes, accounted for 33 per cent of gross fixed investment.

Dwellings accounted for 20 per cent of gross fixed investment. Other new buildings and works, including factories, offices, shops, roads and airfields, accounted for 34 per cent of fixed investment.

Besides fixed investment, there is also investment in stocks and work in progress. The stocks consist of unsold finished output, or of unused stocks of fuel, raw materials or components. Work in progress consists of machines, vehicles, buildings or works that have been begun but are not yet ready to be handed over to the ultimate purchaser. This category is very small in size, under 1 per cent of GNP on the average, but is important as a source of instability in total demand because of its extreme volatility.

GROSS AND NET INVESTMENT

A major distinction can be made between investment projects according to whether they involve the creation of new productive capacity, as in the case of a new factory, a motorway or a new hospital, or whether they are necessary to replace existing pieces of equipment that have worn out or become obsolete. The extent of capital consumption, or 'depreciation' of existing capital, is difficult to measure. When existing pieces of capital equipment are 'retired', or physically discarded, e.g. when buildings are actually demolished or machines are scrapped, it is clear that their useful life is over and they have been entirely used up. In many cases however old machines or buildings are not demolished, but are simply left to decay. Because they are inconveniently located, are extravagent in their use of labour, fuel or materials, compared with newer equipment, or are expensive to maintain in working order, they are rarely actually used any more, but are kept in reserve since they might be useful in an emergency. Even when there is a final demolition, a machine, vehicle or building will usually have lost most of its value long before demolition occurs.

There are a number of ways of estimating the gradual loss of their initial value that capital goods suffer during their working lives, through use, or through the mere passage of time. It is possible to 'write down' their value by a constant amount each year, e.g. 10 per cent a year for ten years; this is known as the 'straight line' method of depreciation. Alternatively, a constant percentage of the value remaining at the beginning of each year can be written off during the year; this is known as the 'reducing balance' method. All such methods are to some extent arbitrary.

The matter is further complicated by the fact that, when machines, vehicles or buildings are replaced, they are very rarely replaced with exact replicas of the old ones. The replacement will usually incorporate technical innovations made since the old machine was built. Changes in design may also be made to adapt to changed conditions, which may be economic (as with the effects of the oil crisis on the relative costs of fuel and other inputs) or social (as with more stringent laws about fire and other safety precautions in buildings). It is thus very difficult to assess in practice how much of gross investment should be regarded as replacement.

In spite of all these difficulties, the Central Statistical Office has produced estimates of capital consumption. Over the years 1968–78 the UK economy invested a total of £220b at 1975 prices, of which it is estimated that 51 per cent was required to replace existing capital as it wore out and 49 per cent could be regarded as increasing the capital stock. The record of gross investment, capital consumption and net investment over the period is shown in Table 7.2. Investment is compared with gross national product, since this seems the best measure of total resources to consider in assessing how much of the UK's national income has been put into investing for the future.

Table 7.2 shows that gross fixed investment has changed little as a proportion of gross national product over the period; 20.5 per cent of GNP went into gross fixed investment on the average of 1968–70, and 19 per cent on the average of 1974–78.

Capital consumption has been increasing, both in £b at 1975 prices, because of the continued rise in the capital stock owing to positive net investment each year, and as a percentage of GNP. Capital consumption absorbed 9.3 per cent of GNP on the average of 1968–70, and 10.5 per cent on the average of 1974–78. This increase has been due partly to the steady rise in the ratio of capital to income, and partly to the lag in the rise of real income since 1973.

The result of a slight fall in gross investment relative to GNP and a rise in capital consumption has been a quite marked fall in net investment as a percentage of GNP, from 11.2 per cent on the average of 1968–70 to 8.3 per cent on the average of 1974–78.

THE CAUSES OF INVESTMENT

Because of the variety of agents carrying out investment, and the variety of goods bought, there is room for plenty of variety in its

TABLE 7.2   *Gross Fixed Investment, Capital Consumption and Net Investment,*
1968-78

Year	Gross national product at 1975 prices £b	Gross fixed investment at 1975 prices £b	% of GNP	Capital consumption at 1975 prices £b	% of GNP	Net investment at 1975 prices £b	% of GNP
	(1)	(2)		(3)		(4)	
1968	91.2	18.9	20.7	8.2	9.0	10.6	11.6
1969	92.8	18.9	20.4	8.6	9.2	10.3	11.1
1970	95.0	19.4	20.4	9.1	9.5	10.4	10.9
1971	97.5	19.7	20.2	9.4	9.7	10.3	10.5
1972	99.9	19.8	19.8	9.9	9.9	9.9	9.9
1973	108.6	21.1	19.4	10.2	9.4	10.9	10.0
1974	106.6	20.6	19.4	10.5	9.8	10.1	9.5
1975	104.7	20.5	19.6	11.0	10.5	9.5	9.1
1976	108.9	20.6	18.9	11.4	10.5	9.2	8.4
1977	109.4	20.2	18.4	11.9	10.9	8.3	7.5
1978	113.3	20.5	18.1	12.4	11.0	8.0	7.1
Average 1968-70			20.5		9.3		11.2
Average 1971-73			19.8		9.6		10.2
Average 1974-78			18.9		10.5		8.3
Average 1968-78			19.6		10.0		9.6

Source: Blue Book on *National Income and Expenditure, 1979,* Table 2.1.

causes. When we go on to consider the determinants of investment, it is hard to find any simple answer. There are many reasons for this. First, investment is a process that takes time. Many large investment projects take years of preparation, during which design problems have to be solved, planning permission obtained and finance negotiated. The actual process of construction may then take years. Smaller or simpler projects take somewhat less time, but there is always some lag between the stimulus to investment and the actual expenditures. Thus plans to invest are bound to be based on people's expectations about what capital goods they are going to want in the future, and sometimes in the quite distant future.

The methods used to predict the future vary quite widely between different sectors of the economy, and between different firms within them. In dealing with the future growth of sectors of the economy that already exist, it is possible to observe their past history of growth. In many cases there will be reasons that will make people expect this growth trend not to persist unaltered. For example, a new consumer durable tends to have a fast rate of growth while its use spreads through society, but then slows down once almost every home has got one, so that the demand is mainly for replacement. Expectations are not fully rational; Keynes ascribed most investment to the sheer 'animal spirits' of entrepreneurs. However, while projection of growth trends is known to be unreliable, all the other possible methods of prediction are unreliable too. Thus economists have expected to find that on average the past growth rate of output would affect investment in the same direction; i.e., a high growth record promotes high investment and a low growth record or falls in output promote cuts in investment.

THE ACCELERATOR

This line of argument has given rise to one theory of investment called 'the accelerator', which says that investment at any time will be an increasing function of the past growth rate of demand. Since demand is hard to measure except in so far as it gets reflected in output, the theory usually takes the form that investment will be an increasing function of past changes in output.

In symbols, assuming that the accelerator investment function can be approximated by a linear function, if I_t is investment in period t, and Z_t is the change in output over whatever period before time t is felt to be relevant, the accelerator model of investment predicts that investment will be given by an equation of the form

$$I_t = k + vZ_t$$

where k and v are constants.

When we consider what Z_t should measure, to test this theory, we are left with some difficulties. The level of total output during period t cannot be known at the time when the investment decisions for period t have to be undertaken. If we were dealing with short time periods such as a quarter or a month we would expect to find that the end of the period over which the output change has to be measured came before period t. When we come to deal with annual figures, however, a lot of the facts about 1979's output become known during 1979, so that this lag may be too short to be distinguished in annual figures. When the period of Z_t should start will vary with the industry. If an industry has a long construction period for its investments, and if its output is subject to very large short-period fluctuations, a long averaging period to estimate its normal growth rate is indicated. On the other hand, the use of a very long period may mean missing the effects of changes in techniques or in relative prices happening recently, which may make the prediction misleading. The best period to use will have to be found by trial and error for each industry, and will probably vary between industries. For all these reasons, even if some form of the accelerator function worked for each industry, an investment function based on aggregate figures of output change and of investment over many industries is unlikely to give a very good fit.

In dealing with investment in new industries, there are no past outputs to extrapolate to predict future ones, so other explanations for investment must be sought for.

THE ACCELERATOR AND INVESTMENT: THE FACTS

When we come to look at the facts for investment as a whole, we find that the accelerator model is quite useless as an explanation of what happened. There are however some parts of total investment where it is not too bad, and we shall look at these.

The first case is investment in stocks and work in progress. In the short run, stock changes are a residual, allowing other people's plans to be carried out. When demand rises, some of the initial increase in sales is achieved by running down stocks of finished goods. This will cause the distributors to order replacements, which will cause output to increase. This increase in output will be achieved partly by running down stocks of inputs, which in turn are then reordered. Work in progress necessarily rises, since production of goods has to be started before it can be completed and deliveries can rise. Once the new level of output comes to be expected, holders of stocks of both inputs and outputs will try to replace any stocks they have run down, and to increase their holdings to whatever level is required to give acceptable safety margins at the increased level of output.

If we work on annual figures, this sequence of running down and expanding stocks will not have had time to be completed within a year, so we look for the explanation of stock changes to the increase in output not merely in year t, but also in the previous year. Thus we take the explanatory change in output, Z_t, as

$$Z_t = Y_t - Y_{t-2}$$

where Y_t is the gross domestic product in year t. If S_t is the increase in stocks and work in progress in year t, in £m at 1975 prices, the equation

$$S_t = k + v(Y_t - Y_{t-2})$$

fitted to the years 1959–78 gives values of k and v as shown in

$$S_t = -744 + 0.33(Y_t - Y_{t-2}).$$

This relation explains 85 per cent of the observed variation in stocks and work in progress. Because there was such a lot of variance there to start with, this still leaves substantial errors in prediction of stock-building; the model under-estimates by £411m in 1973, and over-estimates by £752m at 1975 prices in 1972. A more sophisticated accelerator model can do a little better, but not much.

It is clear that the behaviour of stocks and work in progress described here will accentuate any tendency for gross domestic product to grow irregularly, since each unit increase in any other component of GDP will lead within two years to a 0.33 unit rise in stocks, part of which will come from increased imports and part from extra domestic output.

If we try to apply it to fixed investment, the accelerator does a lot less well. Investment in dwellings has a cycle of its own; investment by the social services is a function of government policies; and investment in the oil and gas industries has clearly been made as a consequence of the technical innovations and geographical discoveries that made exploitation of North Sea oil possible. We therefore exclude these sectors from net investment, and consider the net investment figures for the rest of the economy. This includes manufacturing, distribution, transport and construction, i.e. most of the business investment in the economy. This is then compared with past changes in GDP, measuring the changes over the past three years, i.e.

$$Z_t = (Y_t - Y_{t-3}).$$

This gives an investment function of the form

$$I_t = k + v(Y_t - Y_{t-3})$$

which gives a best fit with the figures

$$I_t = 3,043 + 0.18(Y_t - Y_{t-3}).$$

This explains 39 per cent of the observed variations in investment in the sectors concerned.

A much better fit can be obtained using time as a further explanatory variable. The need to include a time trend in a model of this sort usually serves as a warning that the model is not fully explaining what is happening, though time is here probably serving as a proxy for changes in other factors affecting investment, such as the share of profits in national income, tax rates, or monetary conditions. An equation of the form

$$I_t = 3,395 + 0.13(Y_t - Y_{t-3}) - 0.187(t - 1973)$$

explains 90 per cent of the variance in other net investment over the period 1968–78. This is shown in Table 7.3. Column (1) shows three-year changes in GDP, i.e. $(Y_t - Y_{t-3})$, in £b at 1975 prices, for each year. Column (2) shows the actual net investment of the 'rest' of the economy excluding oil, dwellings and social services as explained above. Column (3) gives the value that would have been taken if net investment had been explained by the accelerator model above, modified by inserting a downward time trend in net investment, which improves the fit. Finally, column (4) shows the errors in prediction made by the model, i.e. column (3) − column (2). The model does pick up the fall in investment to 1972, the rise in 1973, the sharp fall after 1974 and the partial recovery in 1978.

What Table 7.3 shows is that, while the accelerator is not a good explanation of investment, it is not completely unrealistic to suppose that people are influenced by past trends in output in their prediction of their future capital requirements.

OTHER FACTORS AFFECTING INVESTMENT

When we look at all the other theories that can be put forward about investment, we can see why there is a lot of scope for any one

TABLE 7.3   *Actual v. 'Accelerator' Investment, 1968–78*

Year	3 years' change in GDP at 1975 prices* £b	Actual net investment at 1975 prices** £b	'Predicted' net investment using accelerator model, at 1975 prices† £b	'Error' = col. (3) − col. (2) (1975 prices)‡ £b
	(1)	(2)	(3)	(4)
1968	7.6	5.0	5.3	0.3
1969	7.1	5.0	5.1	0.0
1970	7.1	5.2	4.9	−0.3
1971	6.1	4.8	4.6	−0.3
1972	7.1	4.2	4.5	0.3
1973	12.8	5.0	5.1	0.1
1974	8.6	4.8	4.3	−0.5
1975	5.2	3.6	3.7	0.1
1976	1.3	2.9	3.0	0.1
1977	4.3	3.2	3.2	0.0
1978	8.7	3.5	3.6	0.1

* Change in GDP at 1975 prices over past three years; i.e., $Z_{68} = GDP_{68} - GDP_{65}$, etc.

** Net fixed investment, i.e., gross fixed investment minus capital consumption, for a set of industry groups excluding petroleum and natural gas, dwellings and social and other public services. The residual group includes manufacturing, distribution, transport and construction.

† The level that col. (2) would take if it had been 'explained' as well as possible by (a) a linear function of col. (1), and (b) a time trend. The need to use the latter shows that something was happening that the model cannot account for.

‡ The difference between actual net investment, col. (2) and the 'prediction' of the accelerator model, col. (3), in £b at 1975 prices (minor discrepancies are due to rounding errors). It is not a very good fit; however it does catch the fall in 1972, the rise in 1973, the sharp fall after 1974 and the partial recovery in 1978.

Source: Blue Book on *National Income and Expenditure, 1979*, Tables 2.1 and 11.8.

simple theory like the accelerator to go wrong. There is not space to explore all the rival theories empirically, though many will be referred to in subsequent chapters.

Other theories of investment include the following.

(1) *Variations in the profitability of current business.* This can affect investment through expectations; if profits now are poor, there is no strict logical reason why low profits should be expected

to occur next year, or in five years time, but there is a psychological connection. If profits now are low, businessmen will tend to be pessimistic about the future and cautious about investment, while if profits now are high they are likely to feel optimistic.

In addition, profits retained by businesses provide a high proportion of the finance for investment. If profits are low, investments may be held back because of a lack of funds to pay for them, however optimistic firms may feel. The connection between profits and investment will be discussed in the next chapter.

(2) *Variations in the ease and cost of getting credit.* This will affect the financing of capital projects, and the prospects for selling the goods that extra capital would enable firms to produce. This will affect many firms, even if they do not currently need to borrow, since if they invest now and then run into financial trouble they may need to borrow later. The effects of variations in monetary conditions will be discussed in detail in Chapter 17.

(3) *Investment in the government sector will be affected by government policy.* The average level of government investment will be based on the government's views on what proportion of the country's income it ought to be spending on public goods such as new roads, schools, hospitals, etc. The exact timing of this average level of government investment will be affected by the government's policies on overall demand management. Net investment in the public sector has been severely cut since 1975. This will be discussed further when we deal with fiscal policy, in Chapter 11.

(4) *The government is also able to influence private investment by changes in the rates and rules of the system of company taxation.* Cuts in taxes on companies will increase the amount companies have to spend, and tax allowances to investors will influence the incentives to invest. These rules have been frequently altered.

(5) *Investment in dwellings will be affected by demographic factors,* such as changes in the growth of total population owing to changes in birth rates, death rates or immigration, and changes in the number of separate households as the consequence of social changes.

(6) *Finally, changes in techniques or in consumer tastes will affect the demand for investment in new industries.* North Sea oil is one spectacular example of this, but similar smaller changes occur in many parts of the economy.

POLICY QUESTIONS

We are left with a number of questions on policies concerning investment:
(1) Do we need more investment for faster growth?
(2) How could we get more investment?
(3) How can investment be stabilized?

The UK economy could clearly increase its income by several percentage points without any appreciable rise in investment; capital has for some years been growing faster than output, and many parts of the present capital stock are under-used. If this growth is to proceed to more than a few per cent, however, investment will be needed to prevent bottlenecks in the availability of particular goods from producing inflation and higher imports, followed by yet another balance of payments crisis. From the past record of industrial investment, however, it appears that a period of faster growth of output would itself lead to additional investment even without any special steps being taken to stimulate it. In the longer run it can be argued that investment is an integral part of the process of growth; if output grows then investment will keep in line.

Some of the possible methods of encouraging investment will be discussed later in the treatment of fiscal and monetary policies. These can be used either to encourage investment, or to restrict it in the interests of stability if its growth is getting too fast. Stabilizing investment does not look like being at all a simple task, because of the variety of factors affecting it and the difficulty of producing reliable forecasts of investment. The accelerator function for stocks does suggest that, if we could succeed in stabilizing the growth of other parts of effective demand a bit, the reaction of stocks would help to smooth total demand a lot more. On the other hand, if mistaken policies were to cause demand to vary more than it has, the reaction of stocks would tend to make instability even worse.

8. Wages and Profits

Wages and profits are the shares of national income going to the two most important factors of production. Wages provide incomes for the majority of the population, and provide the incentives needed to get the country's work done. Profits provide incentives for the private sector of the economy, and are the source of finance for most private sector investment. What happens to wages and profits is therefore of major macroeconomic importance, and we would like to be able to answer the following questions:

(1) How has the share of national income going to labour varied?
(2) How has the share of profits varied?
(3) How are variations in the shares of national income going to different factors connected with the rise in unemployment?
(4) How are the variations in profits related to changes in investment?

THE SHARE OF EMPLOYMENT INCOMES

Table 8.1 shows some facts about employment incomes. The definition of employment incomes used includes both employers' and employees' contributions to national insurance. This is the right concept of employment incomes to use if we want to explain changes in employment, since these contributions are part of the total cost of employing people. Employment incomes in this sense, and including both salaries and wages, are shown in column (1) as a percentage of net domestic product (NDP). NDP is the income concept used here to give maximum comparability with the analysis of the share of profits, which is discussed in the following section. The definition of NDP used here excludes both depreciation of fixed

78

capital, stock appreciation, which is the nominal profit made through the increase in the monetary values put on stocks and work in progress during a period of inflation, and income from abroad.

Table 8.1 shows that the share of labour in the net domestic product was fairly stable up to 1973, varying only between 75.4 and 77.3 per cent of NDP. During the slump after 1974 there has been a marked increase in labour's share; whereas from 1968 to 1973 labour's share averaged 76.4 per cent of NDP, in 1974–78 it averaged 81.5 per cent.

This rise in the aggregate share of labour incomes in NDP could have come about in either of two ways. There could have been a rise in the share of labour incomes in the total value added, i.e. the total

TABLE 8.1   *Share of Employment Incomes in Total Income, 1968–78*

Year	Employment incomes as % of NDP %	Employment income as % of net output in manufacturing	Output gap %
	(1)	(2)	(3)
1968	75.6	77.2	1.0
1969	75.4	78.0	2.2
1970	77.3	81.3	3.1
1971	76.7	81.2	3.4
1972	76.6	80.7	4.8
1973	77.1	82.6	0.0
1974	82.2	95.4	4.2
1975	83.8	92.1	7.8
1976	81.8	91.6	7.2
1977	79.7	87.4	8.6
1978	80.0	87.7	9.1
Average 1968–73	76.4	80.2	2.4
Average 1974–78	81.5	90.9	7.4

Sources Blue Book on *National Income and Expenditure, 1979*; Income from employment, Gross Domestic Product and Capital consumption, Table 1.2; Manufacturing, Income from employment and Gross incomes, Table 3.1; Capital consumption, Table 11.3; Change in value of stocks, Table 12.1 and Real changes in stocks, Table 12.2.

To get Col. (1), Capital consumption was subtracted from GDP to give 'Net Domestic Product' (which the Blue Book does not show), and employment incomes are given in Col. (1) as a % of Net Domestic Product. Col. (2) gives employment incomes in manufacturing as a % of total net incomes in manufacturing, including profits net of capital consumption and stock appreciation. Col. (3) gives the % Output gap, from Table 2.2 above.

factor incomes generated, in particular sectors of the economy. Alternatively, there could have been a shift in the relative size of sectors, away from sectors of the economy where labour's share was relatively low and towards sectors where labour's share was relatively high, including services and government sector activities such as health care, education and administration. As a check on what actually occurred, column (2) of Table 8.1 shows the share of employment incomes in the net value added of the manufacturing sector. It can be seen that labour's share in manufacturing varied between 1968 and 1973 only between 77.2 and 82.6 per cent; labour's share rose after 1974, and its average for 1974–78 was 90.9 per cent, compared with an average of 80.2 per cent between 1968 and 1973. Thus in this very important sector of the economy there was a shift towards labour incomes within the sector, to an even greater extent than in the national figures.

It is of interest to see how the variations in labour's share have been related to variations in the level of output relative to trend. Column (3) of Table 8.1 reproduces the percentage output gap figures of Table 2.2. This is the percentage by which real gross domestic product in each year fell below a 3 per cent growth trend, passing through the 1973 actual GDP. Labour's share tends to be lower in boom years, and higher in slump years. This is in accordance with the observation that unemployment fluctuates in the short run by smaller percentages than output, so that productivity falls relative to trend in slumps and rises in booms.

The Share of Profits

Table 8.2 shows various measures of the share of profits in NNP. Profits, like NNP itself, are measured net of depreciation and stock appreciation. It is argued that it is only on this definition that profits are truly income, in the sense that the owners of firms could in principle consume their profits each year if they chose to without eating into their real capital.

Column (1) shows the net trading profits and rent received by companies. These were falling relative to NNP even before 1973, and fell catastrophically in the slump after 1974, from an average of 9.4 per cent of NNP in 1968–73 to an average of 4.0 per cent of NNP in 1974–78.

Column (2) shows the total profits of the same companies, including those in column (1) but also including income from financial

TABLE 8.2   *Net Profits and Investment, 1968–78*

Year	Net trading profits & rent % of NNP	Companies net income % of NNP	Net trading profits/ fixed assets %	Company taxes/ net profits %	Net investment by companies % of NNP	Output gap %
	(1)	(2)	(3)	(4)	(5)	(6)
1968	10.6	17.6	11.3	27.0	6.0	1.0
1969	10.6	18.3	10.7	27.2	7.2	2.2
1970	9.2	16.9	8.8	24.1	6.8	3.1
1971	9.4	16.8	8.9	19.9	4.6	3.4
1972	9.1	17.0	8.1	21.6	4.6	4.8
1973	7.6	18.1	6.3	26.5	8.2	0.0
1974	3.0	14.2	2.2	20.6	8.2	4.2
1975	2.6	11.3	2.0	20.7	2.8	7.8
1976	3.4	12.9	2.6	24.7	4.9	7.2
1977	5.6	14.4	4.1	24.3	6.3	8.6
1978	5.5	14.5	4.0	28.0	6.1	9.1
Average 1968–73	9.4	17.4	9.0	24.4	6.2	2.4
Average 1974–78	4.0	13.5	3.0	23.7	5.7	7.4

Note Various Blue Book tables used as follows.

Col. (1) gives net trading profits and rent, net of stock appreciation and depreciation, of all companies and financial institutions, from Table 5.3, as % of NNP from Table 1.1.

Col. (2) gives total income of companies and financial institutions, net of stock appreciation and depreciation, from Table 5.3 as % of NNP.

Col. (3) gives net trading profits of companies and financial institutions, from Table 5.3 as % of all fixed assets at current replacement cost held by companies and financial institutions, from Table 11.11.

Col. (4) gives total company UK taxes, from Table 5.1 as % of companies' net income, from Table 5.3.

Col. (5) gives net capital formation by companies, from Table 11.10 and 12.4 as % of NNP.

Col. (6) gives the % output gap from Table 2.2.

Source Blue Book on *National Income and Expenditure, 1979.*

operations and operations overseas. These other profits have held up well, so that the proportional fall in total profits during the slump was very much less severe than for trading profits. They averaged 17.4 per cent of NNP in 1968–73 and 13.5 per cent in 1974–78.

Column (3) shows the net trading profits of companies as a percentage of their total fixed assets. The rate of return has fallen disastrously over the decade, from an average of 9 per cent in 1968–73 to an average of only 3 per cent in 1974–78.

Column (4) shows the total taxes paid by companies as a percentage of net profits. This does not include income tax on distributed profits; though this is paid by the companies direct to the tax authorities, it counts as part of personal taxation. The system of taxation of company profits has been changed considerably during the decade. The effect of the changes was that taxes on profits fell during the slump by a larger proportion than pre-tax profits. It should be noted that they did not have a completely free choice of what to do with their post-tax profits, since the system of tax allowances on investment was so arranged that if they had invested less they would have had to pay a larger tax bill.

Column (5) shows net investment by companies. This includes both net fixed investment and the value of real changes in stocks and work in progress. Net investment by companies fluctuated considerably before 1973, and fell dramatically in the slump, from 8.2 per cent of NNP in 1973 to 2.8 per cent in 1975, when it was lowered by large-scale reductions in stocks. Net investment by companies averaged 6.2 per cent of NNP in 1968–73, varying between 4.6 per cent in 1972 and 8.2 per cent in 1973. In 1974–78 company net investment averaged 5.7 per cent of NNP, and at 6.1 per cent in 1978 it was approximately at the decade average.

Net investment by companies is associated with the share of profits; regressing investment by companies on the share of pre-tax profits in NNP shows that a fall in the share of company pre-tax profits by 1 per cent of NNP is associated with a fall in net investment by companies of about 0.36 per cent of NNP. Only 26 per cent of observed variance in net investment by companies can be explained by variations in profits, which is a very poor fit.

Finally, column (6) shows the percentage output gap. This makes it clear that the share of profits in NNP is related to the output gap; regressing the share of profits in NNP on the percentage output gap shows that the share of profits in NNP falls by about 0.6 per cent of NNP for every 1 per cent increase in the output gap. The relation between the output gap, company pre-tax profits and company net investment is illustrated by Figure 8.1.

It should be noted that the shares of wages and profits in NNP calculated above do not add up to the total of NNP. This is because

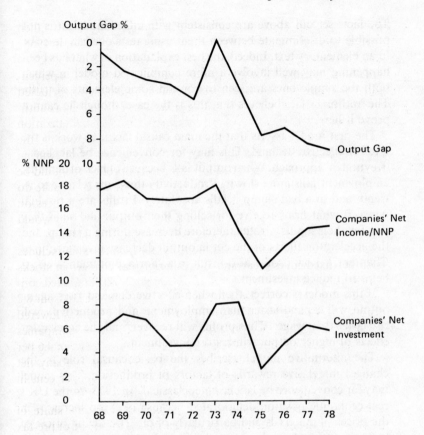

FIGURE 8.1 Companies' net income, net investment by companies and the output gap, 1968–78.

there were other components of income, including government property income, incomes from self-employment and the imputed rents of owner-occupied houses, which do not count as part of either wages or profits. Thus there is no logical necessity that if the share of wages in NNP rises during a slump, the share of profits must fall. In fact, however, these changes do go together.

THE CONNECTION BETWEEN INCOME SHARES AND THE SLUMP

There are at least two possible models of the connection between the slump and the relative income changes that have taken place.

The facts set out above are consistent with either model; it is not possible to discriminate between them using tests one can describe in an elementary text. Indeed, the best explanation of what has been happening may well involve a more complicated model in which both the simple ones are seen to contain some elements of truth. The author in fact believes that this is the case, though he cannot prove it here.

The first model asserts that the main causal factor at work is the level of effective demand. This may for convenience be labelled a 'Keynesian' approach. When output falls because of lack of demand, employment falls more slowly. Productivity thus falls relative to its trend, and in a bad slump it falls absolutely. Profits are a residual between what firms receive for selling their output and what they pay for their inputs. Profits therefore decrease during a slump, and the accelerator effects of the cut in output decrease investment (see Chapter 7). Low profits also result in a shortage of finance which helps to reduce investment.

If this model is correct, then when effective demand rises again, output will expand faster than employment, and productivity will rise faster than wages. Thus profits will recover, and the accelerator effects of higher output will restore investment.

The alternative model ascribes the basic causal role to the changes in relative rewards of factors of production. This model may for convenience be labelled 'neoclassical'. In 1973–74 the UK's real economic position deteriorated because of sharp increases in the prices of materials and particularly of oil. The selling prices of the manufactured goods and services that the UK exports could not be raised in proportion, so the terms of trade deteriorated; i.e., we had to provide more units of our exports for each unit of imported goods. This implies that with unchanged real output the country was several per cent poorer in terms of our ability to buy the goods we wanted to use. This meant that something had to be cut: real government spending was not cut, and the unions refused to recognize that there was any need for part of the real cut to fall on consumption out of labour incomes. The whole burden in the short run therefore fell on profits and investment, to the extent that the real impact was not taken up by allowing the trade balance to worsen, i.e. by keeping up our usage of real goods and services and financing this by borrowing from abroad.

The slump in profit margins made employment less profitable;

this is particularly true of the trading profits of industrial and commercial companies, which account for most private sector employment. If profits were spread evenly throughout industry then a fall in profit margins would have little short-run effect on employment; companies already have their capital in place, and if they are faced with a choice between continuing to operate it on a decreased profit margin and shutting down and making nothing at all they would probably prefer to keep on. They are also motivated by a desire to remain in touch with their customers, so as to be in the market when demand recovers, and by a desire to remain on good terms with their employees.

However, profits are not distributed uniformly between firms, but very unevenly, and they are also distributed unevenly between different parts of the same firm, in the case of conglomerates with sections in different industries. In a boom the lucky or well-run firms make handsome profits and the unlucky or incompetent make mediocre profits. In a slump the better companies make mediocre profits and the worse ones make losses. In some cases, where all parts of a company do badly, the cumulative effects of losses will force them to close down, unless they have enough political pull to get the government to bail them out. In firms with some bad parts, a desire to avoid overall losses will give them an incentive to reduce their labour force in the loss-making sections. Thus in a slump the existing stock of jobs will tend to decline.

In any case the existing pattern of employment is continually getting out of date, under pressure from innovations and from foreign competition. To maintain full employment a continual stream of investment projects leading to new jobs is required. If profits are very low then it is hard for investors to see many opportunities to put their money into ventures where they will not expect to lose it. Thus a slump in profits will lead to a gradual loss of employment opportunities as the less successful existing firms shed workers while others do not expand fast enough to replace the jobs lost. Low profits also cause problems in financing new investment.

If this model is correct, then wage restraint, allowing prices to rise relative to wages, would improve profit margins, leading to more employment and increasing investment, which in turn makes more jobs available when demand expands further.

There is no logical reason why both these models should not have elements of truth in them; both are consistent with the facts examined above concerning income shares, investment and employment changes.

In the long run the shares of wages and profits in total incomes may move either way. Within fairly wide limits a modern capitalist economy can operate with varying rates of profit, provided they are steady enough to be consistent with investors' expectations. In the short run a recovery in output is pretty certain to be associated with a rise in the share of profits in total incomes, and a fall in the share of labour incomes, whatever the causal connection between them.

9. The Government Sector

It is hard to conceive of any advanced economy existing without a government. In the UK, as in most advanced economies, the government plays a major role both in producing and in spending the national income. We shall be interested in examining the following questions concerning this sector:

(1) How large a part does the government play in economic activity?
(2) How does the government get its receipts?
(3) How does it spend them?
(4) How has the government's share in GNP been changing?
(5) What determines the size of the government sector?
(6) Should the government sector get larger, or smaller, or is it currently about right?

THE SIZE OF THE PUBLIC SECTOR

Table 9.1 sets out the size and composition of the government sector in 1977. All the figures are taken from the Blue Book on *National Income and Expenditure, 1979*. The receipts and expenditures shown refer to the whole government sector, including the national government, local government and the National Insurance Fund, but excluding the nationalized industries except for loans and capital grants made to them.

All amounts are shown both in £m, to enable the reader to check the arithmetic, and in £b for indication of orders of magnitude. To compare the importance of various items of government receipts

TABLE 9.1   *Total Government Receipts and Expenditure in 1978**

	£m	£b	% of total government receipts	% of GNP
Government receipts				
Taxes on income	22,321	22.3	31.3	13.7
National insurance contributions	10,023	10.0	14.0	6.2
Taxes on expenditure	23,238	23.2	32.6	14.3
Taxes on capital	898	0.9	1.3	0.6
Total taxes	56,480	56.5	79.2	34.8
Government property income	6,382	6.4	8.9	3.9
Net financial receipts	8,489	8.5	11.9	5.2
Total government receipts	71,351	71.4	100.0	43.9
Government expenditure				
Real goods and services, current	31,654	31.7	44.4	19.5
Grants to personal sector	17,853	17.9	25.0	11.0
Debt interest	7,302	7.3	10.2	4.5
Subsidies	3,598	3.6	5.0	2.2
Grants abroad	1,700	1.7	2.4	1.0
Capital consumption (non-trading)	1,039	1.0	1.5	0.6
Total current	63,146	63.1	88.5	38.9
Real capital formation	4,523	4.5	6.3	2.8
Capital grants and loans	3,682	3.7	5.2	2.3
Total capital	8,205	8.2	11.5	5.1
Total government expenditure	71,351	71.4	100.0	43.9

* 'Government' includes central government, local authorities and the National Insurance Fund; transactions between these are 'netted out'. It exludes public corporations. For comparison, items are shown as a percentage of gross national product at market prices, which was £162,475m in 1978.

Source: Blue Book, *National Income and Expenditure 1979*, Tables 1.1 and 9.1.

and expenditures, they are shown as percentages of total government receipts, and as percentages of the gross national product at market prices. This is chosen as the standard of comparison since it is the widest measure of total national resources available. The market price rather than a factor cost measure is used since the size of the government sector is measured including its receipts from indirect taxes.

Transactions between various levels of government are 'netted out'; for example the central government makes grants both to local authorities and to the National Insurance Fund. These payments do not appear in the table, which shows only dealings between the government sector as a whole and the rest of the economy. The resulting measure of the relative size of the government sector is lower than alternative measures obtained without 'netting out' transactions between various parts of the government sector and then comparing the total with measures of GNP at factor cost. Such methods can produce estimates of the size of the government sector as high as 60 per cent, but these are felt to be misleading.

GOVERNMENT RECEIPTS

The largest category of government receipts in 1978 was from taxes on income (mostly income tax, plus some company taxes). These raised £22.3b, 31.3 per cent of total government receipts, or 13.7 per cent of GNP at market prices. A closely related category was £10.0b of national insurance contributions, from employers and employees. These contributions bear no relation to any possible benefit obtained by employers, and only a hypothetical relation to future benefits to be drawn by employees if they are ever unlucky enough to need them. It is thus probably sensible to regard national insurance contributions simply as an alternative form of taxation of incomes. National insurance contributions brought in 14.0 per cent of total government receipts, or 6.2 per cent of GNP.

The second really large category of government receipts is taxes on expenditure. This includes Value Added Tax, levied on most consumer goods except food, excise taxes on alcohol, tobacco and petrol, and a variety of other taxes including road fund licences for motor vehicles and rates on property levied by local authorities. Taxes on expenditure raised £23.2b, which was 32.6 per cent of government receipts, or 14.3 per cent of GNP.

A final type of taxes is taxes on capital. These have been much altered, and have at various times included estate duties, capital gains taxes, and capital transfer tax. The Blue Book treats these taxes as capital receipts by the government. In many cases, however, the choice between paying income and capital taxation is made by taxpayers to manipulate their tax liabilities, so they are here simply treated as taxes. Their yield was relatively small; £0.9b in 1978, which was 1.3 per cent of government receipts, or 0.6 per cent of GNP.

Total taxes raised were thus £56.5b, which was 79.2 per cent of total government receipts or 34.8 per cent of GNP.

In addition to taxation, the government received quite a substantial income from property it owned, a well-known example being the rent on council houses. The government received £6.4b of gross property incomes in 1978, 8.9 per cent of its total receipts or 3.9 per cent of GNP.

Finally, the government has in most recent years spent more than it could raise in taxes or from its own property income, and the resulting borrowing appears in its accounts as 'net financial receipts'. They are shown net because in any one year the government pays off many loans, and raises others. The amount of 'net financial receipts' is not exactly the same as the much discussed 'public sector borrowing requirement', because it uses a slightly different definition of the public sector, but its economic significance is very similar. In 1978 net financial receipts came to £8.5b, which was 11.9 per cent of total government receipts or 5.2 per cent of GNP.

GOVERNMENT EXPENDITURE

The largest item of government expenditure was 'real current goods and services'. These included spending on defence, health, education and many other public services, which will be discussed in more detail below. In 1978 they took £31.7b, 44.4 per cent of total government spending or 19.5 per cent of GNP.

The next largest item was grants to the personal sector; this includes pensions, unemployment benefits and student grants, and again will be discussed in more detail below. In 1978 grants took £17.9b, 25.0 per cent of government spending or 11.0 per cent of GNP.

Debt interest paid by the central government and local authorities on past borrowing took £7.3b, 10.2 per cent of total government spending or 4.5 per cent of GNP.

Subsidies are used to make certain goods cheaper for consumers than the cost of producing them; housing and some foodstuffs are the main examples. In 1978 subsidies used £3.6b, 5.0 per cent of government spending or 2.2 per cent of GNP.

Grants abroad, i.e. foreign aid to Commonwealth countries and via the United Nations, took £1.7b in 1978, which was 2.4 per cent of government spending or 1.0 per cent of GNP.

Finally, the accounts contain a notional item of £1.0b for capital consumption on non-trading government properties; this was 1.5 per cent of government spending or 0.6 per cent of GNP.

The total current spending of the government sector was thus £63.1b, which was 88.5 per cent of total government spending, or 38.9 per cent of GNP.

Besides its current spending, the government was also responsible for some spending on capital account. 'Real capital formation' includes such items as new council houses, motorways, schools and hospitals. In 1978 this used up £4.5b, 6.3 per cent of government spending or 2.8 per cent of GNP.

Besides investing itself, the government made loans or capital grants to other bodies, mainly nationalized industries. It is open to argument whether some of these loans should be treated as true capital items, since there is a suspicion that some government-financed investments are unlikely ever to prove economic, and are really undertaken to maintain current employment. However, much government-financed investment in the telephone system or the electricity industry, has clearly been economically essential, and the Blue Book's convention of accepting all these capital items as genuine is probably not far from the truth. In 1978 these capital grants and loans absorbed £3.7b, 5.2 per cent of government expenditure or 2.3 per cent of GNP.

Total capital items in the government sector were thus £8.2b, 11.5 per cent of government expenditure or 5.1 per cent of GNP.

CHANGES IN THE PATTERN OF GOVERNMENT RECEIPTS

It is often argued that the level of taxation in the UK has been increasing, is now excessive, and ought to be cut. To comment on the factual part of this set of assertions we make use of Table 9.2. This shows various items of government receipts during each year from 1968 to 1978. Because of some real growth in GNP, and rapid inflation, especially in the later years, the amounts in money terms at current prices are not very illuminating. They have therefore all been expressed as percentages of GNP. The figures for all eleven

TABLE 9.2 *Changes in the Pattern of Government Receipts, 1968–78**

Year	Taxes on income %	National insurance contribs %	Taxes on expenditure %	Taxes on capital %	Total taxes %	Govt property %	Financial receipts %	Total govt receipts %
	(1)	(2)	(3)	(4)	(5)	(6)	(7)	(8)
1968	13.3	4.9	15.5	1.0	34.8	3.7	3.2	41.8
1969	13.8	4.8	16.5	1.3	36.4	3.9	0.0	40.3
1970	14.3	5.2	16.3	1.3	37.1	3.9	−0.6	40.5
1971	13.9	4.9	15.2	1.1	35.1	3.9	1.6	40.6
1972	12.7	5.2	14.5	1.2	33.7	3.8	3.8	41.2
1973	12.5	5.3	13.7	1.2	32.7	3.9	4.6	41.2
1974	14.9	6.0	13.7	1.2	35.7	4.4	6.5	46.6
1975	15.9	6.5	13.5	0.8	36.8	4.2	8.3	49.3
1976	15.1	6.8	13.3	0.7	35.9	4.2	6.7	46.8
1977	14.3	6.7	14.2	0.6	35.8	4.2	3.4	43.4
1978	13.7	6.2	14.3	0.6	34.8	3.9	5.2	43.9
Average 1968–70	13.8	5.0	16.1	1.2	36.1	3.8	0.9	40.9
Average 1971–73	13.0	5.1	14.5	1.2	33.8	3.9	3.3	41.0
Average 1974–78	14.8	6.4	13.8	0.8	35.8	4.2	6.0	46.0
Average 1968–78	14.0	5.7	14.6	1.0	35.3	4.0	3.9	43.2

* All items are shown as percentages of gross national product at current market prices.

Source: As for Table 9.1.

years are shown to bring out the considerable stability of the pattern for most items. To allow for quick description of trends, averages for three groups of year, and for the period as a whole, are shown at the foot of the table.

The groups of years are separated by wider vertical spaces, and correspond to the averages below. The grouping is based on the fact that there were general elections followed by changes of government in 1970 and in February 1974. It can thus be argued that the first and third groups mainly reflect the policies of Labour governments, and the second group reflects the policies of a Conservative government. There is some time lag before any new government's policies can actually be implemented, and in any case many changes reflect not changes of economic policy but the unforeseen results of fluctuations in the economy, such as those following the oil crisis in 1973–74. This view of the grouping of years is thus open to some criticism, but if there is going to be a political criterion for choosing any groups of years this arrangement is probably better than any alternative.

Column (1) of Table 9.2 shows taxes on income. These have fluctuated, with peaks in 1970 and 1975; the second period, from 1971 to 1973, showed a decrease and a slightly lower average than the other periods, but 1978 was close to the average for the decade. The peak in 1975 probably reflects the effect of unprecedentedly rapid inflation pushing people into higher tax brackets, rather than any deliberate policy.

Column (2) shows national insurance contributions. These have shown a steady upward trend.

Column (3) shows taxes on expenditure. These have shown a downward trend, though again 1978 is very close to the decade average.

Column (4) shows taxes on capital. These have been small throughout, and were lowest in the third period. This may well have been due more to the depressed state of the capital market, which lowers receipts from capital gains tax, than to any deliberate policy.

Column (5) shows total taxes; these have been fairly steady, though the second period was 2 per cent lower on average than the others.

Column (6) shows government property income; this has been fairly stable over the period.

Column (7) shows net financial receipts, i.e. government borrowing. This was the only item to show really large changes. In 1970 the government sector was a net lender, repaying its previous borrowings to an extent equal to 0.6 per cent of GNP. Government borrowing then rose rapidly to a peak of 8.3 per cent in 1975, but has more recently been coming down again; 1978 was still above average. This fluctuation in borrowing resulted from the fact that government spending has fluctuated considerably more than government income, from taxes or its own property.

Column (8) shows total government receipts, which are the same as total government spending because they include borrowing. These were very steady for the first two periods, rose very rapidly to a peak in 1975 of almost half GNP, and then fell again sharply. It is arguable that the peak of government spending in 1975 arose partly because of the unexpected decrease in GNP, to which the government sector reacted only after a time lag.

CHANGES IN GOVERNMENT SPENDING

To examine changes in government spending we turn to Tables 9.3 and 9.4.

Table 9.3 shows the main categories of government expenditure for each year from 1968 to 1978, as percentages of GNP.

Column (1) shows expenditure on real goods and services. This was fairly steady over the first two periods, but has been considerably higher in the third. There appear to be two main causes for this. Real spending continued to rise after 1974 when GNP declined; also, a lot of government services, such as health and education, are very labour-intensive, and during the last period wages have been higher relative to other costs than earlier, as seen in Chapter 8.

It is impossible to discuss sensibly whether the increase in the proportion of GNP spent on current goods and services could or should be reversed without seeing in some more detail what goods and services are involved. For some further details we use Table 9.4. The first four columns give the main categories or real goods and services. Column (1) shows military expenditure. This has varied little, and was marginally lowest during the second period.

Column (2) shows expenditure on the National Health Service; this has risen steadily relative to GNP, which may surprise some readers in view of widespread comments on the depressed state of the health service.

Column (3) shows expenditure on education. This rose steadily up to 1975, but has since fallen back. This is mainly due to a relatively generous salary settlement for teachers in 1975, of which the Treasury has since repented. The proportion of GNP spent on education in 1978 was however still considerably above its level in the 1960s.

Column (4) shows 'other' expenditure on real goods and services; these are many and varied, including the police, prisons, roads, parks and Parliament. Between them these have increased substantially.

TABLE 9.3 *Changes in the Pattern of Government Expenditure, 1968–78**

Year	Real goods and services %	Grants to persons %	Sub-sidies %	Debt interest %	Total** current %	Real invest-ment %	Loans and capital grants %	Total capital %	Total govt expen-diture %
	(1)	(2)	(3)	(4)	(5)	(6)	(7)	(8)	(9)
1968	16.9	8.4	2.0	4.1	32.4	5.0	4.3	9.4	41.8
1969	16.4	8.4	1.8	4.1	31.6	4.9	3.9	8.8	40.3
1970	16.9	8.4	1.7	3.9	31.8	4.8	3.9	8.7	40.5
1971	17.1	8.3	1.6	3.6	31.5	4.5	4.5	9.0	40.6
1972	17.7	9.2	1.8	3.6	33.1	4.4	3.8	8.1	41.2
1973	17.4	8.7	1.9	3.7	32.8	5.0	3.4	8.4	41.2
1974	19.1	9.5	3.6	4.3	37.4	5.3	4.0	9.3	46.6
1975	21.3	9.8	3.5	4.0	39.8	4.8	4.7	9.6	49.3
1976	20.7	10.2	2.8	4.3	39.4	4.4	3.0	7.4	46.8
1977	19.8	10.6	2.3	4.5	38.7	3.5	1.2	4.7	43.4
1978	19.5	11.0	2.2	4.5	38.9	2.8	2.3	5.1	43.9
Average 1968–70	16.7	8.4	1.8	4.0	31.9	4.9	4.0	9.0	40.9
Average 1971–73	17.4	8.7	1.8	3.6	32.5	4.6	3.9	8.5	41.0
Average 1974–78	20.1	10.2	2.9	4.3	38.8	4.2	3.0	7.2	46.0
Average 1968–78	18.4	9.3	2.3	4.1	35.2	4.5	3.5	8.0	43.2

* All items are shown as percentages of gross national product at market prices.
** Total current expenditure includes some minor items, so adds to more than the components shown.

Source: As for Table 9.1.

The last two columns of Table 9.4 give some further detail on the composition of grants to persons. Column (5) shows expenditure by the National Insurance Fund on retirement pensions; these have increased steadily over the decade. Column (6) shows payments of unemployment benefit. These were not a large item, being under 0.5 per cent of GNP each year, but show very sharp variations between the 0.22 per cent of the boom year of 1973 and 0.46 per cent in the slump year of 1976. Unemployment benefits do not cover all payments to the unemployed, since many of the unemployed, such as school-leavers, are not insured under the National Insurance Fund,

TABLE 9.4 *Selected Items of Government Expenditure, 1968–78**

	Real goods and services				National insurance fund	
Year	Military %	Health Service %	Education %	Other** %	Pensions %	Unemployment %
	(1)	(2)	(3)	(4)	(5)	(6)
1968	5.4	3.4	3.1	5.0	3.5	0.31
1969	4.8	3.4	3.1	5.1	3.4	0.28
1970	4.7	3.5	3.3	5.4	3.5	0.29
1971	4.7	3.6	3.3	5.6	3.4	0.38
1972	4.7	3.7	3.6	5.7	3.7	0.39
1973	4.6	3.6	3.5	5.7	3.7	0.22
1974	4.8	4.2	3.8	6.4	4.2	0.27
1975	4.9	4.6	4.7	7.2	4.3	0.38
1976	4.9	4.5	4.2	7.1	4.4	0.46
1977	4.8	4.4	4.0	6.6	4.5	0.45
1978	4.6	4.4	4.0	6.5	4.5	0.41
Average 1968–70	5.0	3.4	3.2	5.2	3.5	0.29
Average 1971–73	4.7	3.6	3.5	5.7	3.6	0.33
Average 1974–78	4.8	4.4	4.1	6.8	4.4	0.39
Average 1968–78	4.8	3.9	3.7	6.0	3.9	0.35

* All items are shown as percentage of GNP at market prices.

** Composition of the 'other' category or real goods and services: there are too many of these for a complete list; the largest categories are as follows (each as per cent of GNP in 1978):

Personal social services	0.81	Employment services	0.33
Police	0.80	School meals and milk	0.28
Roads and public lighting	0.59	Water, sewerage and	
Finance and tax collection	0.53	refuse	0.26
Social security (i.e. costs		Parliament and law	
of running it)	0.45	courts	0.23
Miscellaneous local govern-		Parks, etc.	0.23
ment services	0.41	External relations	0.19

Source: Blue Book on *National Income and Expenditure, 1979;* GNP from Table 1.1, cols. (1)–(4) from Table 9.2, cols. (5)–(6) from Table 7.4.

but receive supplementary benefit, which is paid under a different service.

Returning to Table 9.3, column (5) shows total current spending by the government sector. This showed a substantial increase over the decade, from 31.9 per cent of GNP in 1968–70 and 32.5 per cent in 1971–73 to 38.8 per cent in 1974–78.

On the capital expenditures side, column (6) of Table 9.3 shows that government real investment was fairly steady up to 1975, and was cut back sharply during 1977 and 1978. Governments under pressure to decrease their total spending have found capital items easier to cut than current ones, possibly because the government is not the direct employer of many of the people working in the construction and investment goods industries.

Column (7) shows loans and capital grants by the government. These were steady up to 1975, and were cut back sharply in 1976, 1977 and 1978.

Column (8) shows that government capital expenditure, which was fairly steady up to 1973, peaked in 1975 and was sharply cut down in 1976 and 1977.

Column (9) shows total government expenditure. It will be seen that, out of the total cut in government expenditure from 49.3 per cent of GNP in 1975 to 43.9 per cent in 1978, under 1 per cent of GNP was cut from current spending, while total capital spending was halved, from 9.6 per cent to 5.1 per cent of GNP.

SHOULD GOVERNMENT EXPENDITURE BE CUT?

It is clear that the various objects on which government money is spent command very widespread support in modern society. Any individual will doubtless believe some items to be excessive or even unnecessary, but each individual will similarly have some pet scheme that would involve increased spending.

The proper extent, and the exact composition, of government expenditure is necessarily and rightly the subject matter of politics. Serious politicians realize however that major cuts in public expenditure cannot be contemplated lightly. If they involve any reduction in the levels of service that electors have come to expect they are liable to arouse great resentment, both from consumers and from those employed in providing the services. Even improvements in the efficiency with which the same services are provided are liable to be resisted by public employees who are worried about any danger to their security of employment.

When the post-1974 slump comes to an end and the economy starts to catch up on arrears of real growth, there will be a serious choice to be made between raising standards of public provision, and keeping up the percentage of national income used by the government sector, or holding back public services so that the relative size of the public sector can fall and the level of taxation can be reduced. This decision will have to be made through political processes.

THE PUBLIC SECTOR AND STABILIZATION POLICY

Having seen something of how the government raises its revenues and what it does with them, it is possible to ask the question, can this vast body of taxes and public expenditure be used for short-run macroeconomic purposes? How can the government use its vast activities to try to influence the level of activity in the economy as a whole? Such a use of the government sector is called 'fiscal policy', which is the subject of Chapter 11.

10.　Government Debt

As the UK government has not balanced its budget every year, it is now a large debtor. Budget deficits have to be financed by borrowing, and they lead to increases in the size of the total government debt. This gives rise to some questions:

(1) How much has the government had to borrow?
(2) Is the size of the government debt a cause for concern?

THE GROWTH OF GOVERNMENT DEBT

For some of the facts about the growth of government debt we can make use of Table 9.2, which shows the net financial receipts of the government sector each year. These figures are reproduced as column (1) of Table 10.1. This shows that from 1968 to 1978 the government sector was a net borrower in every year except for 1970, when it repaid debt to an extent equal to 0.6 per cent of GNP. On average over these eleven years the government borrowed an amount equal to almost 4 per cent of GNP each year. Government borrowing showed very strong fluctuations, rising from a negative figure in 1970 to 8.3 per cent of GNP in 1975, falling again to 3.4 per cent of GNP in 1977 and rising to 5.2 per cent in 1978.

Before passing any judgement on the wisdom or otherwise of extensive government borrowing, it should be noted than in every year except 1978, even including 1975, the government's borrowing was less than its capital expenditures, as shown in Table 9.3. On the average for eleven years, government borrowing was only half of its capital spending. Provided the capital expenditures were sensible, borrowing half the finance for them would not in itself seem to be strong grounds for criticism.

TABLE 10.1   *Government Debt, 1968–78*

Year	Government borrowing* %	Debt interest* %	Balance of payments on current account*† %
	(1)	(2)	(3)
1968	3.2	4.1	−0.6
1969	0.0	4.1	1.1
1970	−0.6	3.9	1.5
1971	1.6	3.6	2.0
1972	3.8	3.6	0.3
1973	4.6	3.7	−1.2
1974	6.5	4.3	−3.9
1975	8.3	4.0	−1.5
1976	6.7	4.3	−0.7
1977	3.4	4.5	0.2
1978	5.2	4.5	0.6
Average 1968–70	0.9	4.0	0.7
Average 1971–73	3.3	3.6	0.4
Average 1974–78	6.0	4.3	−1.1
Average 1968–78	3.9	4.1	−0.2

* As a percentage of GNP at market prices.
† Negative figures indicate a deficit, i.e. national borrowing from abroad; positive figures a surplus.
Source: Blue Book on *National Income and Expenditure, 1979:* Col. (1) as Table 9.2, col. (2) as Table 9.3, col. (3) from Blue Book Table 1.1 and 1.7.

It is possible to measure the total size of the debt in two ways: securities can be valued at their market prices, or at their redemption prices, i.e. the amount the government will ultimately have to repay. The market method valuation is strongly influenced by changes in interest rates, for security prices fall as interest rates rise. The market value of the total debt varies widely within each year. Redemption value is not of much present importance when the securities concerned are not due for redemption for a long time; in any case some government securities have no definite redemption date.

As both measures of the total volume of debt seem unsatisfactory, and we wish to compare the debt with the current size of the national income, we make use of the proportion of GNP required for debt interest, shown as column (4) of Table 9.3 and reproduced for convenience as column (2) of Table 10.1.

WHY ARE PEOPLE CONCERNED ABOUT GOVERNMENT DEBT?

Many people, including the government itself, are in fact concerned about the growth of the debt. This concern arises from several different sources.

The Interest Burden

If debt increases, interest has to be paid on it. If the increased debt is held by residents of the UK, the interest payments are only transfers of purchasing power between taxpayers and bondholders, and are not a net drain on the economy. However, the more interest the government has to pay out, the higher the taxes it needs to collect. When the level of taxation is already high, it is hard to devise extra taxes that will not create distortions in the economy, as people choose courses of action in order to reduce their tax bill rather than because they are efficient, and that will not create disincentives to working at all. High taxes are believed to be bad for national efficiency, and a high debt is a source of high taxes.

Column (2) of Table 10.1 shows, however, that, in spite of vast government borrowing and high interest rates, debt interest has risen little compared with GNP, though the 4.5 per cent of GNP paid out as debt interest in 1978 was the highest proportion in the decade. The explanation for this relative stability in the real burden of debt interest is that the rapid inflation of the 1970s has greatly reduced the real purchasing power of the interest paid on earlier borrowing. If large-scale government borrowing were to continue while inflation slowed down, then the debt interest could really become a serious problem.

If the government borrows from non-residents, then the payment of interest on the debt will in itself impose real costs on the economy, in addition to the effects of higher tax rates on efficiency.

The Balance of Payments Effects

Although they are both called deficits, the budget deficit of the government and the deficit on current account, or adverse balance of payments of the country as a whole, are entirely different entities, both in their definition and their size. Column (3) of Table 10.1 shows the UK balance of payments on current account each year as a percentage of GNP. Negative figures indicate a deficit, i.e. that the country was spending more on imports of goods and services than it was receiving in payment for exports of goods and services to foreigners. Positive figures indicate a surplus of current receipts over expenditures. The balance of payments will be discussed in more detail in Chapter 24. On the average of the years from 1968 to 1978, the UK payments deficit was equal to 0.2 per cent of GNP, while the government's borrowing averaged 3.9 per cent of GNP.

It is thus a complete fallacy to equate the budget deficit and the foreign payments deficit. They must be distinguished; but it is none the less a fact that they have been quite strongly associated. Regressing the payments deficit as a percentage of GNP on government borrowing as a percentage of GNP shows that over the years from 1967 to 1977 the country's payments deficit tended to worsen by 0.44 per cent of GNP for each increase in government borrowing of 1 per cent of GNP; this accounted for 55 per cent of the observed variance in the external deficit. If time is included as a second explanatory variable, each additional 1 per cent of GNP borrowed by the government corresponded to a worsening by 0.65 per cent of GNP in the current account, 70 per cent of the total variance in the balance of payments being explained.

Thus, while a budget deficit is not itself a payments deficit, they do tend to move together, a rise in government borrowing going with increased national borrowing from abroad. In some cases the government has itself borrowed abroad; in other cases its increased borrowing at home may have made other people borrow abroad.

Monetary Effects of Government Borrowing

When the government borrows from residents this increases the amount of paper assets they hold. Some of these assets may themselves actually be money; others are securities of types that the banks can use as backing for money. When the government has to borrow on a large scale to pay for its expenditures, this makes it difficult to control the growth of the money supply. Other government securities can be sold to raise cash for spending, or they can be used as collateral to enable people to raise loans. A monetary expansion permits total spending to rise, and increases in government debt are thought to play an important part in the monetary causes of inflation. This is discussed further in Chapter 13.

For all these reasons, even economists who have no objection in principle to the government's financing some of its expenditures by borrowing, particularly those of a capital nature, are worried if the extent of government borrowing rises as high as it has done at times over the past decade. This accounts for the importance assigned by the government to keeping down the Public Sector Borrowing Requirement.

11. Fiscal Policy

In this chapter we will consider the interactions between the government sector and the rest of the economy. These may arise in two ways: the government may itself actively initiate changes in its spending or taxing activities, which produce changes elsewhere in the economy; or the government may by its reactions affect the results of changes originating elsewhere.

In each case there will be changes in total incomes, in the balance of trade and in the budget deficit. All of these will be investigated.

CHANGES INITIATED BY THE GOVERNMENT

These can take three forms.

Changes in Real Expenditure on Goods and Services

It is difficult to increase real expenditures quickly because of the planning needed; once projects are under way it is often costly to cancel them. Any cutback in existing spending commitments will provoke political opposition, both among the public who use the service and among government employees who are concerned with job security. Pay increases for public sector employees can be implemented rapidly, but they are unlikely to be adopted for reasons of short-run demand management since they have embarrassing implications for the future when fiscal needs may be different. Thus changes in real expenditures are normally used only on a fairly small scale for short-run purposes.

Changes in Transfer Payments

Where large numbers of recipients are involved, as with pensions, there are some administrative lags in increasing transfers. The main snag with increasing transfer payments for short-run reasons is that there is bound to be political opposition to any reduction in transfers if circumstances change. The only real scope for considerations of demand management to influence transfer payments is in the exact timing of changes, such as increases in pensions, which the Treasury is satisfied that the government can afford on a permanent basis.

Changes in Taxation

This is the method of fiscal policy that is employed most frequently, and on the largest scale. Taxes affect both people's ability and their incentives to spend; for simplicity we will stick to considering the effects on their ability to spend.

Indirect taxes are mostly proportional to spending, as with VAT. A change thus requires altering the marginal tax rate.

Direct taxes are mainly proportional, but only to incomes above some minimum level of tax allowances related to household circumstances, such as the number of dependants, the amount of mortgage interest and the amount of life insurance premiums paid. Direct taxes thus take the form

$$T = t(Y - H) \qquad \text{if} \quad Y > H,$$
$$T = 0 \qquad \text{if} \quad Y < H,$$

where T is the total taxes collected, t the marginal tax rate, Y is income and H is the level of allowances beyond which income tax is payable. There are also some very complex rules for taxing higher incomes at progressively higher marginal rates; these collect little extra revenue and we will for simplicity ignore them.

If the Chancellor of the Exchequer wants to increase people's spending power then he can do this either by lowering the marginal tax rate t, or by increasing the allowances H. Each of these changes raises people's post-tax or disposable incomes. For any given loss of tax revenue, the people with incomes only a little above H will benefit most from a rise in allowances, while people with very high incomes will benefit most from a fall in the tax rate t.

If the Chancellor wants to restrain consumption he can either raise t or cut H, or he can fail to raise H by enough to compensate for the last year's inflation.

How much and how soon people's consumption will adjust when their disposable incomes change will vary. In what follows it will be assumed that lags in the adjustment of consumption can be ignored.

Passive Changes in the Government's Activities

We will now consider what happens to the government's receipts and expenditures when incomes rise elsewhere. We will take first the case where the increases are real, and not simply the result of inflation of prices and wages. If incomes rise in real terms, both direct and indirect tax receipts will rise. Expenditures on unemployment pay and other means-tested benefits will fall. The existence of the government sector therefore helps to limit any changes in incomes due to changes in spending elsewhere in the economy, for example changes in investment or in exports.

This damping down of changes originating elsewhere does not depend on the government taking any positive decisions, but merely on the continued application of the same rules about marginal rates of taxation and entitlement to benefits when incomes alter. This type of stabilizing action is called a 'built-in' stabilizer because it does not require conscious decisions. It thus avoids the various time lags and uncertainties that are introduced whenever decisions are required.

Before any active decision can be taken there is a delay while information, for example about levels of output, employment or the balance of payments, is collected. There is then a need for debate, either in public or within government bodies up to the level of the Cabinet, which takes time and introduces uncertainty about the way the decision will go. Even when the decision is taken, there will then be a further lag before whatever is decided, for example an increase in public works, can actually be carried out.

Thus built-in stabilizers can be distinguished from the use of changes in real expenditures, or in rates of tax or benefits, which require conscious decisions and are known as 'discretionary policies'.

INFLATION AND FISCAL DRAG

All the income changes discussed so far have been real changes. Often however in recent years incomes have risen not because of real changes but because inflation in prices and wages has increased the monetary values of the same set of real transactions.

Many indirect taxes, for example VAT, are fixed in percentage terms, so that their real yield is unaffected by inflation. Many direct taxes, however, especially income tax, are 'progressive', so that the larger a person's income, the larger the percentage of it that they have to pay in tax. With a system in which $T = t(Y - H)$ when $Y > H$, where the level of allowances H is fixed in money terms,

$$T/Y = t[1 - (H/Y)]$$

T/Y rises as Y rises, since (H/Y) falls. When prices and wages rise, more people have incomes above the level where they become liable to tax, and those above this level pay tax on a higher proportion of their incomes. This is accentuated by the taxation of very high incomes at marginal rates above t. The proportion of income collected in tax thus rises with inflation; this is known as 'fiscal drag'.

There are some taxes that are fixed in money terms, for example the road fund licence, and some types of national insurance contribution have upper limits fixed in cash terms. For these taxes the proportion of income collected in tax is decreased by inflation. On the average of all taxes, however, fiscal drag is positive. Every year or two the Chancellor raises tax allowances, and increases lump-sum taxes like the road fund licence, but these changes require discretionary decisions, while fiscal drag is built into the system.

The levels of some tax allowances are indexed to inflation. Any extension of this is likely to be resisted by Chancellors, on the economic grounds that it would remove a relatively easily used tool of discretionary policy, and on the political grounds that raising allowances is one occasion when the Chancellor can be seen to be making concessions to the taxpayers, and he would rather keep the credit for it.

How Stabilizing has the Government Sector Actually Been?

It may well be asked whether the government sector has in fact helped to stabilize the UK economy. Over the period 1968 to 1978 there is no correlation between changes in real government expenditure and changes in the total of other parts of final demand. Total final demand would have been slightly more stable if real government expenditures had simply grown steadily from year to year.

A net stabilizing effect of real government expenditure would require that it varied inversely with the other components of final demand, rising more than usual if they rose less than usual, and vice versa. This would be very difficult to organize since the other elements are so hard to forecast, and we have already seen the difficulties in making short-term changes in real government spending.

Any stabilizing effect of the government sector must therefore be sought on the tax side. It is clear that, if tax rates were kept constant, the government would tend to reduce fluctuations in the rest of the economy by absorbing more leakages when they boomed and less when they slumped. Changes in tax rates and allowances have however been very frequent, and there has been no stable relation between changes in national income and in total tax receipts, in real terms.

Fiscal Policy and the Multiplier

Any change in fiscal policy, whether on the tax or the expenditure side, will have multiplier effects on other parts of the national income, provided only that the economy is not so fully employed as to make the multiplier inapplicable.

The following section examines two examples of this process, using values of parameters which, while they have not actually been fitted statistically, do seem to be of plausible orders of magnitude for the modern UK economy.

The method used is to take a change in fiscal policy, and trace its effects round the economy. Both examples work in units of £m. Unstarred symbols represent changes at the first round of the multiplier, and starred symbols represent the effects of adding up all the rounds. We choose an initial change of £100m, because this seems to be a realistic maximum for any actual current change on the real expenditure side; large programmes of 'cuts' usually refer to what the government merely promises not to start spending in some years' time. Model A will consider a £100m tax cut, assumed to be effected by raising allowances so that the marginal tax rate is unchanged. Model B will consider a £100m rise in real expenditure.

Model A: Tax Cuts

The immediate effect of the £100m tax cut is a rise in disposable incomes, denoted by $D = 100$ (£m signs will be omitted throughout). D has to be split between savings and consumption. With a marginal propensity to save of 0.2 and a marginal propensity to consume of 0.8, private savings rise by $S = 20$ and consumption rises by $C = 80$.

The rise in consumption has three effects: a rise in indirect taxes, V; a rise in imports, M; and a rise in the domestic output of goods and services, and thus of the factor incomes of their producers, F. If the marginal rate of indirect taxes is 0.15, $V = (0.15)(80) = 12$. If the marginal propensity to import is 0.3, imports rise by $M = (0.3) \times (80) = 24$. Thus factor incomes rise by

$$F = C - V - M = 80 - 12 - 24 = 44.$$

The rise in factor incomes has three effects: a rise in direct tax receipts, T; a fall in payments of unemployment benefit and other means-tested transfer payments, U; and a rise in disposable incomes, D'. This rise in disposable incomes is labelled D' to distinguish it from the original rise in disposable incomes owing to the tax cut with which we started. If the marginal direct tax rate, including national insurance contributions, is 0.3, the rise in direct taxes is $T = (0.3)(44) = 13.2$. If payments of unemployment and related benefits falls by 0.2 for every unit increase in factor incomes, $U = -(0.2)(44) = -8.8$. The rise in disposable incomes arising from this round of the multiplier is thus

$$D' = F - T + U = 44 - 13.2 - 8.8 = 22.$$

We have now got back to disposable incomes again, with $D' = (0.22)D$. We could continue to go round the multiplier process, with each round 0.22 times the round before, or we can cut the process short by using the multiplier formula (see Chapter 6),

$$D^* = (1 + 0.22 + 0.22^2 + 0.22^3 + \cdots)D$$

$$= \frac{D}{1 - 0.22} = \frac{D}{0.78} = (1.282)D$$

The change in each element of the national income will thus eventually be 1.282 times its change at the first round of the multiplier. Using * to distinguish these final states, we have

D^* = total rise in disposable incomes

= (1.282)(100)

= 128.2.

S^* = total rise in private savings

= (1.282)(20)

= 25.64.

C^* = total rise in consumption

= (1.282)(80)

= 102.56.

V^* = total rise in indirect taxes

= (1.282)(12)

= 15.38.

M^* = total rise in imports

= (1.282)(24)

= 30.77.

F^* = total rise in factor incomes and output

= (1.282)(44)

= 56.41.

Check: $F^* = C^* - V^* - M^*$

$\qquad = 102.56 - 15.38 - 30.77$

$\qquad = 56.41.$

$\qquad U^* = $ total change in transfers to the unemployed

$\qquad\quad = -(1.282)(8.8)$

$\qquad\quad = -11.28.$

T^* and D^* include the original tax cut of 100.

$T^* = $ total rise in direct taxes

$\quad = -100 + (1.282)(13.2)$

$\quad = -83.08.$

Check: $D^* = F^* - T^* + U^*$

$\qquad = 56.41 + 83.08 - 11.28$

$\qquad = 128.2.$

We can check these results for consistency. In this model investment and exports are assumed not to change, nor does government expenditure apart from transfers, U^*. Applying the test that for equilibrium total leakages equal total injections,

$$\text{leakages} = S^* + M^* + T^* + V^*$$
$$= 25.64 + 30.77 - 83.08 + 15.38 = -11.28$$
$$\text{injections} = U^* = -11.28.$$

As the result of all these changes, the budget deficit rises by

$$U^* - (T^* + V^*) = -11.28 + 83.08 - 15.38$$
$$= 56.42.$$

The foreign trade deficit rises by $M^* = 30.77$.

Whether the government is able to undertake an expansionary fiscal policy on the lines of model A depends on whether it can allow these results.

Model B: Real Expenditure

We now consider the effects of a rise of £100m in real government expenditure. It is assumed for simplicity that the expenditure is measured net of any indirect taxes, and has no direct import content; these could be allowed for if desired. All the parameters of the economy are assumed to be the same as in model A; the only difference is that the government's injection of 100 enters the economy at a different point, buying real domestic output and increasing factor incomes by $F = 100$ at the first round.

When $F = 100$, direct taxes rise by $T = 30$ and payments of unemployment and other benefits fall, so $U = -20$. The rise in disposable incomes is thus given by

$$D = F - T + U = 100 - 30 - 20 = 50.$$

The rise in disposable incomes leads to a rise in private savings, $S = (0.2)(50) = 10$, and a rise in consumption of $C = (0.8)(50) = 40$.

The rise in consumption gives an increase of indirect taxes of $V = (0.15)(40) = 6$, and a rise in imports of $M = (0.3)(40) = 12$.

Thus we get a further rise in factor incomes of $F' = C - V - M = 40 - 6 - 12 = 22$.

We are thus round to factor incomes again, and can go round the multiplier process again with each element in income 0.22 times its size in the round before. Alternatively, we again apply the multiplier formula, and find the final level of the rise in each element of income by multiplying its rise in the first round by $1/(1 - 0.22) = 1.282$.

$F^* =$ total rise in factor incomes and output

$\quad = (1.282)(100)$

$\quad = 128.2.$

$D^* =$ total rise in disposable incomes

$\quad = (1.282)(50)$

$\quad = 64.1.$

$S^* =$ total rise in private savings

$\quad = (1.282)(10)$

$\quad = 12.82.$

C^* = total rise in consumption

$\quad = (1.282)(40)$

$\quad = 51.28.$

V^* = total rise in indirect taxes

$\quad = (1.282)(6)$

$\quad = 7.69.$

M^* = total rise in imports

$\quad = (1.282)(12)$

$\quad = 15.38.$

T^* = total rise in direct taxes

$\quad = (1.282)(30)$

$\quad = 38.46.$

U^* = total change in transfers

$\quad = -(1.282)(20)$

$\quad = -25.64.$

Applying our check for consistency,

$$\text{injections} = 100 + U^* = 100 - 25.64 = 74.36$$
$$\text{leakages} = S^* + M^* + T^* + V^*$$
$$= 12.82 + 15.38 + 38.46 + 7.69 = 74.36$$

so the results are consistent.

The budget deficit will rise by

$$100 + U^* - T^* - V^* = 100 - 25.64 - 38.46 - 7.69$$
$$= 28.21.$$

The foreign trade deficit will rise by $M^* = 15.38$.

Whether the government is able to undertake policy B depends whether it can allow these results.

LAGS IN THE MULTIPLIER PROCESS

Note that, in the fairly realistic models considered here, the eventual result is in fact approached quite closely in the first few rounds of the multiplier. The variables directly affected by government action, that is D in model A and F in model B, reach 78 per cent of their eventual value at the first round. Each further round covers 78 per cent of the distance still to go, so that each variable attains 95 per cent of its eventual change at the second round and 99 per cent at the third round. This type of rapid convergence will be found for any multiplier process involving parameters that are realistic for a modern economy.

PROBLEMS

(1) *Either*: Work out the result of policy A, a £100m tax cut, and policy B, a £100m rise in real expenditure, on an economy with the following characteristics.

(The results should include the effects on factor incomes, disposable incomes, consumption, the budget deficit and the foreign trade deficit. Worked answers are provided below, but the reader is urged to do the problems himself and check them for consistency before consulting the answers section.)

s = marginal private propensity to save out of disposable income

= 0.3

m = marginal propensity to import out of consumption spending

= 0.05

v = marginal indirect tax rate on consumption

= 0.10

t = marginal direct tax rate on factor incomes

= 0.35.

u = marginal change in transfers as factor incomes rise

= −0.3

(2) *Or* If you do not like these parameters, work the model through using ones you prefer.

WORKED ANSWERS TO PROBLEMS

Policy A

A £100m tax cut gives $D = 100$

$$s = 0.3 \quad \text{so } S = 30$$

$$c = 0.7 \quad \text{so } C = 70$$

$$m = 0.05 \text{ so } M = 3.5$$

$$v = 0.1 \quad \text{so } V = 7.$$

Factor incomes thus rise by

$$F = C - V - M = 70 - 7 - 3.5 = 59.5$$

$$t = 0.35 \text{ so } \quad T = (0.35)(59.5) = 20.82$$

$$u = -0.3 \text{ so } \quad U = -(0.3)(59.5) = -17.85.$$

The further rise in disposable income is thus

$$D' = F - T + U = 59.5 - 20.82 - 17.85 = 20.83.$$

$$D' = (0.2083)D$$

so the multiplier is given by

$$D^* = (1 + 0.2083 + 0.2083^2 + \cdots)D$$

thus

$$D^* = \frac{D}{1 - 0.2083} = \frac{D}{0.7917} = (1.2631)D.$$

Total changes are given by

$$D^* = (1.2631)(100) \qquad\qquad = 126.31$$

$$S^* = (1.2631)(30) \qquad\qquad = 37.89$$

$$C^* = (1.2631)(70) \qquad\qquad = 88.42$$

$$M^* = (1.2631)(3.5) \qquad\qquad = 4.42$$

$$V^* = (1.2631)(7) \qquad\qquad = 8.84$$

$$F^* = (1.2631)(59.5) \qquad\qquad = 75.15$$

$$U^* = -(1.2631)(17.85) \qquad = -22.55$$

$$T^* = -100 + (1.2631)(20.82) = -100 + 26.3$$

$$= -73.7.$$

Check:

$$\text{injections} = U^* = -22.55.$$

$$\text{leakages} = S^* + M^* + V^* + T^*$$

$$= 37.89 + 4.42 + 8.84 - 73.7$$

$$= -22.55.$$

The budget deficit rises by

$$U^* - T^* - V^* = -22.55 + 73.7 - 8.84 = 42.31.$$

The external trade deficit rises by $M^* = 4.42$.

Policy B

£100m of government expenditure on real domestic product raises factor incomes by $F = 100$.

$$t = 0.35 \quad \text{so } T = 35$$

$$u = -0.3 \text{ so } U = -30.$$

Disposable incomes thus rise by

$$D = F - T + U = 100 - 35 - 30 = 35$$
$$s = 0.3 \text{ so } S = (0.3)(35) = 10.5$$
$$c = 0.7 \text{ so } C = (0.7)(35) = 24.5$$
$$v = 0.1 \text{ so } V = 2.45$$
$$m = 0.05 \text{ so } M = 1.22.$$

Thus the next round of increases in factor incomes is

$$F' = C - V - M = 24.5 - 2.45 - 1.22 = 20.83.$$

Again, this is 0.2083 times the previous round, so the multiplier is $1/(1 - 0.2083) = 1.2631$. Thus

$$F^* = 126.31$$
$$T^* = (0.35)(126.31) = 44.21$$
$$U^* = -(0.3)(126.31) = -37.89$$
$$D^* = (0.35)(126.31) = 44.21$$
$$S^* = (0.3)(44.21) = 13.26$$
$$C^* = (0.7)(44.21) = 30.95$$
$$M^* = (0.05)(30.95) = 1.55$$
$$V^* = (0.1)(30.95) = 3.09.$$

Check:

$$\text{injections} = 100 + U^* = 100 - 37.89 = 62.11.$$
$$\text{leakages} = S^* + M^* + T^* + V^*$$
$$= 13.26 + 1.55 + 44.21 + 3.09 = 62.11.$$

The budget deficit rises by

$$100 + U^* - T^* - V^* = 100 - 37.89 - 44.21 - 3.09$$
$$= 14.81.$$

The foreign trade deficit rises by $M^* = 1.55$.

12. Money

Money plays a central role in the network of transactions that make up the modern economy. Many economists believe that an unsatisfactory monetary system can hinder the attainment of high and stable levels of activity, and that sensible monetary policies could give substantial help in achieving economic stability.

This chapter will consider some elementary facts and theories about money. There follow chapters on the quantity of money, banks, a model of the whole economy incorporating a monetary sector, a discussion of non-bank financial intermediaries in the UK economy, and finally a chapter on monetary policy.

First we consider some basic questions about money:
(1) What is money?
(2) Why hold money?
(3) What are the functions of money?
(4) How much money is it worth-while holding?
(5) How much money have people in the UK been holding?

WHAT IS MONEY?

Money is anything that is generally accepted as a means of making payments. It could consist of something that is itself of value apart from its monetary use, such as gold or silver; but in a modern economy money is mostly paper, or exists only as book entries in bank ledgers.

The definition of money can be tightly or loosely drawn. Two definitions in particular will be used here. Cash is defined as notes and coin held by members of the public, including both firms and individuals but excluding banks. M1 is the total of notes and coin in

118

circulation with the public, plus sterling demand bank deposits held by the private sector. Demand deposits, or current accounts, are deposits with banks that can be withdrawn on demand, without any requirement to give notice. There are other, wider, definitions of money, including for example deposit accounts, i.e. accounts where withdrawal requires written notice an agreed period in advance, or non-sterling deposits. M3 is a commonly used wider definition of money; it includes notes and coin in circulation with the public, plus all sterling and other currency deposits held by UK residents, including bank deposits held by the public sector. There is no limit to the number of possible wider definitions of money, including various types of 'near money' such as deposits with building societies or with the Trustee Savings Bank. The argument for the M1 definition is that it includes the main types of money that can actually be used for making payments.

It should be noted that, whereas in everyday language 'money' is frequently used as a synonym for wealth in general, this usage is not employed here. Money in this book, as in most economics texts, means a particular form of asset. A person with assets in the form of diamonds, land or equity shares may well be worth a lot of money, but these assets are not themselves money.

WHY HOLD MONEY?

Money, considered as an asset, has two clear disadvantages: it yields no income, and it loses its real purchasing power over time through inflation.

The advantages of money as an asset are convenience and safety. These give rise to the transactions motive for holding money. Most transactions in the economy are settled in money; even when credit is used, money is generally used later when paying off the loans. Everybody thus finds it convenient to hold some money. By a careful arrangement of the timing of transactions, any individual can reduce the average amount of money he needs to hold to a low level, but the cost in convenience is considerable. This is accentuated by uncertainty; firms and individuals are unable to forecast their transactions perfectly.

Holding money assists in coping with emergencies. This gives rise to the precautionary motive for holding money. Individuals may fall sick, lose or break their possessions or need to move house. Firms may have to cope with a sudden need for the repair or replacement of equipment, sudden rises in the prices of their inputs or delays in payment by their customers. Money holdings help to reduce the cost and inconvenience caused by such emergencies. Money holdings also allow people to take advantage of unforeseen opportunities, such as a chance to buy goods at bargain prices for cash down.

It should be noted that if you lend money to somebody else the interest received will normally be subject to income tax, but if you hold the money yourself and take your reward in the form of increased convenience and safety, and decreased trouble and worry, these benefits are tax-free.

THE FUNCTIONS OF MONEY

Money has several functions; notably, it is used as a medium of exchange, a store of value and a unit of account.

A Medium of Exchange

Most transactions in a modern economy are settled in money. There are generally several transactions for each unit of income; the services of most factors of production are sold to firms, and most final products are sold to customers. The parts of income that do not require a monetary transaction, such as the use of an owner-occupied dwelling, are exceptional and account for only a small percentage of total income. Most firms also buy large quantities of intermediate goods, i.e. fuels, materials and professional services, which all add to their transactions. The level of money transactions in the economy each year is thus several times the national income.

For some transactions there is a legal requirement that settlement be made in types of money specified by law, and known as 'legal tender'; weekly wage-earners for example have to be paid in legal tender. The denominations of notes or coin that are legal tender for any transaction will depend on the value of payment to be made. Creditors are entitled to demand payment in legal tender, but will usually prefer to receive payment in a more convenient form, e.g. by cheques drawn on a bank account. If a debtor offers payment in legal tender and the offer is refused, he cannot then be sued for failure to pay up on time.

A cheque is a written instruction to a bank to transfer a stated amount of a deposit kept with it to somebody else, usually the person named on the cheque. Though cheques are used in the majority of transactions, they are not themselves money. A bank deposit is money, but a cheque is not, because there is no guarantee to the person who is offered a cheque that there will be money in the account to meet it.

There is no logical reason why the cheques of very famous people or firms, e.g. ICI, should not circulate in the same way as banknotes, though in fact they do not. The actual circulation is left in England to notes issued by the Bank of England, and coins issued by the Royal Mint. (Scotland and Ireland have special arrangements about note circulation which will not be discussed here.)

A Store of Value

In many transactions the parties do not carry out their sides of the bargain simultaneously. Goods are sold on credit, work for employers is done before being paid for, and loans specify the amount of interest and redemption payments to be made in terms of money. In all of these transactions a deferred payment is being made, the amount to be paid being specified in terms of money.

Also, people work for others, or hire their property to others, for payment in money, which they can use when they choose to consume or buy other assets. In real terms the consumption is a payment for the work done, but it does not have to happen at the same time. Money is thus used to allow the timing of income and expenditure to be independent. Because money is used as a standard of deferred payment and is held as an asset, stability of its value is of great importance.

A Unit of Account

Money is used as a unit of measurement in drawing up accounts by three groups of people. The managers of a business use accounts of the values of sales and purchases in terms of money when taking decisions concerning output, employment and investment. Accountants use monetary values to audit the accounts of businesses, i.e. to try to check that the accounts give a true and fair account of what the business is really worth.

Having reliable accounts is of great importance to people who are considering lending a business money, or supplying it with goods on credit. Finally, the tax authorities use money in valuing the profits or losses of a business to assess how much it is liable to pay in taxes. All these functions of money as a unit of account make it very important that it should have a reasonably stable value; they do not however provide any motive for holding money.

How Much Money Is it Worth-while Holding?

The transactions and precautionary motives for holding money are mainly related to the money incomes of individuals and to the money value of the turnover of firms. They are also related to the expected level of turnover on capital markets. Thus demand for money is expected to be approximately proportional to total money incomes.

There are however other factors that could change the desired ratio of money holdings to incomes. If credit is expected to be readily available, there is little point in holding money, but if credit is expected to be difficult to get then the motive for holding money is strengthened. A high degree of uncertainty about the outlook for business also makes for greater money holdings.

The rate of interest measures the opportunity cost of holding money rather than lending it to somebody else; the higher the rate of interest, the less money it is worth-while holding.

All these influences refer to the transactions and precautionary demand for money. It is also possible that the demand for money holdings will be influenced by changes affecting the attractiveness of money as a store of value.

The Speculative Motive

One such influence is a change in expectations about interest rates. If interest rates are expected to fall, security prices will be expected to rise, which will give capital gains to holders of securities that will not be made by holders of money. Conversely, if interest rates are expected to rise and security prices to fall, this makes money relatively more attractive as a store of value since those holding securities will suffer capital losses that holders of money will avoid. The dependence of willingness to hold money on the way in which security prices are expected to move is known as the 'speculative motive'.

SECURITY PRICES AND INTEREST RATES

The reason why security prices move inversely with interest rates is that the market price of an existing security with a given yield must be the same as that of a newly issued security with the same yield. If interest rates fall, the yield on newly issued securities will fall, so old securities with unchanged yields increase in value.

In mathematical terms, suppose Z is the annual interest on a security, with the first payment due in one year's time, V is its market value and r is the interest rate. The present value of Z in one year's time is $Z/(1 + r)$. The present value of the Z due in two years' time is $Z/(1 + r)^2$. The present value of a stream of payments going on for ever is given by

$$V = \frac{Z}{1 + r} + \frac{Z}{(1 + r)^2} + \frac{Z}{(1 + r)^3} + \cdots = \frac{Z}{r}.$$

Thus if r rises, V falls, and vice versa.

ARE THERE 'TRANSACTIONS' AND 'SPECULATIVE' BALANCES?

It is not sensible to regard money holdings as being divided into two distinct parts, 'transactions balances' and 'speculative balances'. So long as money is held it is an asset, regardless of the motives for holding it, and it can be used for transactions, which are indeed the only way of getting rid of it. Thus there are no separate speculative balances. If security prices are expected to rise people will be tempted to hold less money than they would normally want, given their transactions, taking some increased risks of being left short of money in an emergency for the sake of the capital gains they can make by holding more securities. If security prices are expected to fall people will be tempted to hold more money than they would normally want, because the loss of interest and low gain in convenience from holding extra money when they have a lot already is more than compensated for by the reduced expectation of capital losses.

The second factor affecting the demand for money as a store of value is the expected rate of inflation. If rapid inflation is expected, this means that the purchasing power of money over real goods and services will be reduced; this makes money relatively unattractive as an asset, and capital goods or stocks of commodities more attractive. If goods prices were expected to fall, this would make money relatively more attractive since its purchasing power would be increasing.

How Much Money Have People Been Holding?

Table 12.1 shows some of the facts about holdings of money balances in the UK from 1968 to 1978. Column (1) shows the GNP, in £b at current market prices each year; we assume that the amount of transactions is roughly proportional to GNP.

Column (2) shows the level of M1, i.e. the public's holdings of notes and coin plus current account bank deposits, in £b, average of figures at the end of each quarter.

Column (3) shows the level of notes and coin held by the public, which was included in (2), in £b, average of figures at the end of each quarter.

Column (4) shows M1 as a percentage of GNP. This has fallen somewhat over the decade, from 18.2 per cent in 1968–70 to 15.0 per cent in 1976, though it recovered slightly to 15.8 per cent in 1978.

Column (5) shows the public's holdings of notes and coin as a percentage of GNP. This too has been falling, from 6.3 per cent in 1968–70 to 5.3 per cent in 1974–78.

Column (6) looks at the composition of the money supply, giving notes and coin held by the public as a percentage of M1. This has been fairly stable, varying only between a minimum of 32.8 and a maximum of 35.4 per cent. This shows that people's monetary habits are fairly stable.

TABLE 12.1   *Money in Britain, 1968–78*

Year	GNP £b	M1 £b	Notes and coin £b	M1 % of GNP	Notes and coin % of GNP	Notes and coin % of M1	Treasury bill rate %	Rate of inflation %
	(1)	(2)	(3)	(4)	(5)	(6)	(7)	(8)
1968	43.8	8.5	2.9	19.3	6.5	33.8	7.0	3.0
1969	47.1	8.4	2.9	17.9	6.2	34.7	7.6	3.7
1970	51.6	9.0	3.1	17.5	6.1	35.0	7.0	7.5
1971	57.8	10.2	3.4	17.7	5.9	33.7	5.6	10.9
1972	63.8	11.9	3.9	18.6	6.1	32.8	5.5	9.8
1973	74.1	12.9	4.3	17.4	5.8	33.3	9.3	7.5
1974	84.0	13.5	4.8	16.1	5.7	35.4	11.4	17.1
1975	104.7	16.2*	5.5	15.5*	5.2	33.8*	10.2	27.3
1976	124.6	18.7	6.3	15.0	5.1	33.8	11.1	13.7
1977	142.3	21.4	7.2	15.0	5.1	33.7	7.7	11.9
1978	162.5	25.7	8.4	15.8	5.2	32.8	8.5	10.7
Average 1968–70				18.2	6.3	34.5	7.2	4.7
Average 1971–73				17.9	5.9	33.2	6.8	9.4
Average 1974–78				15.5	5.3	33.9	9.8	16.1
Average 1968–78				16.9	5.7	33.9	8.3	11.2

* The method of calculating M1 used by the Bank of England was changed in 1975; at the time this change made a 4.8 per cent increase.

Notes: GNP, £b at current market prices. M1 = public's holdings of notes and coin plus current banking accounts in sterling, average of figures at the end of each quarter. Notes and coin in hands of the public, £b, average of estimated amount at the end of each quarter. Treasury bill rate, weekly average. Inflation is measured by percentage rise over previous year in the GDP deflator, as in Table 2.2.

Sources: For GNP and inflation, as in Table 2.2. For Notes and coin, M1 and Treasury Bill Rate, *Bank of England Quarterly Bulletin*, December 1979.

Columns (7) and (8) show measures of two factors that could have affected the demand for money. Column (7) shows the rate of interest on Treasury bills, a form of government borrowing for three months at a time, giving the average rate during each year. Treasury bill rate was 7.0 per cent on average from 1968 to 1973, and was very much higher in 1974–78, with an average of 9.8 per cent, though 1978 was very close to the decade average.

Column (8) shows the rate of inflation, as measured by the price deflator for GNP (see Table 2.2). This gives the actual rate of inflation; the rate relevant to the incentive to hold money is the expected rate. This was probably not exactly the same as the actual rate in each year, but on the assumption that people learn by experience expected rates of inflation must have been much higher during the period 1974–78 when the actual inflation rate averaged 16.1 per cent than they were during 1968–70 when the actual inflation rate averaged 4.7 per cent.

Thus both the rate of interest and the rate of inflation were much larger during 1974–76 than they had been earlier in the decade, and the proportions of M1 and notes and coin to GNP were appreciably lower. In 1978 both the Treasury bill rate and the rate of inflation showed a considerable reduction towards the previous levels, while the ratios of M1 and notes and coin to GNP recovered slightly. If one fits an equation giving (M1/GNP) as a linear function of the rate of inflation and Treasury Bill Rate, the equation

$$(M1/GNP) = 20.67\% - 0.095(\text{inflation}) - 0.328(\text{TBR})$$

explains 66 percent of the total variance in (M1/GNP).

The facts are thus consistent with the view that the ratio of money holdings to GNP would be a decreasing function of both interest rates and the rate of inflation. However the movements in the M1 and notes and coin to GNP ratios are quite small compared with the very large changes in interest rates and rates of inflation during the decade. It thus appears that the demand for money balances was a fairly stable function of the level of money incomes.

MONETARY POLICY

The stability of the relation between the money supply and national income provides the basis for an analysis of the ways in which monetary policy can be used to influence the real working of the economy. Before we can go to this, however, we need to consider both the economic theory of money and the working of the monetary institutions in the UK in more detail. Chapter 13 will deal with the quantity of money, Chapter 14 with banks, Chapter 15 with a model of the economy incorporating a monetary sector, Chapter 16 with some of the more important non-bank financial intermediaries; and finally, Chapter 17 will deal with monetary policy.

13. The Quantity of Money

It has long been believed that if the quantity of money changes this will have important effects. In this chapter we will consider how these come about, attempting to answer the following questions:
(1) How does the quantity of money change?
(2) How does the demand for money change?
(3) What happens if people have more or less money than they want to hold?

CHANGES IN THE QUANTITY OF MONEY

The quantity of money can change through three causes.

(1) The government's fiscal actions can affect the quantity of money. If the government borrows newly created money from the banking system and puts it into circulation by spending it, then leakages into taxation will bring some of it back to the government; leakages into imports will cause the foreign rather than the domestic money supply to increase; but leakages into savings will leave somebody in the economy holding more money.

(2) If the balance of payments with the rest of the world is in surplus, including both the current account balance and any net foreign borrowing, which for this purpose can best be regarded as sales of securities to foreigners, then the money supply will tend to rise.

(3) The rules of the banking system may be changed so as to allow the banks to lend people newly created money. This will be considered further in Chapter 14.

127

CHANGES IN THE DEMAND FOR MONEY

The amount of money people want to hold will tend to increase when money incomes rise, whether the rise in money incomes results from an increase in real activity, from higher prices and wages or from any combination of these. The ratio of desired money holdings to incomes can also change; for example, the wider use of credit cards may reduce people's need for money. There may also be changes in the demand for money to finance transactions in capital markets, where the turnover varies greatly over time.

If the quantity of money changes while the demand for it does not, or if the demand for money changes when the quantity does not, then there will be either an excess of the supply of money over the amount people want to hold, or an excess of the demand over the supply.

WHAT HAPPENS IF PEOPLE HAVE MORE OR LESS MONEY THAN THEY WANT TO HOLD?

Individuals or firms get money by selling labour, goods or securities, and they dispose of money by buying them. An individual or firm with perfect foresight would of course never be caught in a position where he was holding more or less of any asset than the amount he wanted. As none of us does in fact possess perfect foresight, it seems sensible to discuss what we will do when we find ourselves in the wrong asset position. What we do then will presumably be much the same as what those blessed with perfect foresight would have done earlier, to avoid getting into an undesired situation.

Too Much Money

Individuals or firms holding too much money, i.e. more than they want to hold, given their overall assets, their present income and their prospects for the future, will try to spend it.

There are two models of how they spend their surplus money. The monetarist model says they spend it on goods, which may be for either consumption or investment purposes. The Keynesian model says that they will in the first instance spend it on buying securities. Trying to buy securities will not in the short run bring any more securities into existence; it will lead to increases in their prices, so that interest rates become lower. There will also be a better market for newly created securities; i.e., credit will become easier to obtain. These changes in monetary conditions mean that spending by borrowers will tend to increase.

In either model, if there is more money than people want to hold, spending will rise. The increase in spending may cause the level of real output to increase, or there may be increases in prices and wages; but in either case the level of money incomes and the money value of total transactions each period will rise. Money incomes will tend to go on rising until somebody is willing to hold all the stock of money.

When people buy labour, goods or securities from each other this does not decrease the stock of money; it just shifts its ownership about. The expansion of money incomes must go on until incomes have expanded so far that people now feel they need to hold all the money stock. The stock itself may be depleted by leakages into balance of payments deficits or into budget surpluses caused by fiscal drag.

If the desire for money balances were sensitive to the rate of inflation that people expected, then an initial excess supply of money could lead to a vicious circle, in which attempts to spend it caused rapid increases in prices and wages, following which more inflationary expectations made people want to hold less money rather than more, so that they tried to spend even faster. This could in theory lead to runaway inflation, but this does not seem very likely. The experience of the past decade (see Table 12.1) suggests that the response of desired money holdings to changes in the rate of inflation is quite small, and in any case leakages into imports and taxes would tend to reduce the money supply. Historically, actual cases of runaway inflation have been caused by reckless increases in the money supply, not by instability in people's demand for money.

Too Little Money

If people have less money than they would like to hold, given their incomes and expectations, they will try to increase their money holdings, i.e. to 'hoard' it. In a monetarist model they will cut their spending on real goods and services, whether for consumption or investment purposes. In a Keynesian model they will initially try to sell securities. This will not decrease the actual stock of securities, but their prices will fall and interest rates will rise. It will become harder to sell newly created securities; i.e., credit will become harder to obtain. This will tend to reduce spending by other people.

On either model spending on goods and services will tend to fall, though the pattern of time lags may be slightly different. The lags in a contraction may also be different from those applying when spending expands. The fall in spending may cause a decrease in the real level of activity, or it may cause falls in prices and wages, or both real activity and the price level may fall. In any case, the level of money incomes will fall. The fall in spending does not increase the total stock of money; it only alters the distribution of money holdings. The fall in money incomes must thus go on until people are satisfied with holding the actual stock of money. The money supply will itself be increased if the fall in incomes brings about an external payments surplus or a government budget deficit.

There is no need to assume that either the monetarist or the Keynesian model is completely true or completely false. It would in fact seem odd for people to become more willing to spend money on goods or services because it had become cheaper or easier to borrow, but not to become more willing to spend as the result of owning the additional money themselves. It would seem equally odd if people holding more money than they wanted did not consider buying securities as one means of disposing of the excess. Thus it seems reasonable to suppose that there is some sense in each model. In any case it does not matter much which is right, since they both predict that if people have more money than they want to hold total spending will rise, and if people have less money than they want total spending will be cut.

The Quantity Theory of Money

The reader may perhaps wonder how all this is related to 'the quantity theory of money'. This is a theory that looks at the new equilibrium position to which an economy will eventually come in the very long run if the quantity of money changes. The prediction of the quantity theory is that in the very long run the economy will settle down to a new equilibrium where the level of real activity reverts to its original level, and the price and wage levels increase or decrease in proportion to the change in the money supply.

This very long-run prediction may well be true, but our interest in this chapter has been not in looking at where the economy will ultimately arrive, but at how it will change in the rather short run as the result of changes in the supply of money. Even if the quantity theory is true, it does not give much help in predicting where the economy will be next year as the result of a change in the money supply this year. This chapter has been concerned with the monetary side of processes of change in the short run, not with where the economy will ultimately get to.

14. Banks

All financial institutions operate by borrowing from one set of people and lending to another. Banks are financial institutions whose liabilities are in major part regarded as money by the lenders. Deposits on current account, which are loans to banks that can be withdrawn on demand or transferred to other people by cheque, are regarded as money on almost any definition.

WHY IS BANKING PROFITABLE?

It is very convenient to hold bank deposits as money; for many transactions cheques are as good as cash, and indeed for some they are superior. The use of cash for large transactions involves handling costs and risks of robbery or loss that are not present when cheques are used. Provided that a cheque is 'crossed', i.e. made out so that it can only be paid into a bank account, it is very difficult to get hold of the actual money even if you can successfully steal a completed cheque, so few people bother to try.

Because of the convenience of holding bank deposits, people are willing to lend to banks by depositing their money in current accounts bearing less interest than can be obtained elsewhere. In the UK demand deposits are in fact interest-free, though it can be argued that the provision of chequing and accounting services gives depositors a form of real yield tax-free. In countries where interest is paid on current accounts, it is at relatively low rates.

How Can Banking Be Made Safe?

There are some obvious risks in running a bank. If all money borrowed by the bank is kept as cash, there is no income to pay the bank's operating expenses. If the money is lent out, then there is a danger that, if too many depositors were to ask for their money back at the same time, the banker would be unable to pay them and would be forced out of business. To avoid this danger, bankers require three attributes.

Commercial Prudence

There is no such thing as a perfectly safe loan. If loans are made only to relatively safe borrowers then only a very small proportion of them can be expected to default. If loans are made to more risky customers, who are willing to pay higher rates of interest, the risk of default is greater. If several borrowers default, or even if there is a single well-publicized failure of a large borrower, this is liable to undermine the confidence of depositors. Because banks borrow short and lend long, if all a bank's depositors were to try to withdraw their money at once the bank would suffer a severe financial crisis which could end in bankruptcy. This sort of risk can be minimized by sticking to relatively safe borrowers, and by not lending too much to any one borrower.

Adequate Reserves

It is statistically very unlikely that all depositors will want their money back at once. If the bank holds some money, this should suffice to meet all likely demands for withdrawals. If in addition it holds some highly liquid assets, i.e. securities that can be turned into money with a minimum of delay or risk of loss, this will allow it to replenish its actual money holdings quickly if necessary. Loans vary in their maturity date, i.e. the time when they are due for repayment. The most liquid assets are those that have short maturities, so that their market value is not altered much by changes in interest rates; those that are widely traded, so that they can be sold without affecting the price much; and those that are as safe as possible from risks of default. Short-dated UK government securities, such as Treasury bills, fit this description very well, as do overnight or seven-day loans to discount houses.

Reputation

If any financial institution has a reputation for being run with commercial prudence and holding adequate reserves, it is unlikely to run into problems over the confidence of its depositors. If it does get into financial difficulties, it is very likely that other financial institutions will help to maintain its solvency, if only for their own protection. If on the other hand it has been lending to dubious customers, and running on very low reserves, the other banks may very well resent its competition, which makes it harder for them to earn profits. If a badly run bank gets into financial trouble the other banks may take the opportunity of the crisis to let it go bankrupt.

BANK ASSETS

In choosing its portfolio of assets, a bank will thus need to hold some cash, and some other very liquid assets. Suitable assets would include:

(1) deposits with other banks – in the UK, with the Bank of England;
(2) very short-dated government securities, such as Treasury bills, which are issued with maturity after only ninety-one days, or other government securities that, while they were originally issued with a more remote redemption date, have in the course of time come close to maturity;
(3) 'call loans' to discount houses or other financial institutions that can be relied to be able to pay off their loans promptly if they are 'called in', because they in turn are holding relatively liquid securities.

These are all good for safety, but they are not the most profitable bank assets. For profit, a bank will also want to hold some proportion of its assets in the form of longer-dated securities, or to make loans or 'advances' to its customers. These will be charged interest, at a relatively low base lending rate for borrowers who are thought to be very unlikely to default and at higher rates, which are individually negotiated, for customers who are thought to be liable to have difficulty in the prompt repayment of loans, or where there is thought to be any possibility of default.

CONTROL OVER BANKS

Some form of regulation of banking operations, by the central bank or the government, has long been thought to be necessary. This is for several reasons.

(1) It is desired to protect depositors from the risk of default. Many depositors are small firms or individuals, who cannot be expected to be fully informed about the risk they are running in depositing their money with a badly run bank.

(2) It is desired also to protect financial institutions as a whole against loss of public confidence, which might occur if some of them failed. In the past whole banking systems have been wrecked through the failure of particular firms, since this sets up a panic among depositors. Expectations of failure in finance tend to be self-justifying. If depositors were to try to withdraw all their deposits at once the banks would all go bankrupt, while if all the banks tried to call in their advances at once their customers would all be unable to pay, so would become bankrupt also.

In the modern UK economy the major banks are so large and so conservatively managed that default is almost inconceivable, but numerous financial problems have arisen in smaller financial institutions, ending in some cases in a take-over by a sounder concern, and in other cases in bankruptcy.

(3) Regulation serves as an anti-monopoly device, reducing the power and profits of bankers by requiring them to hold safe but unprofitable assets.

(4) It also serves as an instrument of macroeconomic policy, designed to influence the money supply and through it the level of real spending in the economy.

RESERVE RATIOS

One of the commonest forms of regulation of banks has been the imposition of minimum ratios on the share of liquid assets in their total portfolios. These minima have usually been based on extending to all banks what the more prudent ones were already doing in any case.

The current UK system of bank regulation was introduced in 1971 under the title 'Competition and credit control'. Its main feature is a minimum ratio of 'reserve assets' to 'eligible liabilities'. Both are complex concepts whose precise definition need not concern us. 'Eligible liabilities' are, generally speaking, liabilities payable in sterling to people or firms outside the banking sector. 'Reserve assets' include deposits at the Bank of England, Treasury bills and other very short-dated UK government securities, and some classes of 'trade bills', which are very short-dated obligations of private firms. Actual cash held at branches is not counted as a reserve asset, though every bank will clearly need to hold some. If a bank has more cash, or 'till money', than it needs, it can always turn this into reserve assets by depositing it at the Bank of England. Conversely, if it has not enough till money it can always get more, provided that its reserve assets ratio is high enough to permit a reduction in its deposits at the Bank of England. Some banks hold significantly more 'reserve assets' than the minimum requirement, presumably because they feel this to be commercially prudent.

CAN BANKS CREATE MONEY?

The answer to this question is clearly 'yes'. If a bank has more reserve assets or till money than it needs for its minimum requirements, it can buy securities or make loans to its customers. The people selling the securities or receiving the loans will presumably spend most of the money they receive. If the people who supply the goods, services or securities that are bought with the borrowed money hold accounts with the original bank, it will once again have excess reserves and will be able to lend some more. If the recipients of the expenditure hold accounts with other banks, the other banks will find that their reserves and deposits have gone up equally, so their reserves-to-deposits ratio will have risen. These other banks will now have excess reserves, and in turn can afford to buy securities or make loans. The process of making loans and buying securities, so that total bank deposits rise, can go on until some bank needs to hold the available quantity of reserve assets and till money. This process is known as the 'credit multiplier'.

Conversely, if a bank feels short of reserve assets or till money it can get hold of more by selling securities or by reducing its loans. If it is in a great hurry it can call in existing loans, but this is not regarded as a sensible policy; the kind of customer whose credit elsewhere is good enough for him to be able to pay off a loan at short notice is the sort a banker would rather not lose, while the less desirable customers could not pay up quickly if called on. If the bank has more time, it can let its total loans go down by not making new ones as fast as the old ones are paid off. The reduction in loans or sale of securities lowers deposits, with the original bank or with other banks; the process of shrinkage of deposits must go on until the banks as a whole are satisfied with the ratio between their deposits and the amount of reserve assets and till money that they are holding.

How Do Reserve Assets Change?

The actual amount of reserve assets may rise in three ways.

(1) Budget deficits may be financed by the sale of assets suitable to act as reserve assets.

(2) A balance of payments surplus leads to purchases of foreign currency by the Bank of England, in its capacity as holder of the country's foreign exchange reserves. It may pay for the foreign currency it receives with money, or by selling securities suitable to be held as reserve assets.

(3) The central bank or the government may conduct what are called 'open-market operations', in which securities that do not count as reserve assets are bought, and the funds to pay for them are raised by selling securities that do count as reserve assets.

In each case the opposite process will reduce reserve assets.

The connection between these changes and changes in the supply of money is not precise. This is because many financial institutions other than banks also hold reserve assets such as Treasury bills. The banks can therefore always get hold of more reserve assets if they really want them by bidding up their prices; this however will cut into banks' profits.

UK BANKS

There are a great many banks that operate in the UK. The largest single group is the 'London clearing banks', including the 'Big Four', Barclays, Lloyds, Midland and National Westminster, and a number of smaller banks. Table 14.1 gives some particulars of the assets and liabilities of the London clearing banks in August 1979. If more detailed figures are required these can be found in the *Bank of England Quarterly Bulletin*.

In August 1979 the London clearing banks had £35.0b of deposits in sterling, £6.8b of deposits in other currencies, and other liabilities,

TABLE 14.1   *The London Clearing Banks, 15 August 1979*

Liabilities	£b	Percentage of total liabilities %	Comments
Sterling deposits	35.0	69.6	
Deposits in other currencies	6.8	13.5	
Other (including capital)	8.5	16.8	
Total liabilities	50.3	100.0	
of which 'Eligible liabilities'	28.7	57.0	
Assets			
Reserve assets	3.6	7.3	Reserve asset ratio = 12.7%
of which Money at call	1.6		
Deposits at Bank of England	0.5		
Treasury bills	0.5		
Other bills	0.7		
British government securities under 1 year from maturity	0.4		
Non-reserve assets			
Notes and coin	0.9	1.7	
Special and supplementary deposits	0.2	0.5	These are explained in Chapter 17
Loans and bills (not reserve assets)	5.9	11.8	
Sterling advances: UK	20.5	40.7	
other	3.1	6.2	
Sterling securities	2.9	5.7	
Non-sterling assets	6.8	13.5	Note that they almost balance non-sterling deposits
Miscellaneous (including buildings)	6.4	12.7	

Source: Bank of England Quarterly Bulletin, September 1979, Tables 3.2 and 4. This gives assets and liabilities on 15 August 1979.

including their capital, of £8.5b. Their total liabilities were thus £50.3b, of which £28.7b were 'eligible liabilities', against which they were required to hold a minimum reserve assets ratio of $12\frac{1}{2}$ per cent.

Turning to their assets, actual reserve assets were £3.6b, equal to 12.7 per cent of eligible liabilities. They included £1.6b of 'call money', £0.5b of deposits at the Bank of England, £0.5b of Treasury bills, £0.4b of other British government securities within a year of maturity, and £0.7b of other bills.

Non-reserve assets included £0.9b of notes and coin, or 1.7 per cent of total liabilities. £0.2b was held in 'special' or 'supplementary' deposits at the Bank of England, which do not count as reserve assets, and are required by the Bank of England as an instrument of monetary policy; these will be discussed further in Chapter 17.

Loans and holdings of bills not counted as reserve assets accounted for £5.9b. Sterling advances to borrowers in the UK accounted for £20.5b, and sterling advances to overseas borrowers for £3.1b. Sterling investments were £2.9b. Clearing bank advances were made to every sector of the economy, as well as to individuals.

Other currency assets were £6.8b; this is very close to foreign currency deposits. As exchange rates are liable to serious short-term fluctuations, a policy of keeping foreign currency assets and liabilities approximately equal reduces risk for the banks.

Finally, there were £6.4b of miscellaneous assets, including bank premises.

MONETARY POLICY

If the government can find ways of influencing the activities of the banking system, this will give it considerable influence on the total real spending in the economy. This chapter should be regarded as background to the discussion of monetary policy in Chapter 17.

15.   General Equilibrium

A general equilibrium model is one that looks at the economy from several different viewpoints. This can be contrasted with a partial equilibrium approach, in which one agent or one market at a time is considered, assuming when considering each one that 'other things are equal' in the rest of the economy.

In this chapter we will consider the simplest possible general equilibrium model of the economy, with two markets only, one for goods and the other for money. This clearly involves suppressing a lot of interesting aspects of the economy; for example, the real side of the model outlined below has no explicit labour market, and the monetary side has no explicit bond market.

The model is presented both in an algebraic form, into which any desired values for the parameters can be substituted, and as an arithmetic example, with income measured in £b and the interest rate in percentage terms.

The use of the interest rate as an indicator of monetary conditions in the economy is somewhat controversial. Actual credit markets do not work via interest rates alone, but through a package of measures including the time that borrowers are allowed for repayment and the collateral they are required to produce for loans (the collateral for a loan is the asset that has to be pledged; for example, in a mortgage the lender is given a claim against your house). When credit gets tighter it is likely that the period of loans will shorten and lenders will demand better collateral for loans, as well as charging a higher rate of interest. When credit becomes easier, it is likely that loans will be available for longer periods and on easier conditions, as well as being cheaper. The rate of interest is thus used in this model as an indicator of all these factors, rather than simply as a measure of the cost of borrowing.

THE MODEL

The Market for Goods

In the goods market, Y is real output, assuming a given price level. Demand for output comes from consumption, C, investment, I, and real government expenditure, G. We assume that linear approximations can be found to the functions determining consumption and investment, and that government expenditure is fixed. Thus

$$C = a + bY \qquad C = 10 + 0.5Y$$
$$I = e - fR \qquad I = 20 - 0.5R$$
$$G = g \qquad G = 25$$

For simplicity a closed economy is considered. A similar model applied to an open economy with foreign trade would require the inclusion of terms for imports and exports. This would add to the complexity of the model without adding to the main point it is being used to make.

Effective demand, Z, is given by

$$Z = C + I + G \qquad Z = C + I + G$$
$$= a + bY + e - fR + g \qquad = 10 + 0.5Y + 20 - 0.5R + 25.$$

so, letting

$$k = a + e + g \qquad k = 10 + 20 + 25 = 55$$
$$Z = k + bY - fR \qquad Z = 55 + 0.5Y - 0.5R.$$

For equilibrium $Z = Y$, so, letting $s = 1 - b$,

$$sY + fR = k \quad (15.1) \qquad\qquad 0.5Y + 0.5R = 55. \quad (15.1')$$

The Money Market

For equilibrium in the money market, the amount of money, M (measured in £b), must be equal to the demand for money holdings, L (for liquidity preference). L is assumed to be an increasing function of Y and a decreasing function of R, so as a linear approximation

$$L = n + qY - uR \qquad L = 10 + 0.2Y - R.$$

For equilibrium in the money market, $L = M$, so

$$M = n + qY - uR \qquad M = 10 + 0.2Y - R$$

or

$$qY - uR = M - n \quad (15.2) \qquad 0.2Y - R = M - 10 \quad (15.2')$$

General Equilibrium

We now have two equations: (15.1), which tells us what combinations of Y and R are consistent with equilibrium in the goods market, and (15.2), which tells us what combinations of Y and R are consistent with equilibrium in the money market. For equilibrium in both markets we require that both equations are satisfied:

$$\left.\begin{array}{l} sY + fR = k \\ qY - uR = (M - n) \end{array}\right\}; \text{ if } M = 20, \left|\begin{array}{l} 0.5Y + 0.5R = 55 \\ 0.2Y - R = 20 - 10 = 10. \end{array}\right.$$

Thus

$$Y = \frac{ku - fn + fM}{fq + su} \tag{15.3}$$

$$Y = \frac{(55)(1) - (0.5)(10) + (0.5)(20)}{(0.5)(0.2) + (0.5)(1)}$$

$$= \frac{55 - 5 + 10}{0.1 + 0.5} = \frac{60}{0.6} = 100 \tag{15.3'}$$

and

$$R = \frac{ns + kq - sM}{fq + su} \tag{15.4}$$

$$R = \frac{(10)(0.5) + (55)(0.2) - (0.5)(20)}{0.6}$$

$$= \frac{5 + 11 - 10}{0.6} = \frac{6}{0.6} = 10 \text{ per cent.} \tag{15.4'}$$

Graphical Solution

Equation (15.1) gives the conditions for $S = I$ where S is the total savings in the economy, and its graph is usually known as the *IS* curve. Equation (15.2) shows the conditions for $L = M$ and its graph is usually known as the *LM* curve. General equilibrium implies that both (15.1) and (15.2) are satisfied, so that general equilibrium occurs where the *IS* and *LM* curves intersect. This is shown at *E* in Figure 15.1, which has *Y* on the horizontal and *R* on the vertical axis.

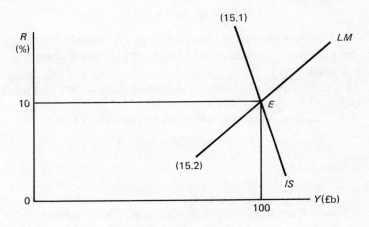

FIGURE 15.1   The *IS/LM* model

Given the signs assumed for the parameters, along the *IS* curve, from (15.1) we have

$$\partial Y/\partial R = -f/s < 0;$$

i.e., the *IS* curve is downward-sloping. An increase in *Y* will tend to raise *S*, and equilibrium in the goods market thus requires a higher *I* which can be brought about by a lower *R*.

Along the *LM* curve, we know from (15.2) that

$$\partial Y/\partial R = u/q > 0$$

so *LM* is upward-sloping. A rise in *Y* requires a higher *L*, but *M* is fixed, so to keep *L* down a higher *R* is needed.

Because *IS* and *LM* have opposite slopes, the equilibrium *E* where they cut must be unique.

The Effects of Changes in Parameters

Any change in the parameters of equations (15.1) and (15.2) will alter the positions of *IS* and *LM* and will thus affect the equilibrium position, *E*, in Figure 15.1.

A rise in *a, e* or *g* will increase *k*; this moves the *IS* curve upwards, and the equilibrium values of *Y* and *R* will be increased. From (15.3),

$$\partial Y/\partial k = u/(fq + su) > 0$$

and from (15.4),

$$\partial R/\partial k = q/(fq + su) > 0.$$

The relative values of the changes in *Y* and *R* depend on the slope of the *LM* curve; the flatter the *LM* curve, the more any changes are concentrated on *Y*.

In the arithmetic case above, if *k* rises by £1b, *Y* rises by £1.67b and *R* rises by 0.33 per cent.

A rise in *M* will shift the *LM* curve to the right. From (15.3),

$$\partial Y/\partial M = f/(fq + su) > 0$$

and from (15.4)

$$\partial R/\partial M = -s/(fq + su) < 0.$$

This will increase the equilibrium value of *Y* and decrease that of *R*. The relation between the changes in *Y* and *R* will depend on the slope of the *IS* curve; the steeper *IS* is, the more changes will be concentrated on *R*.

In our arithmetic example, an increase in *M* by £1b will increase *Y* by £0.83b and decrease *R* by 0.83 per cent.

CRITICISMS OF THE *IS–LM* MODEL

The *IS–LM* model is open to criticism on various grounds. The combined force of these criticisms suggests that it cannot seriously be applied direct to real-world economic policy problems. It has been presented here because it is the simplest available general equilibrium model of the whole economy, and more realistic models can be built up from it. It does have the merit that it looks at the economy from two different points of view, the real and the monetary sides, and shows how these can react upon each other. It is helpful to have it summarized since many more advanced economics texts use it, and assume that references to it will be understood. The criticisms themselves are of considerable economic interest.

(1) It is very aggregated; a more realistic model would need to include a separate treatment of the labour market, and an extension to cover foreign trade, at the very least.

(2) It is static; it considers the conditions required for equilibrium in the economy, but not the process through which the economy will change after an alteration in parameters. This implies ignoring time lags, which may be long and imply major real effects.

(3) It ignores the problems of inflation, by taking the price level as given. This is related to the final criticism:

(4) It assumes that the effects of economic policies are reversible; as a guide to practical economic policy this is probably its most serious defect. This is best shown by an example.

The formal model set out above assumes that, if M is first increased by a very large amount and later decreased again to its original level, the economy will finish up where it started. This may well be approximately true for small changes, but nobody believes it for large ones, unless in a very remote long run.

If M were to be increased by any large proportion, for example if it were to be doubled, it is generally believed that the effects would include a sharp rise in money prices and wages. If M were subsequently lowered again to its original level, it is generally believed that the effects would include a serious slump in the real level of activity. Thus a large rise in M followed by a fall would probably leave the economy with higher levels of prices and wages, and lower levels of real activity and employment, than in the original position.

Conversely, if M were first cut drastically, for example if it were halved, and then increased again, it is equally doubtful whether the economy would finish where it started. Any major fall in M would involve a slump, during which both industrial and financial firms would suffer losses and probably bankruptcies. A subsequent expansion of M would not automatically reconstruct the organizations, reputations and public confidence that would allow real activity to resume its old level. Thus again the economy would probably finish with higher prices and lower real incomes than it started with.

This is an example of the care with which it is necessary to treat very simple macroeconomic models before applying their conclusions to the real-world economy.

16. Financial Institutions

Before going on to consider monetary policy, it is necessary to consider the financial institutions through which monetary policy in the UK has to work. This chapter will therefore give brief descriptions of some of the main financial institutions in the UK, and of the assets that they hold.

The main point of general economic interest that this chapter seeks to make is the fact that the various financial markets of the UK economy are all interconnected. Not all institutions hold assets of any given type, and not all possible assets are held by each institution, but each institution has several possible assets between which it can shift, and each asset has several possible holders. The financial markets are thus all connected; there is always some financial institution prepared to switch between any pair of assets, and monetary pressures are thus transmitted right across the economy.

The connections between various financial markets will be illustrated by Table 16.1 below, which shows the net flow of various assets between different sectors of the economy in 1978.

THE BANK OF ENGLAND

The Bank of England was founded at the end of the seventeenth century. It was nationalized after the Second World War, but this made little difference to its activities, since it had been acting as a central bank for the UK for a century already. The Bank of England has several functions.

Note Issue

The Bank has a monopoly of note issue in England and Wales, though other banks' notes still have a limited circulation in Scotland and Ireland.

Government's Banker

The Bank of England is the government's banker. It is because the government does not bank with the clearing banks that a budget surplus will tend to restrict the money supply: the government's balances with the Bank of England do not count as part of the money supply.

Bankers' Bank

Other banks maintain balances at the Bank of England, and transfer deposits there as a method of final settlement of net claims between them.

Lender of Last Resort

The Bank of England has traditionally acted as lender of last resort. This means that in a financial crisis it is prepared to buy securities from other institutions that might otherwise not be able to meet their obligations. Its rules about what sorts of assets it will buy are normally very strict, but in a serious financial crisis they could be relaxed, as was done during the nineteenth century.

Exchange Reserves

The Bank of England administers the country's foreign exchange reserves for the government.

Leadership

The Bank of England acts as a leader of monetary opinion. It sets a minimum lending rate (MLR), the rate at which it is willing to act as lender of last resort; before 1971 this was known as 'Bank rate'. The minimum lending rate is conventionally used as a standard when setting other rates, for example the rate charged on bank overdrafts, normally at higher rates than MLR.

The Governor of the Bank can also help to shape financial opinion, either by public statements on policy questions or by informal contacts with the leaders of other City institutions. The Governor is appointed by the government, and is nominally subject to government directives; but he is in a strong bargaining position over any policy issue on which he feels very strongly, since his resignation would have a marked adverse effect on foreign confidence in sterling. The Bank thus enjoys a considerable degree of *de facto* independence.

BANKS

The London clearing banks have already been considered in Chapter 14. There are many other banks in the UK; these include Scottish and Irish banks, and various American, European and Japanese banks that have offices in the UK, mainly in London. Since 1971 these other banks have had their reserve asset ratios governed by the same rules as the clearing banks, though only in respect of their operations in sterling. It can be seen from Table 16.1 that the overseas operations of the banking sector have been growing rapidly, and it will be seen in Chapter 23 that banking makes a considerable contribution to the UK balance of payments.

DISCOUNT HOUSES

These are specialist firms, which borrow money for very short periods from banks and other financial institutions such as insurance companies, and use it to hold Treasury bills, other bills, and other very short-dated securities.

MERCHANT BANKS

These are specialist institutions, dealing in the financing of overseas trade, share issue and the negotiation of mergers, take-overs and other forms of industrial finance.

THE STOCK EXCHANGE

This is the institution in which government stocks and the shares of UK and foreign companies are traded. Prices are determined by a relatively competitive process. In the very short run prices are set by 'jobbers', who will buy or sell shares at prices they name. The jobbers' total funds however are far too limited for them to have much effect on prices, so that changes in outside opinion about firms make share prices fluctuate by large amounts in quite short time periods.

INSURANCE COMPANIES

These collect premiums from the public in return for insurance against fire, theft and accidents. They also insure people's lives and provide endowment insurance, selling the promise of lump sums on death or at retirement age, or annuities after retirement.

Life insurance and the provision of funded superannuation schemes for private companies have been growing rapidly, and in recent years the insurance sector has had very large funds for investment. Table 16.1 shows that in 1978 the purchase of life insurance policies and participation in superannuation schemes absorbed £7.7b of personal savings.

BUILDING SOCIETIES

These are the largest group of 'other financial institutions'. They borrow money from the public, mainly from individuals, repayable at short notice, and lend it on mortgage to finance house purchase and a very limited amount of other building. In 1978 building societies came second to insurance companies as outlets for personal savings.

INVESTMENT AND UNIT TRUSTS

These are institutions whose principal activity is to hold government securities or company shares. Investment and unit trusts are used both by small savers and by other financial institutions, partly as a method of hiring the special financial expertise of the trusts' managers, and partly to achieve a spread of risks by holding a stake in a wide variety of companies without incurring the high transactions costs that would result from holding large numbers of very small batches of shares.

ASSETS

Treasury Bills

These are government bills, payable after three months, i.e. ninety-one days. They are regarded as extremely safe, both from risks of default and from extreme variations in price. Their short date stabilizes their value, for the present value of a right to receive £100 in three months' time will fall by only 0.25 per cent for every one per cent rise in the rate of interest. A rise in interest rates from 6 to 10 per cent would thus be required to knock one per cent off the price of a Treasury bill with the full three months to run, and the price becomes even less sensitive to interest rate variations as the bills move closer to maturity.

Trade or Commercial Bills

These are issued by companies to finance trade, particularly foreign trade, and they generally run for three or six months. They are similar to Treasury bills in their relative insensitivity to changes in interest rates, but do suffer from some default risk, which leads to the practice of 'acceptance'. This means adding a signature to a bill, to guarantee that it will be paid by the acceptor should the original debtor fail to meet it. This makes the bills safer to hold and easier to sell, provided that the acceptor has a sufficiently sound reputation for solvency. As the acceptor is taking a risk, he will charge a small premium. When a bill is sold before maturity, it will be at a price lower than the amount payable on maturity, or a discount; hence the term discounting for the purchase of such a bill.

Bonds

These are longer-dated government securities, bearing fixed interest until a set of redemption date, e.g. the year 2000. There are also bonds without a set redemption date, where the Treasury has the right to redeem them at par at any time. These are known in full as 'consolidated fund annuities', and for short as 'consols'. Bonds with remote or indefinite redemption dates can fluctuate severely in price, as the price of a bond with a fixed return will be inversely proportional to the interest rate that can be obtained on a newly created security.

Ordinary Shares

These are issued by companies. They do not have any fixed return, but their owners are the residual beneficiaries of any profits in a firm after all other types of shareholders have been paid, and they may get nothing at all if the firm is unsuccessful. Companies are not compelled to distribute any profits they make to their equity shareholders. Whether profits are distributed or not may well depend on tax considerations. Retained profits are not subject to personal taxation, so shareholders with very high marginal tax rates find that they do better if the profits accumulate in the companies whose shares they hold, leaving them to take their benefits in the form of capital gains when the shares are sold. Ordinary share prices are liable to very large fluctuations, and shares are not very attractive to individuals, who sold £1.5b of shares in 1978.

Debentures

These are fixed-interest securities issued by companies. They have priority over all other types of shares for dividends, which have to be distributed. Debentures carry no voting rights or control over the management of the company so long as their interest is paid, but if it is not paid then the debenture holders have the right to replace the company's directors with their own nominees.

Managements like to do some borrowing on debentures, since this is a method of obtaining more capital without parting with control. If the amount of debentures is large, however, a large part of the profits in a normal year will be required to pay the debenture interest, and there is a risk that in a bad year it will not be possible to pay the debenture interest and control will be lost. A firm with a high ratio of debentures to total capital employed is said to be highly geared. The equity shares in a highly geared firm will be even more risky than the firm itself.

Mortgages

These are loans secured on building and land. They are usually for a long period; twenty years is common for house purchase. They are widely used both for the purchase of owner-occupied houses, and for business premises.

National Savings

These are loans with both fixed interest and a government guarantee of withdrawal rights at fixed prices. Holdings are restricted in amount, and are permitted only to persons and non-profit-making bodies. Most national savings are at fixed interest, but there are securities whose price is 'index-linked' to the retail price index available in restricted amounts to pensioners and under save-as-you-earn schemes.

THE NETWORK OF ASSET MARKETS

Table 16.1 is used to give an idea of the way in which various asset markets are connected. It shows the net acquisition of various forms

TABLE 16.1 *Net Acquisition of Financial Assets in 1978*

Sector	Personal* £b	Industrial companies** £b	Banks £b	Insurance† £b	Other financial‡ £b	Public sector§ £b	Overseas £b
Type of Asset◆	(1)	(2)	(3)	(4)	(5)	(6)	(7)
Money§§	3.8	2.6	−25.7	0.5	0.8	−1.4	19.5
Bank loans	−1.6	−2.9	26.0	−0.2	−0.6	0.3	−21.0
Government securities	0.2	−0.1	−0.3	3.8	0.4	−3.9	—
Savings banks†	2.1	—	—	−0.1	−0.5	−1.5	—
Company shares††	−1.5	0.4	−0.2	2.2	−0.1	0.5	−1.3
Life assurance	7.7	—	—	−7.5	—	−0.2	
Building society deposits	4.8	—	—	—	−4.8	—	—
Loans for house purchase	−5.4	—	0.3	0.1	5.1	−0.1	—
Retail and trade credit	−0.4	0.4	—	—	—	−0.1	0.1
Exchange reserves	—	—	—	—	—	−2.3	2.3
IMF	—	—	—	—	—	0.7	−0.7
Other identified assets	−0.2	−0.3	0.6	0.2	0.4	0.1	−0.7
Total identified assets‡‡	9.6	0.1	0.6	−0.9	0.6	−8.1	−1.8
Unidentified assets‡‡	1.5	−2.3	−0.1	−1.1		0.2	0.8
Total net acquisition of financial assets‡‡	11.0	−2.2	0.5	−1.4		−7.9	−1.0

* Personal sector includes unincorporated businesses.
** Industrial and commercial companies.
† Life insurance companies and superannuation funds.
‡ Other financial institutions, including building societies.
§ Including Bank of England.
◆ Acquisition of assets or reduction of liabilities is positive; increase of liabilities or sale of assets is negative.
§§ Money = notes, coin and bank balances.
†† Company shares and unit trust units.
‡‡ All rows add to zero, apart from rounding errors, except for unidentified assets, and total net acquisition of financial assets, which both add to a residual error owing to discrepancies between various sources of information.
Source: Blue Book on *National Income and Expenditure, 1979*, Table 13.2.

of financial assets in 1978 by different sectors of the economy. Positive figures show acquisition of assets or reduction of liabilities; negative figures show increase of liabilities or reduction of assets. All are in current market prices, in £b. Column (1) shows the net transactions of the personal sector; column (2) the net transactions

of industrial and commercial companies; column (3) refers to the
banks; column (4) to insurance companies and superannuation
schemes; column (5) shows 'other financial institutions', mainly
building societies and savings banks; column (6) shows the public
sector; and column (7) the overseas sector, i.e. the rest of the world.

The various rows show net changes in particular types of assets.
The rows sum to zero, as they logically must since one sector's asset
is another sector's liability. This applies to all rows except for the
last two; if the Central Statistical Office's information were perfect,
there would be no transactions in unidentified assets, but these have
to be assumed to exist to reconcile the flows of security holdings
with other information in the national income accounts. The
column sums including these unidentified assets sum not to zero,
but to a 'residual error' which is the name given to the sum of
discrepancies in information available from various sources. The
transactions of companies, of the overseas sector, and of insurance
companies and other financial institutions, in particular, are subject
to residual errors so large that they cast doubt on the reliability of
all the figures.

The first asset shown is money; money holdings of both persons
and companies increased, and there was a large increase in overseas
deposits with banks operating in the UK. The second asset is bank
loans; these were made to most other sectors. The third asset was
government securities, which were mainly acquired by insurance
companies.

The next asset is company shares, including shares in unit and
investment trusts. The main feature here is that company shares
were being sold off by individuals, and bought by insurance companies and superannuation funds. The shift of individuals' interest
in companies from direct shareholding to using insurance companies as intermediaries is mainly a consequence of the tax concessions given on life insurance. Life insurance policies, the next asset,
were sold by insurance companies to persons.

Building society deposits were made by persons. Loans for house
purchase were made mainly by building societies; in 1977 the building societies lent for house purchase £0.3b more than they received
in deposits.

Considering the sectors, a few important features may be noted.
The personal sector increased the outstanding value of its life insurance policies and rights in superannuation schemes by £7.7b, and

increased its deposits with building societies by £4.8b. The total of mortgages outstanding increased by £5.4b, and net sales of £1.5b of company shares were made. For the personal sector as a whole, bank loans of £1.6b were less than increases in money holdings. The remaining increase in total assets was financed from personal savings.

Industrial and commercial companies borrowed heavily from banks, and also increased their money holdings.

The banks increased both their deposits and their loans considerably; most of the increased business was with the overseas sector.

Insurance companies received £7.5b in the excess of premiums on policies over claims paid out, and used the proceeds to acquire £3.8b of government securities and £2.2b of company shares.

Other financial institutions, including the building societies, lent for house purchase £5.1b more than they received as mortgage repayments.

The public sector sold £3.9b of securities, and decreased its holdings of foreign exchange reserves by £2.3b.

The really important lesson from Table 16.1 comes not from the particular items, which in any case fluctuate from year to year, but from the way in which the various financial markets of the UK are interconnected, both to each other and to financial markets in the rest of the world. This makes it a mistake to consider particular sections of the overall financial market in isolation. This chapter thus provides the background against which monetary policy has to work.

17. Monetary Policy

We have seen that the quantity of money and the availability of credit can have important effects on real activity. In this chapter we will examine the ways in which the monetary system can be used by the government and the central bank as deliberate means of policy. It will be convenient to refer to the government and the Bank of England, acting in consultation, as 'the monetary authorities'.

THE AIMS OF MONETARY POLICY

The main aims of monetary policy are threefold.

Control of Aggregate Demand

The monetary authorities may wish to increase the amount of money or make credit more readily available to increase the real level of effective demand if they think that it is too low, or they may wish to reduce the quantity of money and restrict the availability of credit if they think the level of aggregate demand is too high.

The actual level of effective demand at which the monetary authorities aim will depend on three factors:

(1) the level of real output relative to trend, or the level of unemployment relative to whatever percentage they regard as normal:

(2) the state of the balance of payments: if the country is spending more on imports than it receives from the sale of exports, a cut in effective demand is a quick and simple way of correcting the imbalance (the balance of payments will be discussed further in Chapter 24);

(3) the rate of inflation: if prices and wages are rising too fast, the authorities may feel obliged to restrict the level of effective demand as part of their efforts to control inflation (this will be discussed further in Chapters 18 and 19).

The Balance of Payments on Capital Account

In addition to any influence monetary policy may have on the balance of payments on current account, the authorities may wish to use interest rates to influence movements of private funds on capital account. If borrowing is more expensive in the UK than abroad, there will be an incentive for firms with a choice of markets to borrow abroad rather than in the UK, and to lend in the UK rather than abroad. This applies whether the firms are themselves UK-based, foreign or multinational. For any given level of foreign interest rates, a rise in the UK interest rates will tend to produce a move towards surplus on capital account, and a lowering of UK interest rates will tend to move the capital account into deficit. The same sort of change will result if changes in credit conditions make it harder or easier to obtain loans in the UK.

A Stable Monetary Environment

The authorities would like to be able to provide a stable financial environment to help people make efficient and consistent plans for their own future activities. Stability of financial markets is desired by the Treasury itself in the interests of economical management of the national debt. Large increases in interest rates may impair the solvency of financial institutions, increasing risk for everybody. Firms that are undertaking long-term investment projects would like to be sure that their financing arrangements will not suddenly be upset, and may be unwilling to start on projects if they do not feel this assurance. Individuals buying their homes on mortgage also prefer to avoid sudden large increases in the interest that they have to pay. For all these reasons there is a general public interest in stability of financial markets.

ARE THE AIMS OF MONETARY POLICY COMPATIBLE?

The various objectives of monetary policy may well not all be compatible. For example, if the economy has a year of sharp inflation but also high unemployment, the authorities have to decide whether to aim at high interest rates and a restriction of the money supply to restrain inflation, or at lower interest rates and easier credit to try to cure unemployment. Similar problems arise if a domestic recession coincides with an adverse balance of payments on current account: should the authorities aim at low interest rates to help cure unemployment, or at high interest rates to induce an inflow of private capital, which will allow the balance of payments deficit to be carried without running down official foreign exchange reserves?

There may well be problems also over the speed of policy reactions. If there is a sudden change in the economic climate, the authorities have to weigh the advantages of a sharp shift in their own position to deal promptly with the changed conditions against the arguments for avoiding sudden changes in monetary conditions with their adverse long-term effects on confidence in financial institutions.

It is widely believed that the monetary authorities have not in fact followed any consistent set of policy objectives, but have switched their objectives from time to time, according as the balance of payments, the rate of inflation or the level of unemployment seemed at the moment to be the most urgent problem.

THE MEANS OF MONETARY POLICY

There are several possible instruments of monetary policy; these are usually employed in combination, but can be analysed separately. They include the following.

Interest Rates

The Bank of England sets a minimum lending rate (before 1971, Bank rate), which is the rate at which it is prepared to act as lender of last resort on sufficiently high-class securities. The MLR is used as a reference point by banks and other financial intermediaries in setting the rates at which they will lend or borrow. There is an incentive for lenders to ensure that they are not lending at rates below the MLR, for if they should run short of liquidity and have to borrow they will be liable to make losses if they are holding assets with a yield below the cost of borrowing. If other financial institutions do not follow the Bank of England's lead over interest rates they can have pressure put on them to comply with the Bank's wishes by use of the open-market operations, or of changes in reserve ratios.

Open-Market Operations

'Open-market operations' is the name given to a switch in asset holdings by the Bank of England, acting either on its own account or as an agent for the government. This may involve either a sale of bonds to the public or a purchase of bonds from them.

Sale of Bonds   Bonds sold to the public are paid for by cheques drawn on the purchasers' accounts, normally with a clearing bank. The clearing bank settles with the authorities by transfer of part of its deposits with the Bank of England; thus the government's balances at the Bank go up (assuming it was the government that sold the bonds) and bankers' deposits at the Bank of England go down. The clearing banks' deposit liabilities to their customers and their own deposits at the Bank go down by equal amounts, so the ratio of their reserve assets to their eligible liabilities goes down. If the clearing banks are holding no excess reserves (i.e. no more than the minimum reserve ratio of $12\frac{1}{2}$ per cent), they are compelled to cut credit in some way, by selling securities or reducing their advances. Even if the clearing banks are holding excess reserves, so that they are not forced to cut credit, they will still have an inducement to cut back lending, since they presumably hold excess reserves because they feel that it is prudent to do so, and the prudential motives for holding reserve assets increase, if anything, during a credit squeeze.

Purchases of Bonds   If open-market operations take the form of purchases of bonds from the public, the authorities will pay with cheques, which the vendors will pay into their clearing bank accounts. The authorities will settle with the clearing banks by increasing bankers' deposits at the Bank of England; thus the clearing banks will find that their reserve assets and their own deposit liabilities have risen by equal amounts, and their reserve assets ratio has increased. This will allow but not compel them to expand credit; as loans are profitable, they are likely to be tempted to increase them.

Changes in Reserve Ratios

These have been used explicitly by the banking systems of many countries, especially the USA. The UK has employed a rather camouflaged version. A rise in the required minimum reserve ratio will compel banks that are not holding excess reserves either to restrict their lending, or to incur capital losses through having to sell securities that do not count as reserve assets in order to be able to buy more securities that do count as reserve assets. A lowering of the required reserve assets ratio would allow but not compel banks to expand credit.

The Bank of England has, and makes use of, powers to require the clearing banks to hold 'special deposits' equal to a given percentage of their deposit liabilities. These special deposits are deposits at the Bank of England, but they are not counted as reserve assets. Having to hold special deposits, however, has the same effect as a higher minimum reserve assets ratio would have on the clearing banks' ability to lend.

The Bank of England also has powers to require the clearing banks to hold 'supplementary deposits', which are proportional to the excess of each bank's advances over a target level, usually related to its previous advances; e.g., increases in a given period may be limited to n per cent, after which supplementary deposits are required. This system is designed to penalize lenders who increase their advances too quickly.

Directives to Banks

The Bank of England can issue directives to other banks concerning both the total level and the composition of their lending. The banks may for example be asked not to allow their total advances to rise by more than n per cent during a given period, or they may be asked to show preference in granting credit to some types of customer and denying it to others. Even if directives are not issued, the Bank of England's power to use them lends authority to informal requests made to the other banks.

Directives concerning advances are unpopular with bankers. Banks have obligations to their customers (such as 'standby' arrangements, by which people have access to loans if they need them) that it is embarrassing not to be able to honour. Directives inhibit competition for custom between different banks, and between the banks as a whole and other financial intermediaries not subject to the same controls. It is widely believed that the rapid growth of 'non-bank financial intermediaries' during the past twenty years has been largely owing to the handicaps placed on the banks by controls.

The Bank of England hoped at the time that the 1971 'competition and credit control' rules would enable it to avoid the need to use directives in the future. The need for the system of supplementary deposits, which penalizes particular banks whose lending expands faster than a common target rate, does not seem to be entirely consistent with the aim of avoiding discriminatory controls on the banks.

Priorities   There have been periodic bouts of advice from the monetary authorities to the banks concerning the priority in access to credit to be given to various classes of borrower. Favoured groups have at various times included export and defence industries. Groups to be denied access to credit have included property speculators, and firms wishing to re-finance export credits (i.e. to permit foreign buyers on credit to defer making their payments for a further period after the time originally agreed).

These priorities are very widely disliked; in particular, they are suspected of favouring large and sophisticated organizations, which are more adept than other people at dressing up their applications for credit in whatever form is currently fashionable with the authorities.

Hire Purchase Controls

The government has at various times imposed controls on hire purchase. These have taken the form of minimum proportions of the total price required as a down payment by the customer, and a maximum limit on the period over which the remaining payments can be spread. This type of control discriminates in two ways. It discriminates against those industries that sell a relatively large proportion of their output on hire purchase, especially motor vehicles, electrical goods and furnishings. If hire purchase facilities are restricted because of excess aggregate demand in the economy this imposes additional fluctuations on the industries selling via hire purchase.

Controls on hire purchase also discriminate between various types of customer; in particular, hire purchase controls discriminate against those who do not have access to other forms of credit such as bank loans and credit cards. Thus hire purchase controls are thought to discriminate against the poor. In recent years governments have tried to avoid controls on hire purchase.

SOME COMMENTS ON MONETARY POLICY

A number of general remarks may be made on the use of monetary policy.

Monetary Policy v. Monetary Management

The UK money supply is subject to fluctuations because of seasonal and random variations in government receipts and expenditures, and in foreign trade. For example, there is a strong seasonal variation in the receipts of revenue from taxes on company profits, and from taxes on personal income other than those taxed under 'pay-as-you-earn' arrangements. Many of the Bank of England's actions in the money market are therefore designed for management of the monetary system, smoothing out undesired short-term variations in the money supply, rather than for monetary policy, in which deliberate changes in the money supply are brought about for the sake of their expected effects on expenditure or on overseas finance.

Time Lags

Monetary policies take time to produce their effects. Borrowing and actual spending by the borrowers do not respond instantaneously to changes in the cost and availability of credit. While the monetary authorities are waiting for the effects of their policies to appear, the situation of the economy will be changing.

Some critics of monetary policy, notably Milton Friedman, have argued that, because of defects in the information about the current position that is available to the authorities, and because of time lags in the effects of monetary changes, attempts at detailed short-run control, or 'fine tuning' of the economy, by monetary policy are useless. The lags and uncertainties in the system are so great that 'stabilization' policies, whether by the use of discretionary changes or operating according to previously determined rules, are liable to cause more disturbances than they can cure. The monetary authorities should therefore concentrate on providing a stable financial environment, to allow other people to plan their affairs efficiently.

One possible method of providing a stable monetary system would be to aim at keeping the increase in the money supply to a constant percentage each year, without attempting to react to very short-run situations, which will in any case have changed before any measures based on them have had time to take effect.

Package Deals

The authorities have tended to make use of the measures of monetary policy listed above in combinations, frequently in conjunction with fiscal policy measures also. These combinations of policies are known as 'package deals'; there are two reasons why they are used rather than relying on a large dose of any single policy instrument.

Uncertainty If you are not certain about the exact effects of any single policy measure, like a 1 per cent rise in the minimum lending rate, or about how soon the effects will appear, it seems safer to use several measures in the hope that one of them will be effective.

Side-effects Various monetary measures have 'side-effects'; these are effects that are not deliberately sought, but are the unwanted results for one aspect of the economy of policies adopted to deal with some other aspect. A sudden increase in interest rates, for example, may have a helpful effect in reducing overall excess demand, but it has the disadvantage of impairing the stability of some financial institutions. Tighter restrictions on hire purchase imposed because of excessive total consumption may produce a particularly marked recession in an already depressed furniture industry. The authorities will wish to minimize such side-effects, both because they are concerned about their effects on economic efficiency and because they are concerned about the political consequences of leaving some groups feeling that they have been sharply victimized while other people were left alone. With a package deal the injury to particular sectors can be less, possibly below a threshold level of perception, and if the harm is noticed the fact that other people are suffering too may give some consolation.

Both uncertainty about the effects of policies and a desire to keep any side-effects below a threshold of perception induce the authorities to prefer using packages of policy instruments, each used in moderation, to relying on large doses of any one measure. The fact that the instruments are used in packages makes it hard to sort out the results of each measure, either statistically or by *ad hoc* empiricism. This tends to perpetuate the uncertainty about their effects, so that the temptation to use another package is still strong when the next crisis comes round.

MONETARY POLICY FROM 1968 TO 1978

It is not proposed to give a month-by-month historical account of the use of various policy measures during the decade. Instead of this, in Table 17.1 we have some figures for both the main targets and some of the main measures of monetary policy.

Columns (1) to (3) show the indicators of the main targets of monetary policy. Column (1) shows the percentage output gap, showing how far GDP fell below a 3 per cent growth path (see Table 2.2 above). Column (2) shows the rate of inflation, as measured by the increase in the deflator for GDP over the previous year (again, see Table 2.2). Column (3) shows the balance of payments on current account as a percentage of GNP (see Table 10.1).

Columns (4) to (8) show indicators of the use of monetary policy instruments. Column (4) shows the annual percentage increase in M1 (see Table 12.1). This has varied greatly, from a decrease of 0.5 per cent during 1969 to an increase of 21.4 per cent during 1976.

Columns (5) to (8) are concerned with the Bank of England's minimum lending rate. Column (5) shows the mean MLR in each year, i.e. the average of MLR on the last working day of each calendar month. MLR was at its minimum of 5.9 per cent in 1971, a year in which M1 rose by 13.3 per cent, considerably above the rate of inflation at the time, so that real balances rose. MLR was at its maximum of 11.9 per cent in 1974; this was a year when M1 rose by 4.9 per cent, which was well below the rate of inflation, so that real

TABLE 17.1 *Monetary Policy, 1968–78*

| Year | Indicators for policy | | | Measures of monetary policy Minimum lending rate‡ | | | | |
	Out-put gap* %	Rate of infla-tion** %	Balance of pay-ments† %	Increase of M1 %	Mean %	Max. %	Min. %	Range %
	(1)	(2)	(3)	(4)	(5)	(6)	(7)	(8)
1968	1.0	3.0	− 0.6	—	7.4	8.0	7.0	1.0
1969	2.2	3.7	1.1	− 0.5	7.9	8.0	7.0	1.0
1970	3.1	7.5	1.5	7.0	7.2	8.0	7.0	1.0
1971	3.4	10.9	2.0	13.3	5.9	7.0	5.0	2.0
1972	4.8	9.8	0.3	16.5	6.1	9.0	5.0	4.0
1973	0.0	7.5	− 1.2	8.7	10.1	13.0	7.5	5.5
1974	4.2	17.1	− 3.9	4.9	11.9	12.75	11.5	1.25
1975	7.8	27.3	− 1.5	19.7§	10.7	12.0	9.75	2.25
1976	7.2	13.7	− 0.7	21.4	11.8	15.0	9.0	6.0
1977	8.6	11.9	0.2	14.6	8.2	12.25	5.0	7.25
1978	9.1	10.7	0.6	19.8	9.2	12.5	6.5	6.0
Average 1968–78	4.7	11.2	− 0.2	12.5	8.8	10.7	7.3	3.4

* Percentage by which GDP fell below the 3 per cent trend.
** Inflation measured by percentage rise in deflator for GDP.
† Balance of payments on current account as percentage of GNP: minus signs show a deficit, positive signs a surplus.
‡ Minimum Lending Rate, figures for last working day each month, *Bank of England Quarterly Bulletin;* the range = maximum − minimum is given to indicate the speed of turn-round in monetary policy.
§ In 1975 the Bank of England changed its method of computing M1; this added 4.8 % to M1 on the date of change-over. Figures shown do not correct for the effect of this.
Sources: Output gap and inflation, as Table 2.2; balance of payments on current account, as Table 10.1; increase of M1, as Table 12.1; Minimum lending rate, *Bank of England Quarterly Bulletin.*

balances fell. The year 1974 also showed a record balance of payments deficit, equal to 3.9 per cent of GNP, which required a high interest rate to allow the deficit to be financed by borrowing.

In 1977 the MLR came down to 8.2 per cent, actually below the average for the decade, and M1 rose by 14.6 per cent. In 1978 the MLR was 9.2 per cent, and M1 rose by 19.8 per cent. The authorities were presumably induced to allow this large monetary expansion by the fact that there was a high output gap, of 8.6 per cent in 1977 and 9.1 per cent in 1978, with correspondingly high unemployment;

while inflation was still 11.9 per cent in 1977 and 10.7 per cent in 1978, it was well down compared with the immediately previous years; and a small surplus on the current account balance of payments and a large capital inflow in 1977 meant that the country did not need high interest rates in order to be able to borrow to finance a deficit.

Column (6) shows the maximum level of MLR each year, and column (7) the minimum level. To give an indication of the speed of turn-round in monetary policy, column (8) shows the range within which MLR moved during each year (i.e., column (8) equals column (6) minus column (7)). From 1968 to 1971 the range between maximum and minimum MLR in each year stayed below 2 per cent. The boom year of 1973 saw a rise in the range to 5.5 per cent. In 1974 and 1975, with record balance of payments deficits and record inflation, the range was small as MLR had to be kept high throughout; but in 1976 to 1978, as inflation came down and the balance of payments became more normal, the Bank of England felt able to lower MLR for parts of the year, and in 1977 MLR attained its maximum range within the year, of 7.25 per cent.

A Judgement on Monetary Policy

While a considered judgement on UK monetary policy would require more information than can be included in a very brief survey, it is very hard to believe that a series of policies that have allowed the rate of increase of M1 to vary between 0 and 21 per cent in a year can possibly have been optimal. A policy of completely uniform percentage increases in the money supply might well be thought unduly rigid, but it does look as if short-term switches in policy objectives have been so violent that Milton Friedman has a point in suggesting that a less irregular growth of the money supply would have been better in the long run for economic stability.

18. Inflation

Inflation is the name given to a general and persistent tendency for prices and money incomes to increase. The prices of *particular* goods rise and fall for specific reasons; for example, agricultural prices will normally rise after an exceptionally poor harvest, and fall after an abnormally good one. Inflation, however, is used to refer to longer-term movements of whole groups of prices, or of incomes in general, as measured by widely based indices. Inflation in this sense has been one of the major features of the UK economy since the Second World War.

There are a number of questions concerning inflation that we need to be able to answer:

(1) How much inflation has there been in the UK?
(2) What harm is done by inflation?
(3) What causes it?
(4) How can it be cured?
(5) If inflation cannot be cured, because we do not know of a cure, or are not willing to bear the costs of any known cure, how can society adapt its institutions so as to make inflation less uncomfortable to live with?

How Much Inflation Has Occurred in the UK?

There are various possible measures of the rate of inflation. One has already appeared in Table 2.2 above; Table 18.1 shows some more measures of inflation, for the years since 1968. Column (1) shows the increase in consumer prices for each year, as a percentage of their level in the previous year. Column (2) shows the increase in the deflator for total domestic expenditure; this includes investment

TABLE 18.1   *Inflation in the UK, 1968–78*

Year	Increase in consumer prices %	Increase in deflator for total domestic expenditure %	Increase in employment incomes per unit of final product %
	(1)	(2)	(3)
1968	4.7	4.8	2.4
1969	5.7	5.6	3.1
1970	5.9	6.7	9.8
1971	8.4	9.2	9.5
1972	6.5	7.5	9.5
1973	8.6	9.0	7.8
1974	17.2	19.9	23.6
1975	23.7	24.8	29.9
1976	15.5	15.0	10.7
1977	15.0	13.5	8.3
1978	8.4	9.2	10.8
Average 1968–70	5.4	5.7	5.1
Average 1971–73	7.8	8.6	8.9
Average 1974–78	16.0	16.5	16.7
Average 1968–78	10.9	11.4	11.4

Source: Blue Book on *National Income and Expenditure, 1979*, Table 2.5.

goods and real government expenditure, as well as consumption. Column (3) shows the annual percentage increase in employment incomes per unit of final product. These all give slightly different figures for inflation in any particular year; in some years, indeed, there is a difference of several per cent between the indices. Over the period as a whole, however, the average rate of inflation comes out very similar on all three measures. It can be argued that, if the choice of which measure of inflation to use made any major difference to arguments about how severe inflation had been, this would in itself be a sign that the problem had ceased to be very serious.

Over the decade, inflation rose from a minimum in 1968, on all three measures, to a maximum in 1975 of 23 to 30 per cent, according to the index chosen. Comparing the parts of the decade, inflation averaged 5 per cent from 1968 to 1970, 8 to 9 per cent in 1971–73 and about 16 per cent in 1974–78. In 1976–78, however, while inflation was still high by the standards of earlier periods, it had come down somewhat from its peak levels in 1974 and 1975, on all three criteria.

WHAT HARM IS DONE BY INFLATION?

It is a commonplace to deplore inflation: however, it cannot be stopped merely by wishing that it would cease. If society is to be asked to incur real costs as the result of restrictive monetary and fiscal policies adopted to try to curb inflation, it is worth-while analysing carefully the amount of harm inflation causes. For this purpose, we will need to distinguish between foreseen and unforeseen inflation.

Unforeseen Inflation

Inflation of prices and wages at rates faster than people foresaw makes efficient decision-taking more difficult for everybody. Most incomes are fixed by some procedure for some time in advance: this is true whether the actual procedure is by contract, as in the case of rents and many forms of debt; by government regulation, as with pensions and social security benefits; or by negotiation, as with wages. For all these, unforeseen inflation in prices implies an unforeseen cut in real income.

Unforeseen inflation makes it hard for firms to predict their profits, for governments to predict their revenues and expenditures, and for individuals to predict their real incomes. Unforeseen inflation makes rational choice of consumption and investment plans even more difficult than it is bound to be anyway in an uncertain world.

There is no logical reason why a higher average rate of inflation, over a period of years, should make it harder to predict the actual inflation rate in any one year than if the average rate of inflation was lower. It has in fact been the case in recent years, however, that as inflation has become faster on the average it has also become more variable. This can be demonstrated in various ways. Two of these are shown in Table 18.2, which takes the three measures of inflation in Table 18.1 and gives two measures of variability for each. The first measure of variability is the average year-to-year change in the rate of inflation, calculated without regard to the sign of the change, for the three periods 1968–70, 1971–73 and 1974–78. This is equal to the average error in prediction that would be made by anybody forecasting on the assumption that inflation each year would be the same as the year before. The second measure of variability is the mean error (or 'average deviation'), regardless of sign, that would be made by assuming that the rate of inflation for each year would be equal to the average rate of inflation over the past three years, which is assumed to determine people's expectations of a 'normal' rate of inflation. For all three measures of inflation, the variability of inflation is considerably greater in the third period than in the earlier two, on both criteria of variability.

Foreseen Inflation

It is possible to argue, on a very theoretical view of the economy, that if only inflation were correctly foreseen, it would make no real difference how fast it was proceeding. There would, on this view, be

TABLE 18.2   *Unforeseen Inflation, 1968–78*

Average over years	Index of consumer prices		Deflator for total domestic expenditure		Increase in employment incomes per unit of final product	
	Average change* %	Average deviation** %	Average change* %	Average deviation** %	Average change* %	Average deviation** %
1968–70	1.1	1.4	1.4	1.7	2.5	3.0
1971–73	2.1	1.6	1.9	1.7	0.7	2.7
1974–78	6.1	7.3	6.3	8.4	9.2	11.9
1968–78	3.6	4.2	3.7	4.7	5.1	7.0

* Average percentage change in rate of inflation for the years concerned (e.g. a rise from 3 per cent to 5 per cent counts 2 per cent), regardless of the sign of the change.
** Average deviation, regardless of sign, of inflation in each year from the mean of the previous three years' figures.
Source: Blue Book on *National Income and Expenditure, 1979*, Table 2.5.

a complete separation between the determination of relative prices, and thus of relative incomes, and the determination of money price and wage levels. This argument has to face considerable difficulties, which it is worth considering in some detail.

Accounting When prices in general are rising, there is a serious problem in measuring the real profitability of firms. This affects a number of important economic judgements: whether particular investment projects are really productive; whether the total assets of a firm are large enough relative to its existing debts to make it safe to provide it with goods on credit; and how much of the firm's total money receipts are really income, which it is legitimate to tax. Various methods of 'inflation accounting' are under discussion, but there are still great difficulties to overcome before these are satisfactory for all purposes.

Taxation   If prices are rising, then people making loans need to get a positive return, in money terms, to keep their real capital intact. Under the present tax system any return on a loan beyond the repayment of the money originally advanced counts as income and is liable to tax. In the case of taxation of 'capital gains', holders of assets whose money price has risen are liable to be taxed on the increase in nominal terms, even though the real purchasing power of their assets may well have decreased. It has not so far been possible to devise a tax system that deals adequately with these problems, though a start has been made on the worst anomalies with regard to taxing stock appreciation in company profits.

Pensions Pensions paid by the state can be adjusted at intervals to compensate for the effects of inflation on the cost of living. In the UK pensions were at one time adjusted every other year; then as inflation got under way they were adjusted annually; in the 1970s there has been pressure to have them adjusted more frequently.

Not all pensions are paid by the state, however. People relying on the pension schemes of private firms, or trying to provide for their own retirement, find that rapid inflation makes provision of adequate retirement income very difficult. With inflation at 5 per cent each year, money saved loses half its real purchasing power in 14 years. If inflation rises to 10 per cent, each year, money loses half its real purchasing power in 7.3 years, and 90 per cent of its purchasing power is lost in 24 years; this is a lot shorter than a normal working life, and many people are retired for such a period. If inflation rises to 20 per cent each year, money loses half its real purchasing power in 3.8 years, and 90 per cent of its purchasing power in 12.6 years. Inflation rates of this order make private provision for decent retirement almost impossible.

Pension funds do not of course simply hold money; they lend it at interest. It could be argued that higher interest rates would allow savers to maintain their real capital by re-investing the interest. During the recent inflationary period, however, it has been hard to find any form of security that has paid a rate of money interest high enough to give a positive real rate of return, even before allowing for taxation. Table 12.1 above for example shows that inflation has exceeded the Treasury bill rate in every year since 1969, except for 1973, so that real returns have been negative, even before tax. Rapid inflation thus creates problems over pensions and life assurance provision for retirement. This is an aspect of inflation that gives anti-inflationary policies a widespread political appeal.

Housing   The standard system for providing one's family with accommodation in modern British society is owner-occupation; more than half the homes in the UK are now owner-occupied, and the proportion is rising each year. The standard method of acquiring a house is to buy it on mortgage, usually borrowing from a building society, though insurance companies and local authorities also do some mortgage business. The normal arrangement for a mortgage is that the original loan is repaid, with compound interest, in equal instalments over a period, normally of twenty years. This system evolved at a time of relatively stable prices, and was convenient for the borrowers, as the real burden of buying their homes was spread out fairly evenly over twenty years of their working lives. With a high rate of inflation, and the high interest rates needed to give lenders partial compensation for the erosion of the purchasing power of their capital, the real burden of interest payments on mortgages is very high in the early years. It will diminish rapidly over time, however, unless inflation speeds up and interest rates rise further. If interest rates are steady, the equal cash payments involve a rapidly falling real burden. The high level of payments relative to income during the early years of a mortgage makes it very hard for the lower-paid to get started on home ownership, though the rapid fall in the real burden makes mortgages a very good bargain for anybody who can afford to get started.

The balance of payments　If it is impossible to get a positive real return on lending in the UK, this makes it very unattractive for foreigners to lend in the UK and very attractive for residents to lend abroad. This would normally lead to an outflow on capital account; until 1979 exchange controls were used to try to prevent this, with some success in the case of residents, though controls could not force non-residents to lend to us. Thus under inflation there is liable to be trouble on the capital account of the balance of payments.

When we consider the balance of payments on current account, with any given exchange rate between sterling and foreign currencies, if inflation is more rapid in the UK than abroad this makes exports harder to sell, and also makes imports more attractive. The current account thus tends to move into deficit. This can be prevented by devaluation, i.e. by making each pound worth fewer units of foreign currencies, but devaluation raises import prices and is thus liable to produce further inflation. The effects of devaluation on domestic inflation will be considered further in Chapter 20, and the effects of devaluation on the balance of payments will be further analysed in Chapter 25. The prospect of future devaluation will also create a strong incentive for outward capital movements.

It is clear that worries about the effects of inflation on the balance of payments are among the main reasons why the government is keen to see inflation reduced, even at the cost of policy measures that are in themselves politically unpopular.

CAUSES AND CURES OF INFLATION

The causes and possible cures for inflation are topics so important that the next three chapters are devoted to considering them in detail. Any very brief description of the causes of inflation risks verging on caricature; accepting this risk, the main theories of inflation can be summarized as follows.

Demand Inflation

This is the theory that prices and wages rise when there is excess demand and fall when there is excess supply. This is a theory about human behaviour, not a mechanical necessity. It gives rise to a model of inflation that does not fit the facts very well when applied to a period that has seen inflation becoming more rapid at the same time as unemployment has been rising. The demand inflation theory is however very important whether or not it is correct, since it is very widely believed in government and banking circles: at least, it is very hard to understand many official policies unless this is what the authorities have in mind. The demand inflation model is examined in detail in the next chapter.

Cost Inflation

This is the theory that rises in particular prices and wages can be explained by previous rises in other wages or prices. This theory effectively says that inflation is somebody else's fault; favourite scapegoats include foreigners, trade unions, monopolists and government extravagence. However inflationary movements originate, the cost inflation model certainly helps to explain why they are so hard to stop once they have started. The cost inflation model is examined in detail in Chapter 20.

The Monetarist Model

This is the theory that changes in the money supply produce changes in prices and wages in proportion, after a time lag during which there are some purely transitory real effects. The real level of activity in the economy then reverts to normal, because in the long run the monetary authorities cannot control the amount of real money balances, i.e. the total real purchasing power of the money supply.

Changes in the quantity of money presumably produce their effects either through their influence on the level of effective demand, or through people's anticipations of this; thus it does not seem necessary to have a separate chapter on this model.

Prices and Incomes Policies

There is a type of explanation of inflation that argues that the real causes of inflation are to be found in political and social factors rather than in purely economic forces. If inflation is really due to efforts by trade unions or by primary producers to attain levels of real income that are higher than is consistent with equilibrium in the economy, inflation will occur irrespective of the state of aggregate demand.

Measures to restrain total demand will not reduce this type of inflation; indeed, they could make it worse, because in a slump productivity falls, while the aspirations of organized labour do not. The argument then goes that inflation needs to be treated by political and social means. Prices and wages have to be controlled, either by law or through bargaining between the government and the representatives of powerful groups in the economy. The aim of such bargaining is to induce groups that have the power to make inflation continue to agree to desist from using it, either by offering them sufficient of what they want to satisfy them, or by using threats to make them realize that they cannot attain their objectives. The use of prices and incomes policies, and some of the difficulties with them, will be discussed in detail in Chapter 21.

LIVING WITH INFLATION

During the past decade the UK economy has had over 10 per cent inflation on average each year, in spite of the fact that throughout this period governments and the monetary authorities have declared it to be their firm aim to reduce inflation, and in spite of the frequent adoption of prices and incomes policies intended to have this effect. It is a reasonable conclusion from this history of continued inflation that it is not at all easy to stop inflation; either the authorities do not know how it could be done, or they do know a cure but are not willing to pay the price in terms of increased unemployment or necessary social changes. It also seems likely that, if we ever do find a long-term cure for inflation, it will take a long time to work, so that we will have inflation with us for some time. Even if inflation could be stopped, there is no obvious way to prevent it from starting again. It is thus tempting to inquire whether, if we cannot prevent inflation, we could find ways of reducing the harm it does, so as to make it less unpleasant to live with. Some of the possible devices that could make life with inflation less uncomfortable are as follows.

Indexed Loans

These would provide a guaranteed real return for savers. Indexed bonds, whose principal and interest were both increased in line with some suitable price index, would be of great assistance to pension funds and to the self-employed and other people providing for their own retirement. An obvious problem with indexed bonds is that it is hard to see how anybody except the government could ever be in a position to provide such a guarantee. If indexed bonds were generally available, they could well prove so attractive to lenders that it would be hard for anybody except the government to borrow at all, as it is so hard to find a positive real return anywhere else.

Indexed Accounts

A system of inflation accounting on an agreed basis that would correct for changes in the replacement cost of fixed capital, for changes in the value of stocks and for changes in the value of money would allow a more realistic assessment of profits and capital gains, and a fairer tax system.

Indexed Wages

If wages could be regularly revised in line with some suitable price index, possibly the retail price index, then unintended cuts in real wages when prices rose could be avoided. It can be argued that, if workers were guaranteed compensation for future inflation, unions would not feel the need to include compensation for expected future inflation in their current wage bargains.

An argument against indexed wages is that, if anything should happen that made a reduction in real wages inevitable, such as an adverse movement in the terms of external trade, so that the country could get fewer units of imports for each unit of its exports, indexing of wages would make inflation harder to stop once it got started.

Indexed Mortgages

The present system of mortgages, with equal cash payments over twenty years, could be replaced by a system in which payments started lower, but rose in money terms according to some convenient index, either of wages or prices. This would spread the real cost of house purchase more evenly over people's working lives than the present system does. Because the pattern of payments would be so much more convenient for the borrowers, house buyers might be able to afford interest rates that over a twenty-year period would give the lenders a better deal than at present.

SHOULD INDEXING BE ADOPTED?

Other devices to make it easier to live with inflation could no doubt be worked out. Whether it would be a good thing to adopt these devices is a matter of current controversy. The arguments for them have already been stated; the general argument against them is that inflation does harm in a great many ways, and there is no reason to assume that indexing devices can cure all this harm. Under a situation where none of the devices has been adopted there are a lot of different groups who lose by inflation, so that there is substantial political support available for policies to reduce it. There is a fear that, if some of the problems caused by inflation were alleviated, this would undermine the political will to resist it. The economy might thus finish up with more inflation, which would do just as much harm as before in spite of the various palliative devices. This is an issue on which readers will have to make up their own minds.

19.   Demand Inflation

In this chapter we will consider the model of inflation that ascribes a causal role to variations in the relation between aggregate supply and demand in the economy.

MICROECONOMIC FOUNDATIONS

There is a widely held belief that, at the microeconomic level, prices and wages tend to react to the pressures of supply and demand. If demand for any particular good exceeds supply at the present price, prices tend to rise. This is possible since purchasers who want the goods urgently are willing to pay higher prices for them, so there is a temptation for sellers to raise their prices. If supply exceeds demand, prices are likely to fall, though this tendency is often thought to be weaker than the tendency for prices to rise in the presence of excess demand.

Prices and wages could in principle be fixed in various ways; these include:

(1) unilateral price-setting by a leading or monopolistic buyer or seller;
(2) negotiation between representatives of buyers and sellers, as in the fixing of wage rates by bargaining between trade unions and associations of employers;
(3) government regulation, either in the form of prices originally being set by government-appointed bodies, or of such bodies monitoring changes in prices and wage rates originally set by other means;
(4) auction markets: these are used for houses, and many agricultural products;

(5) competitive markets: these are hard to find.

Only in the case of auctions or competitive markets are prices adjusted so as to equate supply and demand at all times; even here, part of the supply or demand will come from speculators, whose views on future price movements, if strongly held, may cause them to dominate the market in the short run.

Most markets do not operate either by auction or competition; somebody sets prices, for at least a certain time in advance, and very short-run variations in supply and demand result partly in changes in the actual quantity sold, and partly in various symptoms of excess supply and excess demand.

INDICATORS OF EXCESS SUPPLY AND EXCESS DEMAND

It will help us in understanding the demand inflation model if we consider carefully how excess supply and excess demand are observed. The actual amount of any good bought and sold in any period must by definition be the same. If we talk of excess supply and excess demand, these must be observed through some means other than just looking at the amounts actually bought and sold.

Excess Demand

There are many possible symptoms of excess demand, including the following:
(1) there will be more job vacancies than usual, and it will take longer than usual to fill those that can be filled at all;
(2) overtime working will be more common, and for longer hours, than normal;
(3) goods normally obtainable on demand will be out of stock;
(4) goods that have to be ordered will be subject to more than the usual amount of delay and uncertainty of delivery dates;
(5) queues for scarce goods will occur;
(6) search effort by buyers will be greater than usual; examples of this are personal calls at shops, 'wanted' advertisements in the press, more telephone and postal inquiries than usual, and 'poaching' by employers of other firms' workers.

Excess Supply

There are equally many possible symptoms of excess supply, including the following:
(1) more people than usual will be without jobs, and those seeking jobs will take longer than usual to find them;
(2) short-time working will be commoner than usual, and workers will be temporarily laid off;
(3) 'order books' for goods that have to be custom-made will be abnormally low or even zero;
(4) 'surplus capacity' will occur; firms will have machines, buildings or vehicles that they are not using;
(5) stocks of goods that can be stored will be unusually large;
(6) there will be abnormally large signs of search effort by sellers, such as advertising campaigns.

COEXISTENCE OF EXCESS SUPPLY AND EXCESS DEMAND

The economy is made up of a large number of distinct sectors, differentiated from each other by both products and location. Neither the inputs that they use nor the outputs they produce are perfectly substitutable for one another. Even in the market for the same product and district, the periods of time in which macroeconomics is conducted, such as years or quarters, are composed of many shorter time periods; and both supply and demand are subject to variation between these short periods, whose inputs and outputs are often poor substitutes for each other. Macroeconomic time periods are thus likely to include some shorter periods with excess demand and others with excess supply. Even within very short time periods, symptoms of excess demand and excess supply, such as unemployed people and job vacancies, may coexist simply because the economy is not perfectly efficiently organized. Finally, the sectors of the economy used in macroeconomic models are far from uniform, but are vast aggregates. Thus it is pretty well certain that any sector of the economy defined for macroeconomic purposes will in, say, a year have experienced substantial amounts of the symptoms both of excess supply and excess demand.

Overall economic forces like monetary and fiscal policies will influence the average level of effective demand, but their impact on particular sectors of the economy will appear intermixed with large numbers of random variations, because of factors such as the weather, diseases of men, animals or plants, industrial unrest, accidents, etc.

If the overall level of effective demand rises, the various sectors of the economy are likely to experience more symptoms of excess demand and fewer symptoms of excess supply. The signs of excess supply however will not be reduced to zero by any likely levels of overall demand.

If the overall level of supply rises relative to demand, the symptoms of excess supply will increase and those of excess demand will be reduced; but even in the depths of slumps there are likely to be some sectors and some short time periods with excess demand.

An indicator of excess demand can be constructed from some or all of the measures of its various symptoms; we will call this X.

A measure of excess supply can be constructed from some or all its symptoms; we will call it U, since unemployment has often been used as an index of excess supply.

EXCESS SUPPLY AND DEMAND AND PRICE CHANGES

In markets where the price is not set by a competitive bidding process, the various symptoms of excess supply and demand will influence price movements. People expect that increases in price will draw further supplies into markets, and may induce some customers to buy less and others to withdraw from the market entirely.

For the monopolistic price-setter, quantitative indicators give information on what the market will bear. For negotiated prices, the indicators of excess supply and excess demand give information on the relative bargaining position of the parties. In both cases, signs of excess demand will suggest that a move to a higher price would be relatively safe, and signs of excess supply would suggest price cuts, or at least great caution over price rises.

With prices regulated by government-appointed bodies, the connection between supply and demand pressures and price movements is less direct, but it still exists. Even if it is government policy to set the price at a level that can be expected to give rise to excess demand, there is an incentive not to set the price too low, so as to keep the problems of rationing the available supplies manageable. Even if the policy is to set a price that can be expected to result in excess supply, there is an incentive not to raise the price too far, so as to keep within bounds the problems of disposing of the resulting surpluses.

CAN THE SUPPLY AND DEMAND MODEL BE GENERALIZED TO THE WHOLE ECONOMY?

Many economists have thought that the supply and demand analysis of price determination can be extended to the whole economy. In simple form the argument runs as follows. In each particular market people observe variations in the relation between supply and demand. They have no simple means of telling whether the symptoms of excess supply or excess demand that they observe are particular to their own markets, or are general in the economy. If the symptoms are in fact particular to their market, then price changes will help to restore equilibrium. There is an incentive to raise prices in the face of excess demand to try to draw in more supplies, or to induce customers to ration themselves. If there is excess supply there is an incentive to cut prices to attract more custom, or to induce rival suppliers to withdraw from the market.

If the excess supply or demand is in fact general in the economy, price changes will do little in the short run to remedy it. If all prices are raised, or all are lowered, the effects in shifting real resources between sectors cancel out. In the very long run, all-round cuts or increases in prices and wages may restore equilibrium between supply and demand by their effects on the real purchasing power of the money stock; however, prices would have to rise or fall a great deal to make this of much importance.

In the shorter run, if price rises make speculators expect further rises, they may try to increase their holdings of stocks of goods, accentuating excess demand. If price cuts make speculators expect further cuts, they may hold off goods markets until prices have fallen so far that they are not expected to fall any further. Thus price flexibility may in the short run actually accentuate overall excess supply or demand in the economy.

If there is all-round excess supply or excess demand, nobody stands to gain by price changes. However, nobody can be certain whether or not the symptoms of excess supply or demand that they observe on the markets they know best are typical of other markets; thus it always seems a safe strategy to assume that at least part of the symptoms observed in each market are special to it.

This means that, if there is a general increase in demand, there will be a general increase in the symptoms of excess demand, and a general decrease in the symptoms of excess supply, so that people will be more willing to increase prices and wages. If there is a general decrease in demand relative to supply, there will be a general increase in the symptoms of excess supply and a general decrease in the symptoms of excess demand, so that people will become more reluctant to raise prices and wages, or may even be ready to cut them.

All this gives rise to the simple inflation model, in which, if demand exceeds supply, prices rise and, if supply exceeds demand, prices fall. This is given the name 'demand inflation'.

A MODEL OF DEMAND INFLATION

The basic demand inflation model can be set out as follows. Let $R = (1/P)(dP/dt)$, where R is the rate of inflation, P is some suitable price index and t is time. R is then determined by an equation of the form

$$R = f(X, U)$$

or, if we assume $f(\ )$ to be linear,

$$R = A + bX - cU$$

where $b, c > 0$. Even if the function is not linear, it should still obey the restrictions that $\partial R/\partial X > 0$, $\partial R/\partial U < 0$. A will be a constant, whose value will depend on:
(1) the construction of the indices for X and U (the relation between X and U will depend on how they are constructed; there is no general reason to assume it to be linear);
(2) various social and political factors;

(3) the recent rate of inflation, which will determine the rate of increase in other prices and wage rates expected by the people who have to determine the changes in any particular wage or price.

The Natural Rate of Unemployment

In a model of this type, there is no qualitative distinction between situations of excess supply and situations of excess demand; both types of symptom normally occur, though one rises as the other falls. We define the 'natural rate of unemployment', U^*, as being that level of U at which $R = 0$. If $R = 0$ this means that the factors inducing price- or wage-setters to raise or lower their prices just balance. The level of U^* will depend on the values of A, b and c. If A is high, because of widespread inflationary expectations or widespread social discontent with the existing distribution of incomes, then a low X and a high U will be required for $R = 0$.

A high b will result in a high U^*; if price- and wage-setters react to signs of excess demand by raising prices vigorously, then the natural rate of unemployment, U^*, required to balance this tendency will be high. If price- and wage-setters are cautious about raising prices in the face of excess demand, i.e. if b is low, then U^* will be lower.

Similarly, a high c, which means that price- and wage-setters are strongly influenced towards price cuts by signs of excess supply, will allow U^* to be low; while a low c, meaning that price- and wage-setters are insensitive to indications of excess supply, will mean that U^* has to be higher. The more notice people take of X, the higher U has to be for stable prices, and the more notice people take of U, the higher X can be consistent with zero inflation.

THE PHILLIPS CURVE

The Phillips curve is the name given to an early approach to this type of demand inflation model, made by Professor A. W. Phillips in 1958. His model used as its indicator of inflation the increase in wage rates, and as its indicator of demand conditions the single measure of unemployment. This gave a curve relating the degree of wage inflation to the level of unemployment. The general method was quickly applied to other measures both of the rate of inflation and of supply and demand conditions.

DEMAND PRESSURE AND INFLATION IN THE UK

To investigate how well a Phillips curve fits the facts for recent years in the UK, we could try fitting a relation of the form

$$R_t = A + bZ_t$$

where Z_t is a measure of demand pressure. Before 1970 relations of this form gave a tolerable, though not very good fit. During the 1970s when high inflation has coincided with rising unemployment this type of model clearly does not fit the facts. This is understandable, since prolonged experience of inflation has led people to expect it to continue.

If everybody in the economy is expecting 10 per cent inflation, then 10 per cent inflation will result from the levels of X and U that would have produced zero inflation if everybody had been expecting zero inflation, i.e. from the X and U that would induce price setters to aim at staying in line with other people. Thus in the inflation equation, the term A has to include people's expectations of continuing inflation. A model which does this is known as an expectations-augmented demand inflation model.

AN EXPECTATIONS-AUGMENTED DEMAND INFLATION MODEL

We will thus try fitting an equation which takes account of inflationary expectations. If R_t is the actual rate of inflation, and R_t^* the expected rate, we will fit the form

$$R_t - R_t^* = A + bZ_t$$

where Z_t is our indicator of demand pressure. The material for this is given in Table 19.1. Column (1) gives R_t, measured by the percentage increase in the GDP deflator. Column (2) gives an estimate of R_t^*; this is the average of R_t for the previous three years, which

could well be regarded as 'normal' inflation. Column (3) then gives
'residual' inflation, i.e. the difference between actual inflation shown
in column (1) and 'normal' inflation shown in column (2). It is this
residual which we will seek to explain by a measure of the pressure
of demand.

TABLE 19.1   *Demand Inflation in the UK, 1968–78*

Year	Inflation R_t %	'Normal' inflation R_t^* %	Residual inflation $R_t - R_t^*$ %	Total final expenditure at 1975 prices %	Average TFE (lagged) %
	(1)	(2)	(3)	(4)	(5)
1965	4.0	—	—	—	—
1966	3.8	—	—	0.2	—
1967	2.8	—	—	0.5	—
1968	3.0	3.5	−0.5	2.1	0.4
1969	3.7	3.2	0.5	0.8	1.3
1970	7.5	3.1	4.3	0.6	1.5
1971	10.8	4.7	6.1	0.7	0.7
1972	9.9	7.3	2.6	1.4	0.7
1973	7.5	9.4	−1.9	6.9	1.1
1974	17.1	9.4	7.7	2.5	4.2
1975	27.3	11.5	15.8	−2.7	4.7
1976	13.7	17.3	−3.6	−2.0	−0.1
1977	11.9	19.4	−7.5	−3.8	−2.3
1978	10.7	17.6	−6.9	−3.5	−2.9

Inflation refers to GDP deflator, annual increase. 'Normal' inflation is defined as
average of previous 3 years. Residual inflation is actual − normal inflation for each
year. TFE is given as percentage deviation from trend fitted to 1957–78 data, the
growth rate over the period being just over 3% per annum. Average TFE is the
average of the previous 2 years.

Source: Blue Book on *National Income and Expenditure, 1979.* Inflation from Tables
1.1 and 2.1, TFE from Table 2.1.

It is possible to get an explanation of inflation using various
measures of demand pressure. We could use the 'output gap' calculated in Chapter 2, or deviations of gross domestic product
measured at 1975 prices from its long term trend. It is, however,
possible to obtain a better explanation of variations in the rate of
inflation using the deviation from its long term trend, fitted over the
years from 1957 to 1978, of total final expenditure at 1975 prices.
These deviations, in percentage terms, are shown in column (4).

There is a good reason for expecting that variations in total final expenditure will reflect demand pressure better than figures based on gross domestic product. Neither series actually measures demand, but only those parts of total ex ante demand which people actually succeed in spending. Attempts to spend may be frustrated by supplies of goods and services not being available. These supply constraints affect both total final expenditure, which includes imports, and gross domestic product which excludes them. However, as the UK obtains its imports from a wide variety of sources, the effects of supply constraints on imports are largely unrelated to the pressure of demand in the UK. Thus, because of the ability to obtain marginal requirements of many goods from imports, total final expenditure is less affected by supply constraints than is gross domestic product. TFE is therefore a better reflection of the overall pressure of demand on resources.

The influence of demand pressure on inflation is subject to various time lags. The rate of inflation used here compares average prices in year n with those in year $n - 1$. The rate of inflation is affected by price changes during the whole of year $n - 1$ as well as year n. The decisions of price and wage setters during these years will have been made in the light of opinions about the state of the balance of supply and demand in the markets for their products formed not just at the time concerned, but over the previous months. Thus the demand pressures during year $n - 2$ could well turn out to be relevant to inflation in year n. The best lags to use can only be found by experiment.

When the relation between residual inflation and TFE is calculated, it is found that TFE in year n itself appears to have almost no connection with residual inflation in year n. Inflation in year n is however strongly correlated with demand pressure in both in year $n - 1$ and year $n - 2$. Column (5) gives for each year the average deviation of TFE from its trend during the previous two years.

It is not at all clear exactly why inflation in year n does not seem related to demand pressure in the same year. On possible reason is that as demand rises output increases; where there are fixed overhead costs this lowers average costs for many businesses. In the short run an upturn in the economy raises output by a larger percentage than employment, which lower costs; while in a downturn the percentage decrease in output exceeds that in employment, so that costs rise.

Thus within the year, while the effect of expanding markets is to produce signs of excess demand which induce sellers to aim at setting their prices higher relative to costs, their perceived costs are lower than they would have been without demand expansion. Within the year these influences on prices approximately cancel out. Higher demand pressure during the previous year also makes for optimistic opinions about market prospects and thus for a preference for higher prices relative to costs, without any effects in lowering costs. To check whether such an explanation is correct would demand a more sophisticated model, data related to shorter time periods, and the use of more advanced statistical techniques than it is possible to apply here.

If we regress residual inflation, $(R_t - R_t^*)$ as shown in column (3) of Table 19.1, on Z_t where Z_t is the lagged average deviation of TFE from its long run trend, as shown in column (5), the result is given by

$$R_t - R_t^* = -0.76 + 2.72Z_t.$$

This means that for each extra 1 per cent on the average TFE over two years, inflation the following year will be 2.7 per cent faster. This relation accounts for 82 per cent of the observed variance in $(R_t - R_t^*)$. This is not a very good fit, and it leaves some quite substantial deviations to be explained by cost inflation or other models. It does seem sufficiently good, however, that it is not possible simply to dismiss the expectations augmented Phillips curve model as entirely irrelevant to the recent facts.

If one believes this model, it suggests that expansion in the level of effective demand had a strong effect in speeding up inflation after 1973 and 1974, while deflation of effective demand since 1975 has been quite effective at slowing inflation down. The model also implies that the average level of TFE required for a stable inflation rate in the UK over the past decade would have been very little below the average actually achieved. This implies that the associated level of unemployment need have been little above that actually suffered, and could have been considerably below the levels of 1976–78.

OBJECTIONS TO THE DEMAND INFLATION MODEL

There are two main grounds for objection to the demand inflation model, which have made people look for an alternative. The first is intellectually extremely respectable, and is politically neutral: this is the assertion that the demand inflation does not fit the facts. We have seen that it is not true that the demand inflation model has no relevance to the facts. It is however very likely that it does not contain the whole truth about inflation, so that other models also need to be considered. The second objection is intellectually more controversial: the demand inflation model implies that there is a natural rate of unemployment, U^*, and that any nearer approach than this to full employment cannot be made without ever-accelerating inflation. The demand inflation model is thus politically extremely unattractive to people who believe that there is no human ill that cannot be cured by a sufficiently enlightened and energetic government.

One may comment on this objection that it is foolish not to believe the truth merely because it is unpleasant.

THE IMPORTANCE OF THE DEMAND INFLATION MODEL

It can be argued that, even if it proves in the end to be entirely untrue, the demand inflation model is clearly important because so many government officials and central bankers believe in it.

One view of this belief is that the monetary and fiscal establishment believe the demand inflation model because, being in close touch with practical affairs, they have grasped in an intuitive manner an important aspect of the truth about inflation, even if it has not so far been possible to formulate it in a shape that stands up well to statistical testing. An alternative view is that they believe the demand inflation model because any theory that says monetary and fiscal policies are important has an irresistable attraction for people who earn their living and derive their social prestige from administering monetary and fiscal policies.

Whatever the truth of these conjectures, the world's finance ministers and central bankers have shown considerable willingness to impose, and to some extent even to threaten, credit controls and fiscal measures that increase unemployment in the short run, in the avowed interests of reducing inflation.

We have seen that, even if the demand inflation model contains part of the truth, there is plenty about inflation left to explain; in the next chapters we go on to consider some alternative views of inflation.

20. Cost Inflation

Cost inflation is the name given to the process by which changes in any one price or wage rate lead to changes in other prices. To understand this theory, it is helpful to consider the process of price- or wage-setting.

In view of the uncertainty about the various symptoms of excess supply and excess demand, there is usually no one obviously 'right' price or wage for any particular good or type of labour at any one time. Some levels of prices and wages are obviously 'wrong'; if a price is set too low it will fail to cover the direct costs of production, and if it is set too high it will lead to rapid loss of customers; if a wage rate is set too high it will be impossible to get employers to replace workers who leave, and if it is set too low it will be impossible to recruit anybody suitable for the job. Between these limits, however, there is usually some range of prices or wages within which choice is largely a matter of guesswork.

Also, it is administratively inconvenient to change prices or wages too often. With wages determined by collective bargaining, or prices set by government-appointed control bodies, the actual process of negotiating a change takes time. Even where prices are set unilaterally, price lists take time and cost money to print and distribute, and labels or advertisements may mention prices and would need to be changed. If it is planned that a price or wage rate decided now should remain in force for some period of time, it is necessary in deciding on its level to have some idea of what will be happening to other prices and wages during the life of the new price. There is no certain way of predicting this, which adds to the uncertainty about the right price.

PRICING RULES

Because of all the difficulties in assessing a 'correct' price or wage rate from first principles, people setting wages and prices tend to make use of various 'rules of thumb'. Goods prices will be set in some customary relation to their costs, including labour, materials, fuel and transport, or in a relation to the prices of other goods that experience has suggested is safe. Wage rates will be set in a customary relation to the rates for other workers, or to the cost of living. These rules are not inflexible; they may give different answers, for example when the wage rate of a group with which comparability has traditionally been maintained has risen by more or less than the cost of living. In these cases a choice has to be made between the different rules, and supply and demand signals will to some extent be taken into account. This type of customary relativity is the material of many of the arguments used in collective bargaining, or in negotiation with government-appointed price control bodies.

LAGGED ADJUSTMENTS

When any given price or wage rate is renewed, the new level at which it is set will be affected in two ways by recent changes in other prices and wages. First, the more other prices and wage rates have risen, the lower the price will look now relative to its customary differentials, and the more it will need to rise to restore them. Second, as prices have to be set for some period into the future, the faster other prices and wages have been rising, the more they can be expected to rise during the life of the price now being set; this again argues for a larger increase, if the relative level of the price being set during its period of currency is to be about right on the average.

COST INFLATION

This gives rise to the cost inflation model, in which most price and wage rises are explained by some earlier increases in the prices of other goods, or in other wage rates. The model distinguishes in principle between active and passive participants in the cost inflation process.

Active Cost Inflation

Cost inflation can start with some sector of the economy deciding to shift the existing pattern of prices or wages in its own favour. Possible cases of this include:

(1) a price rise by a monopolist;
(2) a wage increase negotiated by a powerful trade union;
(3) a rise in import prices imposed on the country by a change in world trading conditions;
(4) an increase in the government's claims on the country's real resources, giving rise to higher tax rates and lower real take-home pay. If direct taxes are raised then money take-home pay will be cut; if indirect taxes are used, then the same level of money income will represent less real purchasing power, so that real take-home pay falls. Workers will then demand compensation in the form of a pay rise.

Any of these could start off a process of cost inflation. The model is clearly incomplete, since it does not investigate why a monopolist should choose this particular time to increase the degree of exploitation of his monopoly position, or why a powerful union should choose this particular time to try to improve the living standards of its members relative to those of other people. We would only really be able to claim that we could explain inflation if we could explain the timing of the active parts of cost inflation.

Passive Cost Inflation

Price and wage increases can be passive, or defensive, designed merely to restore some normal relation to other prices or wages rates, which has been disturbed by changes elsewhere. This will indeed usually be asserted by those gaining by the increase, and it is very often possible to find at least some degree of justification for the assertion.

If we had some stable background against which to judge price and wage changes, it might be possible to sort out in practice which are aggressive, or active, and which are merely defensive, or passive. We lack any such stable background, however; prices and wages have been altering their relation to each other for as far back as we care to inquire.

By way of illustrating this instability of price relations, Table 20.1 shows the annual rates of increase from 1968 to 1978 of ten of the main categories of goods included in the consumer price index. Many of these groups, e.g. food, themselves contain numerous components, some of which will have risen in price in any one year by more than the average for the group, while others rose by less. As prices do not rise uniformly within any year, comparisons for particular dates would show up even wider variations in the relative prices of different goods than appear in the annual averages. A very similar analysis can be carried out for the relative wage rates of different types of labour. It is clear from this exercise that almost any increase in any price or wage can be defended as being 'passive', a mere restoration of some previous relativity, given sufficient discretion over the choice of other goods and dates with which to make comparisons.

TABLE 20.1   *Variations in Inflation, 1968–78*

Commodity group	1969 %	1970 %	1971 %	1972 %	1973 %	1974 %	1975 %	1976 %	1977 %	1978 %
Food	5.4	5.0	9.5	6.8	12.3	16.7	23.3	15.7	16.2	8.5
Housing	6.3	8.7	10.5	11.7	15.1	19.8	22.5	15.0	14.9	11.6
Durables	4.2	7.0	7.8	3.4	4.2	15.8	23.9	12.2	17.9	12.3
Alcohol	9.0	3.4	5.8	4.3	3.7	11.7	25.0	16.5	13.7	6.1
Clothing	3.8	5.3	6.8	6.9	9.5	18.0	14.2	10.9	12.6	8.0
Running costs of motor vehicles	8.8	2.6	5.7	4.8	7.7	28.2	29.7	9.7	12.7	1.9
Fuel and light	2.9	3.8	9.5	7.0	2.8	17.5	31.5	24.4	15.6	7.3
Tobacco	8.7	1.7	1.9	1.4	1.3	16.4	28.9	17.1	22.9	−1.4
Travel	4.6	6.7	13.6	4.7	7.3	14.8	28.2	23.4	13.9	9.6
Other household goods	5.3	8.2	7.4	5.3	8.7	19.4	21.2	14.3	15.4	10.9
Average*	5.9	5.2	7.8	5.6	7.3	17.8	24.8	15.9	15.6	7.5
Standard deviation	2.1	2.3	3.1	2.7	4.1	4.2	5.0	4.7	2.8	4.1

* Unweighted average of ten groups above. The consumer price index behaves slightly differently from this average, because it weights the items by expenditure on them, and includes some minor items omitted here.

Source: Blue Book on *National Income and Expenditure 1979*, Tables 4.9 and 4.10.

It should not in any case be supposed that 'passive' participants in the process of cost inflation are thereby freed from blame. If the prices of other goods have gone up because of some special factor, e.g. harvest failure, or if other people's wages have gone up because of improved productivity, those who insist on parallel increases without any similar special justification are more to blame for cost inflation than the 'active' participants they follow. It is only because some groups are willing to accept only partial, or no, price and wage rises to restore past relativities that relative prices and wages can change at all without producing unlimited cost inflation.

LAGS AND DISCONTENT

Suppose that inflation was to proceed at a steady n per cent each year, and that all prices and wages were adjusted once a year, with exactly one-twelfth of them adjusting each month. This means that in the month when your own wages, or the prices of the goods you sell, increase you gain n per cent from your own increase, and lose $(1/12)n$ per cent through the general rise in the cost of living. In each of the remaining eleven months you just lose $(1/12)n$ per cent. On average during the year you will be $(11/24)n$ per cent worse off than in your best month (and, of course, $(11/24)n$ per cent better off than in your worst month). If n is small, say 2.5 per cent a year, on average you are 1.15 per cent worse off than in your best month; this will hardly be noticed. If inflation is rapid, say 25 per cent a year, on average you are 11.5 per cent worse off than in your best month, and at worst another 11.5 per cent below; this will really hurt.

On a philosophical view of this process, people would realize that their best month's real income is intentionally higher than usual, in compensation for the losses they will endure later in the year. However, one has to be quite sophisticated to see this, and it is very easy to come to regard your position immediately after a rise as being the right and natural one, and to come to feel that other people's gains during the rest of the year are being made at your expense. The result is that during a period of rapid inflation people become more and more disgruntled with each other, every group believing that it is bearing more than its fair share of the real cost of inflation.

An End to Inflation

The process by which various prices and wages are adjusted in turn, with each adjusted so as to put it into a preferred relation to those decided earlier, helps to explain why inflation, once started, is very hard to stop. At any moment some prices and wages are seriously below their equilibrium levels. Firms will not be covering their full costs, or workers may not be receiving enough to keep up recruitment to their occupations. Those who are just approaching their turn in the annual cycle of adjustments are most likely to be in this position.

Everybody wants inflation stopped, but we do not all want it stopped at the same moment. Those who have just had their turn want the cycle stopped at once, before other groups overtake them; those whose turn has not yet come want it to go on just a little longer. Each further round of price and wage adjustments, however, raises the average price level and the cost of living, and adds to the group who feel that their present prices or wages are too low to be permanently tolerable.

Examples of Cost Inflation

Table 20.2 gives some basic data on cost inflation in recent years. Column (1) shows the rate of inflation, as measured by the annual percentage increase in the GDP deflator. Column (2) gives the annual percentage increase in the index of import prices. Column (3) gives the index of employment incomes per unit of final product; these are the two main sources of cost increases for firms. Column (4) gives the annual change in the percentage of total personal incomes taken in tax and national insurance contributions each year; this has been widely cited as a contributory factor in cost inflation.

Import Prices and Inflation

In the UK imports account for almost a quarter of total final expenditure. Their prices affect the various price indices in various ways.

TABLE 20.2   *Cost Inflation, 1968–78*

Year	Inflation* %	Increase in import price index %	Increase in employment incomes per unit of final product %	Change in percentage of personal incomes taken in tax** %
	(1)	(2)	(3)	(4)
1968	3.0	11.2	2.4	n.a.
1969	3.7	2.5	3.1	0.4
1970	7.5	6.8	9.8	0.5
1971	10.8	4.1	9.5	0.0
1972	9.9	3.3	9.5	−0.8
1973	7.5	23.5	7.8	0.8
1974	17.1	43.1	23.6	1.5
1975	27.3	14.3	29.9	1.9
1976	13.7	21.8	10.7	0.3
1977	11.9	14.7	8.3	−1.1
1978	10.7	3.0	10.8	−1.5
Average 1968–70	4.7	6.8	5.1	0.4†
Average 1971–73	9.4	10.3	8.9	0.0
Average 1974–78	16.1	19.4	16.7	0.2
Average 1968–78	11.2	13.5	11.4	0.2‡

* Percentage increase in GDP deflator.
** Including national insurance contributions.
† Average 1969–70.
‡ Average 1969–78.
Source: Column (1) as Table 2.2; column (2), Blue Book on *National Income and Expenditure 1979*, Tables 1.1 and 2.1; column (3), Blue Book, Table 2.5; column (4), as Table 5.2.

The prices of imports of consumer goods, including many food-stuffs, petrol and many manufactured goods, enter directly into the consumer price index. Imports of raw materials, fuels and machinery enter into industrial costs, and therefore affect prices.

The UK imports a sufficiently small part of the total world supply of most of the goods that it buys that their prices in foreign currency can be regarded as fairly independent of conditions in the UK economy. Sorting out the effects of import prices on inflation, however, is complicated by the fact that the price of sterling in terms of other currencies has changed substantially over the past decade. In late 1967 a fixed exchange rate was devalued by 14 per cent; and since 1971 there has been a flexible exchange rate, and sterling has fallen considerably relative to the dollar and the main European currencies. This will be discussed in more detail in Chapter 24.

If there is inflation in the UK, and if in order to keep foreign trade in balance the exchange rate goes down in proportion, this will raise import prices. To avoid the complications this causes, in considering import prices as a source of inflation we will look at the difference between the increase in import prices in any year and the general inflation rate. This is shown in Table 20.3; column (1) gives the rate of inflation, column (2) the percentage increase in import prices, and column (3) the difference between column (2) and column (1).

TABLE 20.3   *Import Prices and Cost Inflation, 1968–78*

Year	Inflation* R_n %	Increase in import price index M_n %	Relative increase in import prices $(M_n - R_n)$ %	Change in inflation $(R_n - R_{n-1})$ %
	(1)	(2)	(3)	(4)
1968	3.0	11.2	8.2	0.2
1969	3.7	2.5	−1.2	0.7
1970	7.5	6.8	−0.7	3.8
1971	10.8	4.1	−6.7	3.3
1972	9.9	3.3	−6.6	−0.9
1973	7.5	23.5	16.0	−2.4
1974	17.1	43.1	26.0	9.6
1975	27.3	14.3	−13.0	10.2
1976	13.7	21.8	8.1	−13.6
1977	11.9	14.7	2.8	−1.8
1978	10.7	3.0	−7.7	−1.2

* Percentage increase in GDP deflator.
Source: as Table 20.2.

From 1968 to 1978 import prices rose by 13.5 per cent a year on average, compared with only 11.2 per cent average domestic inflation. Column (3) shows, however, that there was considerable variation in the relation between import prices and inflation. In 1974 import prices rose 26 per cent faster than the domestic inflation rate, and in 1973 they rose 16 per cent faster. In 1968 import prices rose 8 per cent faster than domestic inflation, following the devaluation of sterling in November 1967. This looked a strong inflationary rise compared with the mild inflation current at that time. In other years import prices rose more slowly than domestic inflation; in 1975 import costs rose by 13 per cent less than domestic inflation, as domestic prices caught up with the import price rises of the previous years.

Column (4) shows the change in the rate of inflation each year. A cost inflation model suggests that, when import prices rise faster than the general rate of inflation, the rate itself will tend to rise, as various price- and wage-setters try to catch up with import prices, or with other prices strongly affected by import costs.

Because of the time lags in the formation of industrial prices, and in the processes of wage bargaining, there will be some lag in the relation between import price rises and changes in the rate of inflation; how long the lag is must be determined empirically. In fact, if we regress the change in the inflation rate, $(R_n - R_{n-1})$, on the difference between import prices and general inflation in the previous year, $(M_{n-1} - R_{n-1})$, where R is the inflation index and M the index of import price rises, for the period 1969–78 we find that each one per cent rise in the rate of increase of import prices relative to domestic inflation in year $n - 1$ was associated with a 0.47 per cent rise in the inflation rate in year n relative to that in year $n - 1$. This relation accounts for 65 per cent of the observed variance of $(R_n - R_{n-1})$. This is not a very good fit, but this is hardly surprising considering all the other influences on inflation, including demand inflation, that are being left out. It should be noted that the inclusion of R_{n-1} on both sides of the regression exposes it to various statistical pitfalls, which means that the result is not very reliable. It does suggest however that, so far as import prices are concerned, the cost inflation model seems to have a solid basis in reality.

In more impressionistic terms, it is often argued that the 1967 devaluation, following on a decade in which the inflation rate averaged 3.2 per cent and never rose above 4.6 per cent, gave the impulse to the speeding up of inflation in the 1970s. As inflation was still only 3.7 per cent in 1969, this does not seem very plausible.

In 1973, even before the oil crisis, import prices rose considerably, and then in late 1973 and 1974 the OPEC countries raised the price of oil by about 400 per cent. This started off a major process of cost inflation in all advanced countries, as various sectors of the economy tried to pass on to each other the impact on their real incomes of a worsening of the terms of trade – by 20 per cent in two years in the case of the UK.

WAGE COSTS AND INFLATION

A second aspect of cost inflation is the impact of wages and salaries on price changes. As wages and salaries account for most of value added, there is bound to be a strong correlation between changes in prices and changes in employment incomes per unit of final product. Table 20.4 provides data for inspecting a form of this model. Column (1) gives the rate of inflation, measured by the increase in the GDP deflator as before. Column (2) gives the increase in employment incomes per unit of final product. Column (3) gives the difference between this and the rate of inflation; i.e. column (3) equals column (2) minus column (1).

The model suggests that, if employment incomes per unit of final product rise faster than prices, so that gross profit margins shrink as a proportion of total output, the rate of price inflation will speed up as employers try to restore their gross margins; while if employment incomes per unit of product rise more slowly than prices, the rate of inflation will come down. Again, we expect this process to be subject to time lags, whose length must be determined empirically. In this case, using annual data we get a better result regressing $(R_n - R_{n-1})$ on $(E_n - R_n)$ than on $(E_{n-1} - R_{n-1})$, where E is the index of increases in employment incomes per unit of final product. The regression shows that for each one per cent by which employment incomes per unit of final product rise faster than prices, the overall rate of inflation speeds up by 1.76 per cent. This relation accounts for 59 per cent of the observed variance in $(R_n - R_{n-1})$, which makes it seem plausible that there is something in the theory. Again, the inclusion of R_n in both sides of the regression exposes it to statistical traps so that the result is not at all reliable.

TABLE 20.4   *Employment Incomes and Cost Inflation, 1968–78*

Year	Inflation* R_n %	Increase in employment incomes per unit of final product E_n %	Relative increase in employment incomes $(E_n - R_n)$ %	Change in rate of inflation $(R_n - R_{n-1})$ %
	(1)	(2)	(3)	(4)
1968	3.0	2.4	−0.6	0.2
1969	3.7	3.1	−0.6	0.7
1970	7.5	9.8	2.3	3.8
1971	10.8	9.5	−1.3	3.3
1972	9.9	9.5	−0.4	−0.9
1973	7.5	7.8	0.3	−2.4
1974	17.1	23.6	6.5	9.6
1975	27.3	29.9	2.6	10.2
1976	13.7	10.7	−3.0	−13.6
1977	11.9	8.3	−3.6	−1.8
1978	10.7	10.8	0.1	−1.2

* Percentage increase in GDP deflator.
Source: as Table 20.2.

PERSONAL TAXATION AND INFLATION

A further cost inflation model suggests that the rate of inflation is affected by changes in personal taxation. The theory is that, if there is a rise in the level of personal taxation, this leaves workers with less take-home pay. If they place less value on increased government expenditure than on private consumption, they will demand higher wages in compensation, and in view of fiscal drag on the increased income, they may need to ask for considerably more before tax.

There is clearly some scope for this to have occurred; column (4) of Table 20.2 shows the annual changes in the percentage of total personal incomes taken in tax and national insurance contributions. Figures for the proportion of tax on labour incomes separately are not available, but as they receive the largest part of total incomes it is probable that the overall figures are not unrepresentative. Over the decade from 1968 to 1978 the share of personal incomes paid in tax and national insurance contributions increased on average by only 0.2 per cent a year; the increase was as high as 1.9 per cent in 1975 and 1.5 per cent in 1974, while there were decreases of 1.5 per cent in 1978 and 1.1 per cent in 1977. The resulting percentage changes in take-home pay would be somewhat larger. Unfortunately the effects of this factor in inflation are impossible to isolate statistically in any simple manner. A piece of casual evidence on this effect is the fact that in 1977 and 1978 the Chancellor used the promise of personal tax concessions as an inducement to persuade the unions to accept wage restraint.

THE COST OF LIVING AND WAGE INFLATION

There is a very widely held belief that increases in the cost of living have an influence on changes in wage rates. In making wage claims, unions demand compensation for past increases in the cost of living, and to some extent for anticipated future increases in prices. The past changes at least are regarded by employers and arbitrators on wage claims as being legitimate arguments for an increase.

When we investigate the facts, we find that there is a high correlation between price rises and increases both in wage rates and in the level of employment incomes per unit of output. Unfortunately, while the correlation between wage and price changes is very high, this is so only when we compare increases in the same year. This tells us nothing about the direction of causation; it could be that wages rise because prices rise, or that prices rise because wages rise, or both could result from some other factor. If we try to explain wage increases by the price changes of earlier years, the statistical results are too poor to be worth quoting. There is in fact no simple relation that gives any help towards explaining the level of wage rises each year.

There are two possible reactions to this. One is that, if no simple relation can be found, then we must search for a more complex explanation, involving several explanatory variables. This is a flourishing line of research, but involves the use of advanced statistical techniques and will not be pursued here. The other alternative is to conclude that the rate of wage inflation is what the unions decide it shall be; if this so, then to control inflation governments must negotiate with the unions. This leads us to the question of prices and incomes policies, which is the topic of the next chapter.

21. Prices and Incomes Policies

In addition to the use of monetary and fiscal policies to control the level of demand, governments over the past decade have adopted a whole succession of 'prices and incomes policies', designed to control inflation by acting directly on the processes of price and wage determination, rather than through the manipulation of effective demand.

It has been widely argued that the government ought to have 'policies' about prices and incomes. This is for three main reasons.

(1) *Income distribution.* The distribution of real incomes depends on the relation between various prices and wage rates; this makes the process of deciding price and wage levels of great political interest.

(2) *Full employment.* The concern of all governments with keeping down unemployment has made them reluctant to see deflation of the level of demand used sufficiently vigorously to prevent inflation, even if they have believed this to be possible.

(3) *Residual responsibility.* The government is nowadays regarded by many people as being responsible in the last resort for everything that happens to the economy. It is therefore thought that it ought to have a policy for every problem.

What Powers Does the Government Have?

There are many channels through which the government can influence inflation, besides demand management. These include:
(1) its position as the largest single employer in the economy;

(2) its position as a major purchaser from many industries;
(3) its overall control of the nationalized industries;
(4) its access to the media to publicize its views on what it would like to see happening to prices and wages;
(5) its control over taxes, tariffs and the exchange rate;
(6) the theoretically unlimited powers of Parliament to pass laws authorizing the control of any aspect of the economy.

What Can Governments Actually Do with These Powers?

There are a large number of policies governments can adopt; UK governments have tried most of them. They include:
(1) tax changes;
(2) the imposition of price controls;
(3) the imposition of wage controls;
(4) the imposition of controls on profits and/or dividends;
(5) the imposition of 'cash limits' on public expenditure.

Any of these measures may be adopted for alternative reasons. They may be used for the sake of their direct effects on prices or wages, or they may be used to 'buy' consent from people affected by other government policies. It may for example be easier to persuade unions to accept wage controls if there are also to be price controls, and easier to persuade firms to accept price controls if there are also to be wage controls.

Tax Changes

Concessions on direct taxes improve take-home pay; concessions on indirect taxes lower the price index. If one believes that the total level of demand is the important variable determining inflation, through a demand inflation model, or that the monetary effects of a budget deficit are the important thing, via their effects on demand later on, then tax cuts are seen as inflationary and tax rises as counter-inflationary measures. If one believes in cost inflation, however, then tax cuts may help to restrain inflation both through their *direct* effects in reducing the price index and through their indirect effects if they can be used to buy consent to other control measures. At a time of 'stagflation', when high inflation rates coincide with high unemployment, tax cuts look tempting as an anti-inflationary device, and have been so used.

Earlier in the postwar era the West German government used tariff cuts as a weapon against inflation; this is now impossible as a national policy as tariffs in Western Europe are set jointly by the EEC.

Cash Limits

Cash limits in the public sector are of course part of overall budgetary policy. They have a role as a measure of wage control because, when a cash limit is in force, if unions believe the government will stick to it they have to face the prospect that, the higher the wage rate they negotiate, the fewer jobs there will be in the public service concerned. Under the previous system, in which it was assumed that if costs rose extra funds would be provided to meet them via 'supplementary estimates', it was argued that the management side had inadequate incentive to resist wage claims. The same argument applies to prices of goods where the public sector is a major purchaser.

Controls on Prices and Wages

Various controls on prices and wages have been resorted to by governments, for two distinct and not entirely consistent reasons:
(1) to try to restrict increases in prices and wages;
(2) to try to influence the relative incomes of different groups in the
    economy, and the relationship between incomes and prices.
The latter aim is also shared by other controlling bodies, including the Monopolies Commission, wages boards and by equal pay legislation.

HOW PRACTICABLE ARE PRICE AND WAGE CONTROLS?

There is no reason to doubt that price and wage controls can have some real influence on both absolute and relative price and wage levels, at least in the short run. This is due partly to the wide range of legal powers and methods of persuasion open to governments. It is due much more to the existence of a range of indeterminacy in the 'right' wage or price at any one time, in the minds of the people who have to set it. If the government introduces legal controls, or simply publicizes 'guidelines' that fall within this range of indeterminacy, there is a very good chance that they will be complied with, at least for a while. If the policies attempt to fix prices or wages outside the limits of what the people concerned regard as tolerable, then they will meet severe resistance, of forms we will discuss below.

The hope of price and wage controls is that, if those fixing particular prices or wages can be induced to plump for figures near the bottom of their range of indeterminacy, this will lower the rate of inflation expected by those deciding the next round. If they in turn can be induced to choose figures near the bottom of their range, inflationary expectations will continue to fall, and in this way the actual inflation rate can gradually be reduced. This hope was actually incorporated in the name of the '$n-1$' policy, in which unions in each 'round' of wage settlements were urged to accept an increase 1 per cent smaller than that in the round before.

While there may be no doubt that price and wage controls *could* work to reduce inflation, there is great doubt as to whether they *have* in fact 'worked'. There are two major difficulties in judging the effectiveness of price and wage controls: the first is that we do not have a well-defined idea of what would have happened to prices and wages in the absence of any 'policy'; the second is that the actual mechanism of the controls has been adjusted so frequently that a statistical study of their effects is extremely difficult, and cannot be attempted here.

There have during the past decade been innumerable boards, committees, 'wise men', 'guidelines', 'stages', 'phases', etc; there is not room here for a chronological account of them. Given the comparative stability of the desire of successive governments to control inflation, the fact that they have changed the mechanism quite so often suggests that the governments themselves have not usually been content with the execution of their general policies. One suspects that if any method of control had been hit upon that did give the desired results, the government would have stuck to it. It is the author's view that, while it is hard to be sure what results controls have had, on the whole they have been disappointing. After all, following ten years of almost continuous experiment with these 'policies', inflation is still with us. It is not suggested that this is the result of ill-will or incompetence; rather, there are some very real difficulties about price and wage controls, which we will now analyse.

ENFORCEMENT OF POLICIES

Problems about enforcement arise whether a policy has legal force or is voluntary. For a policy to be effective three conditions must be satisfied:

(1) there must be some method of deciding what the policy implies in particular cases;
(2) there must be some method of checking whether people are in fact complying with it;
(3) there must be some form of sanction, if only moral, against anybody found to be disobeying the policy.

Price Controls

These are relatively easy to enforce, given sufficient determination, on large and well-known firms selling standardized commodities. Price controls are more difficult to enforce upon small firms, or firms selling non-standardized goods, simply because there are too many of them for infractions to be monitored.

It is impossible to apply price controls to imports, unless we are prepared to suspend foreign trade if international prices rise beyond limits we set; we cannot force foreigners to sell cheaply to us. If import prices cannot be controlled, it is very difficult to refuse to allow increases in costs to be passed on by firms using imported fuels or materials in significant quantities. There are many goods that are partly imported and partly produced at home; any effort to control the price of the home-produced variety when the price of imports rises would produce great problems.

It is also impossible to control prices that are fixed by auction, or in other competitive markets. Difficulties arise in controlling the prices for new products, or modified products, or for goods specially designed and tailor-made for particular customers.

Many goods are normally sold to the public at 'discount' prices, as compared with an official or 'list' price set by the maker that is rarely or never actually charged; it is not clear whether controls should apply to the list price, or to the variety of prices actually charged to customers.

If price controls can be enforced, they are liable to lead to shortages, or to a deterioration of the quality of the good provided. The market in rented housing provides classic examples of both these effects.

All this is not to say that price controls can never have any effect; but they are likely to do so only with some degree of voluntary co-operation on the part of the sellers.

Wage Controls

These again are very difficult to enforce upon small firms, non-unionized firms or subcontractors.

Severe problems arise with control when the pay of some groups of workers is fixed via time rates and the pay of other groups is fixed by piece rates. A comparable problem arises if policies allow 'productivity deals'; these are more practicable for groups whose product consists of something that can be counted than for groups whose product does not lend itself to similar calculations.

Some occupations have incremental pay scales, on which people receive regular additions to their pay as the reward of longer service and greater experience; other groups rely on a less formal system of *ad hoc* reassessment. If a policy disallows contractually fixed increments, it is liable to encounter extreme resistance from those who are affected. If a control does allow increments, it will be regarded as unfair by those on the *ad hoc* system; and if *ad hoc* adjustments are allowed then for these groups control will be non-existent.

Controls can be avoided by changing job descriptions, so that a larger proportion of the labour force is treated as being 'skilled', or 'supervisory'; this type of up-grading is particularly hard to monitor as the average level of skill of the labour force has in fact been increasing anyway. Controls can also be avoided by allowing workers to slack during normal working hours, so that overtime working becomes necessary, or indeed by paying them for overtime or for whole shifts that they do not actually work. Premiums can be paid for quality of product, or regularity of attendance, in excess of that actually achieved.

Finally, 'fringe benefits' can be improved, for example subsidized meals, the private use of the firm's car or leisure facilities. An increase in these benefits is probably bad for the efficiency of the economy, since benefits in kind give worse value for the resources they use than letting workers have more money to spend for themselves. Evidence on fringe benefits is inevitably anecdotal; the author's favourite example is the small firm whose social club contracted, during a pay pause, to take the firm's entire labour force on holiday for a fortnight in Majorca for £1 a head.

All these problems, both with price and with wage controls, are probably tolerable in the short run; firms have their long-run reputation for quality to consider, which will inhibit them in cutting the standard of their products; job classifications have normally required lengthy negotiation to achieve an acceptable situation, and firms will be reluctant to jeopardize such agreements for a purely transient advantage. However, the longer controls remain in force, the more likely it is that they will be evaded in all the ways described above, and others. This is partly because firms will have had more time to devise ways round the rules; as time goes on new products, new techniques or new locations will raise genuine problems of interpretation of any rules, and firms may also be tempted to make changes deliberately so as to raise such ambiguities. They are also likely to become increasingly convinced that other people are breaking or evading the rules, which will probably be true, and the more they believe this the more likely they are to resort to similar ruses themselves.

THE STRUCTURAL EFFECTS OF CONTROLS

It is likely that if controls are effective at all they will produce changes in the structure of relative prices and wages, many of which were neither foreseen nor desired by the authorities. To try to determine the actual levels of all prices and wages would be a fantastic administrative task, as there are literally millions of them. Price and wage controls usually start from the position that the present levels of prices and wages, however they were originally set, should not be increased without permission, or should be raised only subject to a maximum percentage increase.

Price or wage 'freezes' attempt to peg the existing structure of relative wages and prices. Uniform percentage limits on increases have an effect in the same direction, particularly if the maximum increase comes to be regarded as normal. It is in fact rather unlikely that the structure of prices and wages in force at the moment when the control began will have been satisfactory to all parties at the time. Controls are usually imposed only after inflation has begun, and we have seen that prices and wages in different sectors of the economy change in sequence. Even if the structure of wages and prices was acceptable when the controls began, the longer they continue the more likely it is that changes in circumstances will require the structure to change. This may not matter too much for short 'freezes' – very few prices or wages are so bad that people cannot live with them for a month or two more – but as time goes on more and more groups will come to regard a freeze on the existing structure as intolerable.

It is however very likely that controls will be less effective for some sectors of the economy than for others; this is liable to impair the solvency of some businesses. An example of this can be seen in rented housing, where a combination of relatively effectively controlled rents with uncontrolled building costs has meant that many landlords could not afford to keep premises in good repair out of the controlled rent. When controls work unevenly they are liable to produce shortages of goods or types of labour whose prices are effectively controlled, and to lead to a diversion of resources into producing goods and services whose prices are harder to control.

In the case of wage controls, there is an alternative to a uniform percentage limit on increases; this is the 'flat rate limit' to wage rises. Such a policy tends to squeeze 'differentials'; if everybody gets a wage rise of £6 a week this means a 20 per cent rise for a worker on £30 a week but only 5 per cent for a skilled worker on £120 a week. Flat rate limits have operated to diminish the premium placed by pay scales on skill and responsibility.

In both prices and wages, the distorting effects of controls are piling up inflationary trouble for the future, even if the policies achieve their short-run objectives. Sooner or later the prices of strictly controlled goods will have to rise if shortages are to be avoided, and the differentials of the skilled and responsible are going to have to be restored if they are to be replaced with competent successors when they leave. When the distortions are corrected this is liable to start off another round of cost inflation.

Profit controls have been widely advocated, but they are very difficult to enforce, mainly because firms do not know in advance how profitable their operations are going to be. As a substitute for profit controls, governments have restricted the dividends firms can distribute, not so much because anybody believes that this has any appreciable effect on the economy, but as a political sop to induce trade unions to accept wage controls.

All controls on prices and incomes suffer from the disadvantage that they blur responsibility for decisions in the economy. The fact that an increase is not contrary to prices and incomes policy comes to be regarded as adequate justification for it, whatever its effect on employment or resource allocation.

DISAGREEMENTS ON OBJECTIVES

If price and wage controls are used purely as a means of checking inflation, there is some measure of agreement on the objective. Even here, however, there is scope for disagreement on the means. We will consider three such controversies.

(1) Should we rely on price controls or on wage controls? One point of view says: concentrate on controlling prices, and after a short time lag, once price rises slow down, wages will come into line. The other view says: control wages, and once wage inflation stops, price stability will follow. The main difference between these policies is in their short-run effects on income distribution; the wage control policy favours profits, and the price control policy favours labour incomes.

It is not even clear that one can get a fair compromise by the apparently simple expedient of controlling both prices and wages. Employers argue that this is not as impartial as it looks, because price controls can be enforced against firms more than wage controls can be enforced against powerful unions. Firms will obey legal injunctions, and can be fined; but workers, if they are determined enough, can get away with flouting the law. It would be physically impossible to imprison all the miners or dockers, and the attempt would cause vast economic disruption.

(2) A second controversy concerns the speed with which controls

should attempt to reduce inflation. The argument for gradual reduction is that a sudden freeze would make permanent all the temporary disequilibria in the structure of relative prices and wages that arise during inflation. Also, monetary arrangements, for example mortgage interest rates, are geared to the expected rate of inflation. This should therefore be decreased gradually, to get a smooth transition to stable prices. The opposing view says that controls are always unpopular, and will be tolerated only if they are seen to be having results. Also, governments want to have cured inflation before the next election. This view urges that any policy must aim at quick results if it is to succeed at all.

(3) A third point of controversy in any general policy of limits on increases in prices and wages is the question of how much scope there should be for exceptions for 'special cases', and who should decide which groups have a special case. The argument against special cases is that once you start allowing them there is no rational place to stop, and if you let everyone be a special case then the policy collapses. The case for having some 'special cases' is that each round of prices and wages policy builds on the legacy of the ones before it. Any policy is bound to produce some anomalies and exceptionally hard cases; the victims can be expected to put up with it only if there is some prospect that their wrongs will one day be righted. If there is no scope for special cases, the message is that patience will never bring you a remedy, so you had might as well strike when it will cause maximum inconvenience.

OTHER OBJECTIVES

When it comes to the use of prices and incomes policies to influence the structure of prices and incomes, there is even more scope for disagreement on objectives.

Wage Controls

There are several objectives of incomes policy, not all of them consistent:
(1) to raise the living standards of the worst paid;

(2) to provide the incentives needed to make it worth-while acquiring skills and accepting responsibility;
(3) to avoid hurting people by sudden and drastic cuts in their pay and status compared with other groups.

It is pretty clear that there is never going to be complete concensus on the right balance between these objectives, and the right structure of relative income levels of various groups of workers.

Control of Prices and Profits

There is no agreement on the proper view of profits to be taken by those responsible for the control of prices; possible views include:
(1) the view that all profits are robbery of the workers, and that the proper level of profits is nil;
(2) the view that profits are a just and necessary reward for enterprise, and that every business should make fair and reasonable, and presumably so far as possible equal, profits;
(3) the view that, whatever the average level of profits, the proper social function of profits and losses is to transfer control of resources as rapidly as possible from people who waste them to those who organize them successfully. This means that firms run by people who are bad at predicting what processes will work, what goods customers will buy and what subordinates will work efficiently should be making large losses, and firms run by people who are good at these things should be making large profits.

These views are clearly not consistent; the differences between them are essentially political, and there is no reason to suppose that we are likely to see any concensus on these issues.

MISTAKEN PRICES AND INCOMES POLICIES

We have seen that it is hard to tell whether prices and incomes policies have worked in reducing inflation. Equally, it is hard to be sure when they have failed; all that can be done here is to outline some possible failings.

First, it is possible that on occasions the adoption of a publicly announced 'maximum' for price or wage increases may actually have caused some prices or wages to be raised by more than they might otherwise have been. On this view, incomes policies may at times have decreased the effectiveness of demand restrictions as a method of slowing inflation, thereby wasting the only beneficial by-product of unemployment.

Second, it is not obvious that the policy of UK governments in laying down a minimum period between settlements, normally a year, is sensible. This policy implies that any bargain struck now will have to be lived with for a year, during which prices and other wages will rise. Compensation for the full year's prospective inflation is therefore insisted on; unions might be willing to settle for less if they could look forward to an earlier renegotiation.

Third, governments have made a practice of including in packages of policies some elements designed as sops to particular groups in the economy. This applies to packages such as the 'social contract' of 1974, which included rent controls, food subsidies and flat rate wage increases. These inducements contain two sources of trouble for the future: (1) when rents eventually rise, subsidies are cut and pay differentials are restored, this will reactivate cost inflation; and (2) there is every reason to expect that any group that has exacted a price for its consent to anti-inflationary policies in one year will come back for more. This is not to say that measures to help the worst-off are wrong, but that they should be undertaken as part of a long-term policy, not as a bribe to win short-term consent to incomes policies.

SOME UNRESOLVED POLICY QUESTIONS

There thus remain some questions on prices and incomes policies that cannot be resolved entirely objectively, both because they involve political differences over their objectives, and because of very severe statistical difficulties in measuring their effects.
(1) Should the government have a 'policy' at all, and if so, with what objectives?
(2) Should it be permanent or short-run, in which case when does the short run end?
(3) Should it be 'statutory', i.e. enacted by Parliament on a delegated legislation basis and enforced by legal penalties; or

should it be voluntary, relying largely on the Chancellor's powers of persuasion?

Readers will have to decide these issues for themselves. (If they are interested in the author's answers, these are as follows.

(1) No; on the whole these policies have done more harm than good. They tempt governments to risk irresponsible monetary and fiscal policies, and they tempt unions to make bargains that damage employment. At best, they are a means of postponing trouble.

(2) If we must have 'policies', let them be genuinely short-term, with some discernable gaps between them, and let them be short-run in intent, i.e. concerned purely with restraining inflation when it shows signs of getting out of hand, by delaying price and wage rises until expectations are less inflationary.

(3) Given the sheer impossibility of real enforcement of price and wage controls on any uniform basis, they can only really work by consent. Thus if they are voluntary they will do just as much good if well-conceived as if they had legal force, while if they are badly thought out they will do less harm.)

22. Imports

We have seen how imports and exports play a vital part in determining the level of activity in the economy, and how imports are closely linked with inflation. In the next section we will consider how far imports and exports can themselves be explained, and how they interact to determine the balance of payments on current account. In this chapter we will first consider UK imports, including both 'visible' imports, of goods, and 'invisible' imports, of services.

Questions concerning imports include:
(1) What does the UK import?
(2) How have our imports changed?
(3) What determines the level of imports?

WHAT DOES THE UK IMPORT?

Table 22.1 shows the composition of all the debit items, i.e. payments to foreigners, in the UK balance of payments on current account in 1978. The table shows the various payments in £m, in £b and, to indicate their macroeconomic importance, as percentages of GNP at factor cost.

Much the largest category of debit items was visible imports, which totalled £36.6b, or 25.6 per cent of GNP. Of this total, imports of food, beverages and tobacco cost £5.7b, or 4.0 per cent of GNP. This category includes some goods like wheat and butter where a substantial part of our requirements is produced at home, and other goods like tea, coffee and tobacco that we cannot produce at all, so that we have to import all we use.

Imports of basic materials, for example iron ore, cost £2.9b or 2.0

TABLE 22.1 *UK Imports in 1978*

	£m	£b	Percentage of GNP
Visible (i.e. goods) imports*		36,607	36.6	25.6
of which			
Food, beverages and tobacco	5,663	5.7	4.0
Basic materials	2,919	2.9	2.0
Mineral fuels and lubricants	4,536	4.5	3.2
Manufacturers and semimanufactures	22,989	23.0	16.1
Unclassified	500	0.5	0.4
Imports of services		8,596	8.6	6.0
of which			
Sea transport	3,334	3.3	2.3
Travel	1,548	1.5	1.1
Civil aviation	1,100	1.1	0.8
Government	1,015	1.0	0.7
Other services	1,918	1.9	1.3
Other current invisible items			
Property incomes**	4,211	4.2	2.9
Transfers†	3,002	3.0	2.1
Total current account debits	52,735	52.7	36.9

* Visible imports valued f.o.b. (free on board), i.e. cost at foreign port of embarkation, excluding freight and insurance. If these were provided by foreign firms they appear as invisible debits. In 1978 freight and insurance charges on imports totalled £1,963m, or 5.4 per cent of the f.o.b. value of imports.
** Property incomes paid to foreign holders of national debt or owners of foreign firms operating in the UK, net of UK taxes.
† Transfers including government aid, EEC contributions, private charitable donations and family transfers.
Source: *United Kingdom Balance of Payments, 1979*, Tables 1.2 and 2.2.

per cent of GNP. Imports of 'mineral fuels and lubricants', i.e. of oil, cost £4.5b or 3.2 per cent of GNP. Much the largest category of visible imports was £23.0b, or 16.1 per cent of GNP, of imports of manufactures and of 'semi-manufactures', for example copper wire. This group contains a vast number of consumer products and investment goods, most of which can also be made in the UK. Finally, £0.5b of imports were unclassified.

There were also imports of invisibles, or services, of £8.6b or 6.0 per cent of GNP. Invisible imports included £3.3b of payments for sea transport, £1.1b of civil aviation, £1.5b of travel expenditure abroad, £1b of general government expenditure, including expenditure by defence forces stationed abroad, and £1.9b of other services.

There were some further invisible debit items in the balance of payments. £4.2b of property income was paid abroad net of UK taxes, to foreign holders of national debt or foreign owners of firms operating in the UK. £3.0b of transfers were made, including government aid and subscriptions to international bodies including the United Nations, EEC contributions, private charitable donations, family transfers, including remittances by immigrants to their families overseas, and pensions paid to UK citizens in retirement abroad.

The grand total of all these current account debits was £52.7b, equal to 36.9 per cent of GNP.

How Have Imports Been Changing?

Table 22.2 gives details of changes in UK visible imports from 1968 to 1978 (details of changes in invisibles follow in Chapter 24). The imports are classified in two ways: first by commodity, and second by country of origin. To overcome the problems of comparison created by the inflation that has occurred during the decade, all items are given as percentages of GNP at factor cost.

The first section analyses imports by commodity. As imports of food, drink and tobacco, and of basic materials, have both been fairly stable and relatively small, they are combined in column (1). Over the whole period from 1968 to 1978 this group averaged 6.7 per cent of GNP, varying only between a minimum of 5.8 per cent in 1972 and a maximum of 7.5 per cent in 1974.

Column (2) shows imports of mineral fuels and lubricants, i.e. oil. Before 1973 expenditure on these was quite small, varying between 1.5 and 2 per cent of GNP. In 1974 the oil price explosion put this group up to 5.6 per cent of GNP; this has since been reduced, as other prices rose in pursuit of oil prices and North Sea development began to make the UK less dependent on imports for its oil. However, in 1974–78 oil imports averaged 4.3 per cent of GNP.

TABLE 22.2   Changes in UK Visible Imports, 1968–78

| Year | Analysis by commodities | | | Analysis by country of origin | | | | | Total goods % |
	Food & basics* %	Oil** %	Manufac-tures† %	EEC§ %	Other W. Eur‡ %	N. Am & Ot. Dev§ %	Oil §§ %	Rest of world• %	
	(1)	(2)	(3)	(4)	(5)	(6)	(7)	(8)	(9)
1968	7.2	1.8	9.8	5.2	2.6	5.8	1.5	3.7	18.8
1969	6.9	1.7	10.0	5.2	2.7	5.5	1.4	3.8	18.5
1970	6.8	1.5	10.2	5.2	2.8	5.8	1.3	3.4	18.5
1971	6.1	1.8	9.7	5.4	2.8	4.9	1.5	3.0	17.6
1972	5.8	1.7	10.7	6.2	3.0	4.9	1.4	2.9	18.3
1973	6.9	2.0	13.2	7.9	3.6	5.5	1.7	3.6	22.2
1974	7.5	5.6	15.7	10.1	4.1	6.1	4.6	4.0	28.8
1975	6.4	4.2	13.5	9.2	3.3	5.1	3.2	3.2	24.1
1976	6.7	4.7	14.6	10.0	3.6	5.2	3.5	3.7	26.0
1977	6.9	3.9	16.2	10.9	3.7	5.6	2.7	4.2	27.0
1978	6.0	3.2	16.4	11.1	3.6	5.2	2.1	3.5	25.6
Average 1968–70	7.0	1.7	10.0	5.2	2.7	5.7	1.4	3.6	18.6
Average 1971–73	6.3	1.8	11.2	6.5	3.1	5.1	1.5	3.2	19.4
Average 1974–78	6.7	4.3	15.3	10.3	3.7	5.4	3.2	3.7	26.3
Average 1968–78	6.7	2.9	12.7	7.9	3.3	5.4	2.3	3.5	22.3

* Food, beverages and tobacco, and basic materials.
** Mineral fuels and lubricants.
† Manufactures, semi-manufactures and unclassified.
§ EEC refers to the other 8 members throughout (i.e. France, W. Germany, Italy, the Netherlands, Belgium, Luxembourg, Denmark & Ireland).
‡ Other Western Europe.
§ North America, and other developed countries.
§§ Oil producing countries.
• Rest of the world.
All items are given as percentages of the GNP at factor cost.
Source: United Kingdom Balance of Payments, 1979, Tables 2.2 and 2.3.

Column (3) shows the remainder of imports, grouping together manufactures, semi-manufactures and unclassified imports. This group has risen steadily over the decade, relative to GNP. In 1968–70 it averaged 10 per cent, in 1971–73 11.2 per cent, and in

1974–78 15.3 per cent of GNP. In 1978, at 16.4 per cent of GNP, these imports were at their highest ever.

The remaining columns of Table 22.2 show visible imports classified by country of origin. Column (4) shows imports from the European Economic Community (EEC), i.e. from the eight other countries that were members in 1978: these were the six original members, France, West Germany, Italy, Belgium, Luxembourg and the Netherlands, and the two that joined with the UK, Denmark and Eire. The EEC share in UK imports has risen quite dramatically, from 5.2 per cent in 1968–70 to 6.5 per cent in 1971–73 and 10.3 per cent in 1974–78. In 1978, at 11.1 per cent of GNP, imports from the EEC were at their highest ever.

Column (5) shows imports from the other Western European countries, including Sweden, Switzerland, Norway and Finland. These too have risen, though less rapidly than imports from the EEC. As these countries lost former preferential tariffs under the European Free Trade Area when the UK entered the EEC, this is hardly surprising. Imports from other Western European countries rose from an average of 2.7 per cent of GNP in 1968–70 to 3.7 per cent in 1974–78.

Column (6) shows imports from North America, i.e. the USA and Canada, and other developed countries, including Australia, Japan and South Africa. These are grouped together because they have both been relatively stable; imports from this group averaged 5.7 per cent of GNP in 1968–70 and 5.4 per cent in 1974–78.

Column (7) shows imports from the oil-exporting countries, including Iran, Saudi Arabia, Kuwait and Nigeria. These have risen dramatically, from 1.4 per cent of GNP in 1968–70 to 3.2 per cent in 1974–78. These figures are below total imports of oil, as some oil products are imported from refineries in non-oil-producing countries.

Column (8) shows the UK imports from the rest of the world, including the non-oil-developing countries like Hong Kong and India, and also the Soviet bloc. These too have been stable; UK imports from them averaged 3.6 per cent of GNP in 1968–70 and 3.7 per cent in 1974–78.

Finally column (9) shows the total of visible imports, of all types of goods and from all countries. These have risen dramatically, relative to GNP over the period, from an average of 18.6 per cent of GNP in 1968–70, to 19.4 per cent in 1971–73 and to 26.3 per cent in

1974–78. The peak of 28.8 per cent of GNP in 1974 has not been equalled, but at 27 per cent 1977 was not far behind.

The overall trend means that during the decade the UK economy has become far more 'open'. This was partly due to the rise in oil prices, but much more to the increase in the imports of manufactures and semi-manufactures, and, among these, to imports from European countries.

WHAT DETERMINES THE LEVEL OF IMPORTS?

The factors determining foreign trade flows are very similar to those determining the level of sales inside the economy, with a few special features owing to the international nature of the transactions.

Imports and Income

The basic factor determining the demand for imports is the total level of effective demand. It is not obvious to what national income aggregate imports should be related. If imports consisted entirely of final products, like consumer goods or machinery for investment, one would expect total imports to be related to total domestic expenditure. If all imports consisted of intermediate products, like fuel and raw materials, one would expect to find imports related to total final demand, including exports, many of which make use of imported fuels and materials. As actual imports are partly final goods and partly intermediate products, presumably neither approach is completely right. We have chosen here to relate imports to total final expenditure, on the grounds that very few imports go to final users without some processing or at least internal transport and distribution.

Table 22.3 shows the relation between imports and total final expenditure, when both are valued at 1975 prices. Column (1) shows total final expenditure at 1975 prices; column (2) shows actual imports, including both goods and services. If we regress imports on total final expenditure we find that each £1m rise in total final expenditure leads to a rise of £0.32m in imports. Column (3) shows the level of imports predicted by this regression, and column (4) shows the error of this prediction, i.e. column (4) equals column (3)

TABLE 22.3   *Imports and Total Final Expenditure at 1975 prices, 1968–78*

Year	Total final expenditure £b	Actual imports £b	'Predicted' imports £b	Error* = (3) − (2) £b
	(1)	(2)	(3)	(4)
1968	113.0	22.2	22.6	0.4
1969	115.0	23.0	23.2	0.3
1970	118.3	24.2	24.3	0.1
1971	122.0	25.3	25.5	0.1
1972	126.6	27.8	26.9	−0.9
1973	137.6	31.1	30.4	−0.6
1974	136.3	31.3	30.0	−1.3
1975	133.0	29.0	29.0	−0.1
1976	138.0	30.2	30.6	0.4
1977	139.7	30.4	31.1	0.7
1978	144.3	31.6	32.6	0.9

* Error = predicted imports − actual imports. Discrepancies in figures are due to rounding to nearest £0.1b.
Source: Blue Book on *National Income and Expenditure, 1979*, Table 2.1.

minus column (2). This relation explains 96 per cent of the observed variance in imports, which is quite a good fit. It is not perfect, however, with errors in its prediction of imports for particular years up to 4 per cent of the actual level of imports. There is thus something left for other factors to explain, though no statistical fitting for the effects of any other factor can be attempted here.

Relative Prices

Imports may change because of alterations in the relative prices of imported goods or services and home-produced substitutes. Such changes in relative prices can occur for two reasons: the rate of inflation can differ between countries, or the exchange rates between their currencies can alter. Inflation in the UK has on average been faster than in other developed countries in recent years. Sterling has declined in value relative to the US dollar and leading European currencies such as the Deutschemark. As these two processes have not kept in step, there has been considerable variation in the level of UK prices relative to import prices, as was seen in Chapter 20.

The effects of this variation in the relative prices of imports on the total import bill in the short run are doubtful. For many imports, especially foodstuffs and materials, the elasticity of demand is rather low, so that a rise in import prices raises imports relative to GNP. For manufactures the elasticity of demand is much higher, but only in the fairly long run, since sales of many manufactured goods depend on sales effort, quality and after-sales service. Thus in the short run it is not at all clear that higher prices of imports reduce total expenditure on them. The overall effects of relative price changes on the import bill are very uncertain, and quite possibly on balance in the short run higher import prices tend to raise imports relative to GNP.

Trade Policies

A country's imports will be affected by the special controls it places on them, whether by tariffs or by quantitative restrictions. During the past decade there have been major changes in the UK's trading policies. Notably, we entered the EEC in 1973, and UK tariffs on EEC countries' goods have since been removed. This helps to account for the large increase in imports from EEC countries. (It will be seen in the next chapter that exports to the EEC have also grown very fast.)

Trade in an area such as the EEC may increase even before barriers to trade are removed. Once the change is expected, the prospect of open markets makes firms feel that it is worth-while to invest in establishing sales networks and after-sale servicing facilities even before the tariffs are removed.

The increase in manufactured imports, and the rise in unemployment in the UK, have led to demands for protection against imports. In the case of imports from EEC countries, which have been expanding rapidly, nothing can be done about this unless the UK leaves the EEC. There has however been an increase in the use of quota restrictions on imports from some less developed countries, from which total imports have in fact been pretty stable, and 'voluntary export restraint' agreements have been negotiated with their governments to limit their exports to the UK.

Technical Progress and Efficiency

Technical progress affects imports, since countries have to import new and improved goods that they do not have the technical skill to make for themselves. This applies particularly in very research-intensive industries such as computers, aircraft and pharmaceuticals.

General efficiency in business is a great aid in selling in any market. Customers prefer suppliers with a high reputation for the design of their products, quality control in production, early delivery dates and punctuality in meeting them, a reliable supply of spare parts and good facilities for training customers' staff in the use and care of the product. Equally, buyers avoid suppliers who lack these qualities. If any industry finds itself subject to increased competition from imports, it is worth checking on all these points to see whether its own deficiencies are exposing it to increased penetration of its domestic market by foreign suppliers.

POLICY QUESTIONS

The large increase in imports to the UK during the past decade obviously raises some important policy questions: can the country afford so many imports, and what can be done about them if it cannot? It is not really sensible to try to answer these questions, however, until we have seen what has been happening to exports, and how imports and exports interact to determine the balance of payments. Accordingly we will defer them, and go on to consider UK exports.

23. Exports

A country with as many imports as the UK needs comparable exports to pay for them. We can ask about exports the same questions as for imports:
(1) What does the UK export?
(2) How have our exports been changing?
(3) What determines the level of UK exports?

What Does the UK Export?

Table 23.1 shows UK receipts on current account in 1978, in £m, £b and as percentages of GNP at factor cost. Total visible exports were £35.4b, or 24.8 per cent of GNP.

Exports of food, drink and tobacco were £2.9b, or 2 per cent of GNP. This includes some processed foods like biscuits, and some UK specialities like whisky. Exports of basic materials were £1.0b, or 0.7 per cent of GNP. Exports of mineral fuels and lubricants were £2.4b, or 1.7 per cent of GNP; these were mainly refined products.

Much the largest group of visible exports were manufactures and semi-manufactures, which totalled £28.2b, or 19.7 per cent of GNP. These accounted for 80 per cent of total visible exports; they spanned a very wide range of engineering and other industrial products. Finally, £1b of exports were of unclassified goods.

Invisible exports, of services, were £12.2b, or 8.5 per cent of GNP. Services were relatively more important among exports than among imports; invisible exports were 25.6 per cent of the total of visible and invisible exports, whereas on the import side only 19 per cent of the total were invisibles. Invisible exports included £3.2b from sea transport, £1.4b from civil aviation, £2.5b from travel ex-

TABLE 23.1 *UK Exports in 1978*

	£m	£b	Percentage of GNP
Visible (i.e. goods) exports*	35,432	35.4	24.8
of which			
Food, beverages and tobacco	2,865	2.9	2.0
Basic materials	1,006	1.0	0.7
Mineral fuels and lubricants	2,375	2.4	1.7
Manufactures and semi-manufactures	28,175	28.2	19.7
Unclassified	1,011	1.0	0.7
Exports of services	12,204	12.2	8.5
of which			
Sea transport	3,163	3.2	2.2
Travel	2,503	2.5	1.8
Civil aviation	1,448	1.4	1.0
Financial services	1,488	1.5	1.0
Other services	3,284	3.3	2.3
Government	318	0.3	0.2
Other invisible items			
Property incomes**	5,047	5.0	3.5
Transfers†	1,084	1.0	0.8
Total current account credits	53,767	53.8	37.6

* Visible exports f.o.b.
** Property incomes received from debt owned abroad and profits of UK companies from operations abroad, net of foreign taxes.
† Transfers received.
Source: *United Kingdom Balance of Payments, 1979*, Tables 1.2 and 2.2.

penditure by foreigners in the UK, £1.5b from sales of financial services including banking and insurance, and £3.3b from sales of other services, including royalties, commission of consulting engineers and expenditure by foreign students and journalists. Finally, there were £0.3b of government receipts for services.

There were two further invisible items of receipts on current account: £5.0b, or 3.5 per cent of GNP, was received in property incomes from foreign securities or profits earned by UK companies operating abroad, net of foreign taxes, and £0.8b was received in transfers, by the government from the EEC and by the private sector from, for example, remittances to their families in the UK by British expatriate workers in Zambian copper mines.

The grand total of receipts on current account was £53.8b, or 37.6 per cent of GNP.

How Have UK Exports Changed?

Table 23.2 gives details of changes in the pattern of UK visible exports from 1968 to 1978, showing all items as percentages of GNP at factor cost. Exports are analysed first by commodity, then by country of destination.

Column (1) shows exports of food, beverages and tobacco, plus basic materials; these groups have been combined since both are so small. They have grown moderately, from 1.7 per cent of GNP in 1968–70 to 2.3 per cent in 1974–78.

Column (2) shows exports of mineral fuels and lubricants. These have grown from 0.4 per cent of GNP in 1968–70 to 1.3 per cent in 1974–78, and by 1977 had grown to 1.7 per cent; the increase however was largely accounted for by the rise in oil prices.

Column (3) shows exports of manufactures, semi-manufactures and unclassified goods. These grew from 15.7 per cent of GNP in 1968–70 to 19.6 per cent in 1974–78.

Columns (4) to (8) give a geographical analysis of exports. Column (4) shows exports to EEC countries, i.e. to the eight other 1978 members. These rose from 4.9 per cent of GNP in 1968–70 to 5.4 per cent in 1971–73 and 8.3 per cent in 1974–78. In 1978, at 9.6 per cent, they were the highest ever.

Column (5) shows exports to other Western European countries. Here growth was more modest, from 2.9 per cent of GNP in 1968–70 to 3.5 per cent in 1974–78.

Column (6) shows exports to North America and to other developed countries; these were sluggish, averaging 5.1 per cent of GNP in 1968–70 and 4.7 per cent in 1974–78.

Column (7) shows exports to oil-producing countries. These rose rapidly, from 1.1 per cent of GNP in 1968–70 to 2.7 per cent in 1974–78, as the result of the rapid rise in these countries' incomes.

Column (8) shows exports to the rest of the world, which were also sluggish, averaging 3.9 per cent of GNP in 1968–70 and 4 per cent in 1974–78.

TABLE 23.2   *Changes in UK Visible Exports, 1968–78*

| | Analysis by commodities | | | Analysis by country of destination | | | | | |
Year	Food & basics* %	Oil** %	Manufac- tures† %	EEC %	Other W. Eur‡ %	N. Am & Ot. Dev.§ %	Oil §§ %	Rest of world %	Total goods %
	(1)	(2)	(3)	(4)	(5)	(6)	(7)	(8)	(9)
1968	1.7	0.4	14.9	4.5	2.6	5.1	1.0	3.8	17.0
1969	1.6	0.4	16.0	5.0	2.9	5.1	1.1	4.0	18.1
1970	1.8	0.5	16.2	5.3	3.2	5.0	1.1	3.9	18.4
1971	1.7	0.5	16.0	5.0	3.0	5.0	1.2	3.9	18.1
1972	1.7	0.4	14.8	5.1	2.9	4.5	1.1	3.4	17.0
1973	1.9	0.6	16.0	6.0	3.1	4.6	1.2	3.4	18.5
1974	2.1	1.0	18.7	7.4	3.6	5.3	1.6	4.0	21.9
1975	2.1	0.9	17.7	6.7	3.3	4.4	2.4	3.9	20.6
1976	2.2	1.1	19.5	8.1	3.6	4.5	2.8	3.8	22.8
1977	2.5	1.7	21.5	9.5	3.9	4.7	3.4	4.2	25.8
1978	2.7	1.7	20.4	9.6	3.2	4.5	3.2	4.3	24.8
Average 1968–70	1.7	0.4	15.7	4.9	2.9	5.1	1.1	3.9	17.8
Average 1971–73	1.8	0.5	15.6	5.4	3.0	4.7	1.2	3.6	17.9
Average 1974–78	2.3	1.3	19.6	8.3	3.5	4.7	2.7	4.0	23.1
Average 1968–78	2.0	0.8	17.4	6.6	3.2	4.8	1.8	3.9	20.3

* Food, beverages and tobacco, and basic materials.
** Mineral fuels and lubricants.
† Manufactures, semi-manufactures and unclassified.
‡ Other Western Europe.
§ North America and other developed countries.
§§ Oil producing countries.
All items are shown as percentages of GNP at factor cost.
Source: United Kingdom Balance of Payments, 1979, Tables 1.1 and 2.2.

Finally, column (9) shows total visible exports, summed over both commodities and countries of destination. These have risen rapidly, from 17.8 per cent of GNP in 1968–70 to 17.9 per cent in 1971–73 and 23.1 per cent in 1974–78. In 1977, at 25.8 per cent, they were the highest ever. This expansion has been mainly due to increased exports of manufactures and semi-manufactures, with minor contributions from oil and from food, beverages and tobacco. The increase has been concentrated almost entirely on trade with Western Europe and with the oil-exporting countries.

Thus on the export as well as on the import side, the UK economy has become more open; a larger proportion of total sales and therefore of employment is dependent on remaining competitive in foreign markets.

WHAT DETERMINES UK EXPORTS?

Level of Demand in Foreign Markets

Having seen that UK imports are strongly correlated with the level of total final expenditure, it seems natural to investigate whether a similar relation holds between exports and the incomes of our customers. Because of inflation and changes in exchange rates, it is difficult to find a good measure of world GNP. In default of this, column (1) of Table 23.3 shows an index of demand conditions in the UK's overseas markets. This is found by taking an unweighted average of the annual percentage rate of growth of GNP at constant prices of nine of our largest customers; the USA, West Germany, France, Italy, Belgium, the Netherlands, Sweden, Switzerland and Eire. From 1968 to 1978 the real growth of these markets has averaged 3.2 per cent a year; it has varied between a maximum of 5.7 per cent in 1969 and a minimum of −1.7 per cent (i.e. a fall in GNP) in 1975.

Column (3) shows the annual rates of growth of UK exports at 1975 prices. These averaged 5.6 per cent a year over the period, which is 2.4 per cent a year faster than the customers' real rate of growth. As with the UK, our customers' economies have been becoming more open.

The growth of UK exports also varied widely, between a maximum of 13 per cent in 1973 and a minimum of −2.4 per cent (i.e. a fall in exports) in 1975. UK exports on average did better in boom years abroad, and worse during slumps in our markets. A regression of UK exports on customer countries' GNP, both at constant prices, shows that for each 1 per cent increase in customer GNP

TABLE 23.3 *UK Export Markets, 1968–78*

Year	Growth in customers' real GNP* %	Growth in rivals' export volume** %	Growth in UK exports at 1975 prices %
	(1)	(2)	(3)
1969	5.7	13.9	9.8
1970	4.9	10.9	5.5
1971	3.2	8.9	7.2
1972	4.5	10.7	0.4
1973	5.1	11.9	13.0
1974	2.6	8.2	6.5
1975	−1.7	−3.7	−2.4
1976	3.9	12.0	9.1
1977	2.4	4.6	7.0
1978	3.3	4.7	2.1
Average, 1969–78	3.2	7.9	5.6

* Unweighted average of annual percentage increases in GNP (in some cases GDP) at constant prices of USA, W. Germany, France, Belgium, the Netherlands, Italy, Sweden, Switzerland and Eire, nine of the UK's largest export customers.
** Unweighted average of annual percentage increase in export volume of USA, W. Germany, France, Belgium, the Netherlands, Italy and Japan, seven of our main rival suppliers.
Sources: Columns (1) and (2), *International Financial Statistics*. Column (3), Blue Book on *National Income and Expenditure, 1979*, Table 2.1.

there is a 1.43 per cent increase in UK real exports. The fit is not very good, however, only 42 per cent of observed variance in export growth being explained by the growth in customer incomes.

As a check on this approach to export markets, column (2) shows an index of the real export changes of our main competitors as industrial exporters. This is constructed by taking an unweighted average of the annual percentage rate of growth of the volume of exports by seven of our main competitors: the USA, West Germany, France, Italy, Belgium, the Netherlands and Japan. The index shows that their exports grew in real terms at an average of 7.9 per cent a year between 1968 and 1978. This was 2.3 per cent a year faster than the growth rate of UK exports at 1975 prices, so that we were gradually losing our share in world export markets. Our competitors' rate of growth of real exports also varied, between a maximum of 13.9 per cent in 1969 and a minimum of −3.7 per cent in 1975.

The average growth rate of the real exports of our seven competitors in each year is rather well explained by the index of customers' real GNP changes; a regression of column (2) on column (1) shows that 90 per cent of the observed variance in the growth of competitors' exports can be explained by variations in the growth of customers' GNP.

An alternative approach to measuring the influence of the growth of markets on UK exports is to argue that the ease of selling in any year can be measured by the growth in the total export sales of our competitors; this is not of course entirely correct, since we have to sell in competition with them. If we ignore this last point and regress UK real export growth, column (3), on competitors' export growth, column (2), we find that each 1 per cent faster growth in average sales by competitors corresponded to a 0.64 per cent faster growth of real UK exports; this relation explains 51 per cent of the observed variance in UK real export growth.

Thus the level of demand in foreign markets explains part, but by no means all, of the variations in UK export performance. This leads us to ask what other factors affect exports.

Prices and Exports

One factor that might be expected to have an effect on export competitiveness is the price of exports compared with those of our competitors. Inflation has been occurring in all advanced countries during the past decade, and exchange rates have varied considerably. There have thus been quite sharp year-to-year fluctuations in the relative export prices of the different industrial countries. While there are some export goods whose sales are sensitive to price changes in the short run, there are others that are not, owing to contracts fixed in foreign currency, or very long delivery lags. While price changes are helpful in explaining trade in some commodities, for exports as a whole relative export price changes on a year-by-year basis are unhelpful.

It is believed that in the longer run relative export prices do matter, but this theory is hard to test for the past decade because there has been relatively little difference between the UK and her competitors in export prices converted to US dollars at current exchange rates. This is because devaluation of sterling relative to other currencies has offset relatively rapid inflation of UK export prices measured in sterling. From 1968 to 1978 the trend rate of increase of the unit value of UK exports, converted to US dollars, was 10.4 per cent. The figures for the same period for our rivals (obtained from *International Financial Statistics*, published monthly by the International Monetary Fund) were; USA 9.7 per cent, Japan 10.6 per cent, Italy 10.7 per cent, France 11.0 per cent, Belgium 11.1 per cent, Germany 12.4 per cent and the Netherlands 12.5 per cent. The differences are entirely unrelated to differences in the growth rate of export quantities; on average UK exports have tended to become cheaper relative to those of our competitors.

Supply Factors and Exports

It has sometimes been suggested that exports are affected by variations in the pressure of overall demand in the UK. There are two possible theories about this. One theory is that in a domestic boom firms will divert goods to home markets, or may be unable to obtain export orders because of inability to quote acceptable delivery dates, or may be unable to fulfil export orders because of shortages of inputs. The opposing theory is that a boom in the home market is good for exports, as it leads to long production runs and low unit costs, so that firms can export profitably at competitive prices.

Unfortunately, the facts do not support either theory; whether domestic market conditions, as measured by the output gap, are related to the real growth rate of UK exports or to the deviation of export growth from the rate predicted by the index of customers' GNP, the fit is hopeless. One can only conclude either that both theories are wrong, or that each is right for some sectors of exports but that they cancel out in the aggregate figures.

Technical Progress and Efficiency

We have seen that UK exports, while they have been growing, have risen 2.3 per cent a year less rapidly than those of our competitors. Some of this can plausibly be ascribed to supply differences; their GNP on average grew at 3.2 per cent, while over the years from 1968 to 1978 the UK GNP grew at only 2.1 per cent a year. However, this difference of 1.1 per cent a year in the growth rates of total output is only half the difference in export growth rates.

It is not at all clear what has caused the difference between the export performance of the UK and that of other countries; we have seen that it cannot be attributed to export prices. One can only conclude that it must be difficulties of some sort over quality that have resulted in our decreasing share of world markets. We may not be as good as our competitors at designing better products, at mastering the linguistic and other skills necessary to market them, at setting and meeting early delivery dates or at servicing our goods after they have been sold.

This should not be interpreted as saying that UK products are worthless, or that we are too lazy to sell them. We have seen that in 1978 the UK was selling more goods and services abroad than ever before, and over 82 per cent more than a decade earlier. It is not that the UK has been without merit in export performance; it is just that on average we do a small percentage worse each year than our competitors. A detailed investigation of any possible deficiencies of the organization of UK industry that have contributed to this is not possible here.

24. The Balance of Payments

Problems over the UK balance of payments have been so frequent as to become proverbial. In this chapter we will put together the information on imports and exports of the last two chapters, to see how far they account for the persistent problems. There are a number of questions we would like to be able to answer:

(1) What is the balance of payments?
(2) What is meant by a 'balance of payments deficit'?
(3) What is the difference between current and capital account in the balance of payments?
(4) What are 'exchange reserves'?
(5) How has the balance of payments been changing?
(6) What determines the balance of payments?

WHAT IS THE BALANCE OF PAYMENTS?

The 'balance of payments' is a slightly confusing concept because the expression is used in two quite distinct senses. In one meaning, it simply refers to a statement of all transactions between the UK and the rest of the world. These transactions consist of three types:

(1) payments on current account;
(2) non-government payments on capital account;
(3) official payments.

If these three are all considered together, the country's total receipts and expenditures must balance, by definition.

The other meaning of the balance of payments, used when it is said to be a problem, infers that the composition of these items is not satisfactory; usually, that there is a deficit on current account, a loss of foreign exchange reserves, or both. In a more general sense, the balance of payments may pose a problem in that, while the actual amounts of payments are not unsatisfactory, it has been necessary in order to bring this about for the authorities to adopt monetary or fiscal policies that they would on other grounds prefer to avoid. For example, imports may be held down by restrictive fiscal policies, or capital may have to be attracted from abroad by restrictive monetary policies, when on grounds of concern about unemployment the authorities would prefer to be able to expand the economy.

We will first distinguish between the balance of trade, the balance of payments on current account, and the overall balance of payments.

The Balance of Trade

This is sometimes used to refer to trade in goods only, but we will adopt the more modern usage that the balance of trade refers to the difference between exports and imports of goods and services combined. Table 24.1 shows the UK balance of payments on current account in 1978. Receipts, expenditures and the balance on each item are shown in £m, £b and as a percentage of the GNP at factor cost.

Exports of goods were £35.4b, and imports were £36.6b; the balance on visible trade items was thus a deficit of £1.2b, equal to 0.8

TABLE 24.1   *The UK Balance of Payments on Current Account in 1978*

	Receipts			Expenditure			Balance		
	£m	£b	%GNP	£m	£b	%GNP	£m	£b	%GNP
Goods	35,432	35.4	24.8	36,607	36.6	25.6	−1,175	−1.2	−0.8
Services	12,204	12.2	8.5	8,915	8.9	6.2	3,289	3.3	2.3
Trade = goods + services	47,636	47.6	33.4	45,522	45.5	31.9	2,114	2.1	1.5
Property (net of tax)	5,047	5.0	3.5	4,211	4.2	2.9	836	0.8	0.6
Transfers	1,084	1.1	0.8	3,002	3.0	2.1	−1,918	−1.9	−1.3
Total Current Account	53,767	53.8	37.6	52,735	52.7	36.9	1,032	1.0	0.7

Source: United Kindgom Balance of Payments, 1979, Table 1.2.

per cent of GNP. Exports of services were £12.2b, and imports £8.9b, so that there was a surplus on trade in invisibles of £3.3b, or 2.3 per cent of GNP. On goods and services combined, the balance of trade was thus a surplus of £2.1b, or 1.5 per cent of GNP.

The Balance of Payments on Current Account

To the trade figures we need to add property incomes, taxes and transfers to get to the balance of payments on current account. In the case of property incomes, the UK had property incomes net of overseas taxes of £5.0b, and paid out, net of UK taxes, £4.2b; there was thus a net surplus on property incomes after tax of £0.8b, or 0.6 per cent of GNP.

The UK paid out £3.0b in transfers in 1977, and received £1.1b; there was thus a net deficit on transfers of £1.9b or 1.3 per cent of GNP.

Combining all the current account items, reckoned on the basis above, the UK received £53.8b and paid out £52.7b, resulting in a net current account surplus of £1.0b, or 0.7 per cent of GNP.

The Overall Balance of Payments

Figures for the overall balance of payments in 1978 are shown in Table 24.2, again in £m, £b and as percentages of GNP. We start with the current account balance. To this has to be added net

TABLE 24.2   *The UK Overall Balance of Payments in 1978*

	£m	£b	% GNP
Current account balance	1,032	1.0	0.7
Identified non-government capital items	−2,931	−2.9	−2.1
(−means we made more loans than we received)			
Unidentified items	773	0.8	0.5
Balance for official financing	−1,126	−1.1	−0.8
Government capital items	−1,203	−1.2	−0.9
Change in official foreign exchange reserves	2,329	2.3	1.6
(+ means that they *fell*)			

Source: United Kingdom Balance of Payments, 1979, Tables 1.1 and 1.2.

receipts on capital account by non-government bodies. Here borrowing produces a positive entry; this is best understood by thinking of borrowing as the sale of securities to foreigners, and of lending as the purchase of securities from them. The entry of −£2.9b means that in 1978 private lending abroad exceeded private foreign borrowing by £2.9b.

The next item is unidentified receipts of £0.8b. It is not known whether this represents unidentified capital items, or is the result of errors in measuring the various current account items. The fact that the unidentified item is positive means that the authorities found they finished the year with £0.8b more of reserves than they would have had if all the identified items had been correctly measured. By the time this book appears, revisions to the figures may well have been made. The fact that the unidentified item is so large suggests that all the balance of payments data for 1978 need to be treated with some caution.

The current balance, the identified capital items and the unidentified item need to be added to get the 'balance for official financing'. This is the amount of finance the authorities have to find. They can finance a deficit either by government borrowing abroad, or by reducing the official foreign exchange reserves. Government borrowing may be from the International Monetary Fund, from the central banks of other countries or from other sources. In 1978 there was a balance for official financing of −£1.1b. This required the government to increase overseas debt, or decrease the foreign exchange reserves. In fact it chose to lend £1.2b abroad, so that the exchange reserves fell by £2.3b, equal to 1.6 per cent of GNP.

The foreign exchange reserves are held by the Bank of England on behalf of the government. They consist partly of gold, and partly of holdings of US dollars and other convertible currencies. The 'convertible' at one time meant that the currencies were freely convertible to gold, but has now come to mean merely that the currencies are those of countries of sound financial reputation, which do not impose too many restrictions on their use.

How Has the Balance of Payments Been Changing?

To answer this question we will divide it into three parts, dealing with the balance of trade, the balance of payments on current account, and the capital and reserves items separately.

Changes in the Balance of Trade

The facts about changes in the balance of trade over the past decade are summarized in Table 24.3. This shows exports, imports and the net balance between them for each item. The items shown are two categories of goods, oil and non-oil, and services; the total of goods and services combined is shown as the balance of trade. To allow

TABLE 24.3   *The UK Balance of Trade, 1968–78*

	Goods – oil			Goods – non-oil			Services			Total trade		
	Recd	Paid	Bal	Recd	Paid	Bal	Recd	Paid	Bal	Recd	Paid	Bal
1968	0.4	1.8	− 1.3	16.5	17.0	− 0.5	6.8	5.9	0.9	23.8	24.7	− 0.9
1969	0.4	1.7	− 1.2	17.7	16.9	0.8	7.1	6.1	1.0	25.2	24.7	0.6
1970	0.5	1.5	− 1.1	18.0	17.0	1.0	7.8	6.7	1.0	26.2	25.3	0.9
1971	0.5	1.8	− 1.4	17.7	15.8	1.9	7.9	6.7	1.2	26.0	24.3	1.7
1972	0.4	1.7	− 1.3	16.5	16.6	0.0	7.6	6.4	1.2	24.6	24.7	− 0.1
1973	0.6	2.0	− 1.5	17.9	20.1	− 2.2	7.9	6.8	1.1	26.4	29.0	− 2.6
1974	1.0	5.6	− 4.5	20.9	23.3	− 2.4	8.7	7.4	1.3	30.6	36.3	− 5.7
1975	0.9	4.2	− 3.3	19.8	19.9	− 0.1	8.1	6.7	1.4	28.8	30.8	− 2.0
1976	1.1	4.7	− 3.6	21.6	21.3	0.4	9.0	7.0	2.0	31.8	33.0	− 1.2
1977	1.7	3.9	− 2.3	24.0	23.1	0.9	9.2	6.9	2.4	34.9	33.9	1.0
1978	1.7	3.2	− 1.5	23.1	22.5	0.7	8.5	6.2	2.3	33.4	31.9	1.5
Average 1968–70	0.4	1.7	− 1.2	17.4	17.0	0.4	7.2	6.2	1.0	25.1	24.9	0.2
Average 1971–73	0.5	1.8	− 1.4	17.4	17.5	− 0.1	7.8	6.6	1.2	25.7	26.1	− 0.3
Average 1974–78	1.3	4.3	− 3.0	21.9	22.0	− 0.1	8.7	6.8	1.9	31.9	33.2	− 1.3
Average 1968–78	0.7	2.9	− 2.1	19.4	19.4	0.0	8.1	6.6	1.4	28.3	29.0	− 0.6

Note: All items are in percentage of GNP at factor cost.
Source: United Kingdom Balance of Payments, 1979, Tables 1.2 and 2.2.

comparability over the decade all items are expressed as percentages of GNP at factor cost.

Trade in oil products shows a steady deficit up to 1973, a very sharp rise to a deficit of 4.5 per cent of GNP in 1974, and then a gradual fall in the deficit as North Sea oil has begun to help. By 1978 the oil deficit was down to 1.5 per cent of GNP and there are good prospects that it will decline further and turn to a surplus. On average over the decade there was an oil deficit of 2.1 per cent of GNP.

In the non-oil goods items, the balance oscillated during the decade. Starting with a deficit in 1968 of 0.5 per cent of GNP, non-oil goods moved to a surplus in 1971 of 1.9 per cent of GNP, then to deficits of 2.2 per cent in 1973 and 2.4 per cent in 1974, then back to a surplus of 0.9 per cent in 1977. Over the decade trade in non-oil goods was almost exactly balanced.

When we come to services, we find that both imports and exports have tended to increase relative to GNP over the decade, though not as fast as trade in goods. Exports of services have also risen more rapidly than imports. Thus while the UK has had a surplus on invisible trade throughout the decade, this has risen from 1.0 per cent of GNP in 1968–70 to 1.9 per cent in 1974–78. In 1977 the net surplus on services was the highest ever, at 2.4 per cent of GNP.

The balance on goods and services combined, i.e. the balance of trade, has moved from a deficit of 0.9 per cent of GNP in 1968 to a surplus of 1.7 per cent in 1971, then back to deficits of 2.6 per cent in 1973 and 5.7 per cent in 1974. This was then reduced to 2.0 per cent in 1975, and changed to a surplus of 1.5 per cent in 1978. On average over the decade the trade balance showed a deficit equal to 0.6 per cent of GNP.

Changes in the Balance of Payments on Current Account

Table 24.4 gives a summary of the other current account items. Property incomes, net of overseas taxes on them, have been fairly steady, with a peak in 1974 of 4.4 per cent of GNP. Payments of property income, net of UK taxes, have risen slowly. The UK had a surplus on property incomes net of tax throughout the decade, varying between 1.9 per cent of GNP in 1973 and 1974 and only 0.2 per cent in 1977. On average over the decade the surplus on property incomes net of tax was 1.1 per cent of GNP.

TABLE 24.4   *The UK Balance of Payments on Current Account, 1968–78*

	Trade balance	Property—taxes			Transfers			Balance of payments on current account
		Recd	Paid	Bal	Recd	Paid	Bal	
1968	−0.9	2.9	2.0	0.9	0.4	1.1	−0.6	−0.6
1969	0.6	3.3	2.1	1.2	0.5	1.0	−0.6	1.3
1970	0.9	3.3	2.0	1.3	0.5	0.9	−0.4	1.8
1971	1.7	3.0	2.0	1.0	0.5	0.9	−0.4	2.3
1972	−0.1	3.1	2.2	1.0	0.4	0.9	−0.5	0.4
1973	−2.6	4.3	2.4	1.9	0.6	1.3	−0.7	−1.3
1974	−5.7	4.4	2.5	1.9	0.6	1.2	−0.6	−4.4
1975	−2.0	3.0	2.2	0.8	0.8	1.3	−0.5	−1.7
1976	−1.2	3.5	2.3	1.2	0.7	1.4	−0.7	−0.8
1977	1.0	3.2	3.0	0.2	0.7	1.6	−0.9	0.2
1978	1.5	3.5	2.9	0.6	0.8	2.1	−1.3	0.7
Average 1968–70	0.2	3.2	2.0	1.1	0.5	1.0	−0.5	0.8
Average 1971–73	−0.3	3.5	2.2	1.3	0.5	1.0	−0.5	0.5
Average 1974–78	−1.3	3.5	2.6	0.9	0.7	1.5	−0.8	−1.2
Average 1968–78	−0.6	3.4	2.3	1.1	0.6	1.2	−0.7	−0.2

All items are shown as percentages of GNP at factor cost.
Source: United Kingdom Balance of Payments 1979, Table 1.2.

On transfers, receipts have been very steady, while payments have gradually increased. In 1978 transfer payments at 2.1 per cent of GNP were the highest ever. The UK had a net deficit on transfers every year, rising gradually to 1.3 per cent of GNP in 1978.

Adding these items to the balance of trade, the balance on current account started with a deficit in 1968 equal to 0.6 per cent of GNP, moving to a surplus of 2.3 per cent in 1971, and back to a deficit of 1.3 per cent in 1973 and 4.4 per cent in 1974. The deficit was then reduced to 1.7 per cent of GNP in 1975 and 0.8 per cent in 1976, while in 1978 the UK had a current account surplus of 0.7 per cent of GNP. Over the decade the average current account balance was a deficit of 0.2 per cent of GNP.

Changes in the Overall Balance of Payments

Table 24.5 gives the facts on the overall balance of payments. Net identified non-government capital items have fluctuated severely, with no obvious relation to the balance on current account. On average over the decade these items came to only 0.1 per cent of GNP. As a guide to their importance in determining the short-run movements in the overall balance of payments, Table 24.5 gives for

TABLE 24.5   *UK Overall Balance of Payments, 1968–78*

	Current balance	Net non-government capital	Unidentified	Balance for official financing	Government transactions	Change in official exchange reserves
1968	−0.7	−3.0	−0.5	−4.2	3.8	−0.3
1969	1.3	−0.4	0.9	1.7	−1.6	0.1
1970	1.8	1.2	−0.1	2.9	−2.6	0.3
1971	2.3	3.6	0.4	6.3	−3.2	3.1
1972	0.4	−1.2	−1.4	−2.3	1.0	−1.2
1973	−1.3	0.1	0.0	−1.2	1.5	0.3
1974	−4.4	2.0	0.2	−2.2	2.3	0.1
1975	−1.7	0.1	0.0	−1.6	0.9	−0.7
1976	−0.8	−2.7	0.2	−3.3	2.5	−0.8
1977	0.2	3.5	2.1	5.9	1.8	7.6
1978	0.7	−2.1	0.5	−0.8	−0.8	−1.6
Average 1968–70	0.8	−0.7	0.1	0.1	−0.1	0.0
Average 1971–73	0.5	0.8	−0.3	0.9	−0.2	0.7
Average 1974–78	−1.2	0.2	0.6	−0.4	1.3	0.9
Average 1968–78	−0.2	0.1	0.2	0.1	0.5	0.6
Average Change, disregarding sign	1.5	3.1	0.9	3.9	1.9	2.8

All items shown as percentage of GNP at factor cost.
Source: United Kingdom Balance of Payments, 1979, Table 1.1.

each item the average change from each year to the next, regardless of sign. On this basis the average change in the current account balance was 1.5 per cent of GNP, whereas the average change in identified capital items was 3.1 per cent of GNP. The capital items' short-run impact on the balance of payments was thus greater than that of the current account.

The unidentified items in the balance of payments have also oscillated severely, and with no obvious relation to anything else. Their average size over the decade was only 0.2 per cent of GNP, but their year-to-year change, disregarding sign, averaged 0.9 per cent.

Combining the current account, identified non-government capital items and the unidentified item gives the 'balance for official financing'. This has oscillated severely, from a deficit of 4.2 per cent of GNP in 1968 to a surplus of 6.3 per cent in 1971, deficits from 1973 to 1976 with a maximum deficit of 3.3 per cent in 1976, and a surplus of 5.9 per cent of GNP in 1977. On average over the decade the balance for official financing has been only 0.1 per cent of GNP, but the average year-to-year movement, disregarding sign, was 3.9 per cent.

Some of the official financing is done by government lending or borrowing; the lending appears as a negative item in the table, and the borrowing as positive. On average the government has borrowed an amount equal to 0.5 per cent of GNP each year, but with wide variations from year to year resulting in an average year-to-year change, disregarding sign, of 1.9 per cent of GNP.

The change in official foreign exchange reserves is the balance for official financing plus the net receipts on government borrowing. Reserves have in fact been kept fairly steady except for a rise by 3.1 per cent of GNP in 1971 and 7.6 per cent in 1977. In the worst year of current account deficit, 1974, the official foreign exchange reserves actually rose slightly. On average over the decade foreign exchange reserves rose by 0.6 per cent of GNP each year, but this increase is entirely accounted for by 1977. Year-to-year variations in the growth of reserves, regardless of sign, averaged 2.8 per cent of GNP over the decade.

THE CURRENT ACCOUNT BALANCE AND THE OVERALL BALANCE OF PAYMENTS

There has in fact been no detectable relation between the balance of payments on current account and movements in the foreign exchange reserves. There is some relation between identified non-government capital movements and reserve movements, but this accounts for only 57 per cent of observed variance in reserve changes. The year-to-year movements in the overall balance of payments appear to be dominated by capital movements, both private and government.

In view of this, the stress that is frequently laid on current account balance of payments figures requires some explanation. There is undoubtedly a belief among economic commentators, which is shared by the author, that in the long run the state of the current account will be reflected in the overall balance of payments figures. Years like 1974 cannot be repeated at all frequently without exhausting the country's credit abroad and thus its ability to borrow. If the current account is persistently unsatisfactory, nothing else will come right; and if the balance of payments on current account is healthy, then in the long run the capital account can be relied on to look after itself. However, this is a matter of faith and cannot be proved from the figures.

The reasons for capital movements are many and complex; they certainly include differences in the rate of return on loans or real investment available in different countries; expectations about changes in exchange rates; and fears concerning the political and economic stability of various countries. It is not possible to investigate all these factors here, but we must note that the balance of payments in the short run is dominated by their effects.

THE EXCHANGE RATE

The UK exchange rate has been changed for two reasons during the past decade. Up to 1971 the UK had a 'pegged' exchange rate. Under this system the Bank of England was committed to keeping the exchange rate within a narrow margin, by using its foreign exchange reserves to buy in sterling if its price would otherwise have gone down, and selling sterling for foreign currency that could be added to the exchange reserves if the value of sterling would otherwise have gone up. In 1967 sterling was devalued by 14 per cent, from 2.80 to 2.40 US dollars to the pound.

In 1971 the UK adopted a floating exchange rate. Since then sterling has gone down in relative value compared with other leading currencies in every year except 1978. On an index compiled by the IMF sterling fell between 1970 and 1978 at an average rate of 6.5 per cent a year. The actual rate of decline varied between a maximum fall of 15.3 per cent in 1976 and a 1.3 per cent rise in 1978; there is no obvious reason for the variations. As we saw in Chapter 23, the devaluation of sterling has on average been sufficient to offset relatively rapid inflation in the UK and keep UK export prices in line with those of other countries, but the exact timing of the decline is erratic, and the mechanism determining it is unknown.

Changes in the exchange rate appear to have no obvious immediate effect on the balance of payments on current account. Given the very large levels of overall payments each way in the UK economy's international transactions relative to the foreign exchange reserves, the Bank of England cannot long maintain sterling at any exchange rate higher than that expected by other people. These may be the controllers of private capital, or they may be the central bankers of other countries if international credit is to be used to maintain the exchange reserves.

POLICY QUESTIONS

This very brief survey of the balance of payments leaves us with a number of policy questions to which economists are still looking for the right answers. These include the following:
(1) What exchange rate regime should the UK adopt? Should we maintain a floating rate, or join in Western European arrangements for a currency bloc?
(2) How can speculation against sterling be stopped? There appears to be a danger that we will continue for ever in the vicious circle by which we have cost inflation because the exchange rate goes down, and the rate goes down because foreigners regard this as inevitable given our rate of inflation.
(3) Should the authorities be given, and encouraged to use, powers to control capital movements, or are these futile?
It may well be salutory to realize that we do not know all the answers.

Chapter 25 will attempt to pull together the theories that may help in providing answers to some of these questions.

25. Internal and External Equilibrium

In this chapter we will set out in a formal manner the theory of the last three chapters concerning the balance of payments on current account of an economy we will refer to as 'the home country'.

Exports, X, including both goods and services but ignoring property incomes, are determined by the income level of the rest of the world, W, and a parameter representing foreign desire to buy the home country's products, a. Thus

$$X = aW.$$

Imports, M, again including both goods and services, are determined by the total final demand of the home country, Z, and a parameter representing the home country's propensity to buy imports, b. Thus

$$M = bZ.$$

We can assume that $0 < b < 1$.

Z is the total demand for consumption, investment, government spending on goods and services and exports. We assume that the parts of Z other than exports can be represented as the sum of autonomous elements of spending, i.e. those not dependent on the level of income, k, and the sum of parts of spending induced by the level of income, hY, where we can assume that $0 < h < 1$. Thus

$$Z = k + hY + X.$$

Incomes, Y, are total final demand minus imports; i.e.,

$$Y = Z - M = (1 - b)Z$$

so

$$Z = k + h(1 - b)Z + aW$$

and

$$Z = \frac{k + aW}{1 - h(1 - b)}.$$

Income, Y, is given by

$$Y = (1 - b)Z = (1 - b)\left[\frac{k + aW}{1 - h(1 - b)}\right].$$

The current account balance of payments, P (again neglecting possible property incomes), is given by

$$P = X - M = aW - bZ = aW - b\left[\frac{k + aW}{1 - h(1 - b)}\right]$$

or equivalently

$$P = \frac{(1 - h)(1 - b)aW - bk}{1 - h(1 - b)}.$$

It is a simple matter to find the effects on Y and P of any change in the parameters a, W, b, k or h. The signs of these, which do not depend on the exact sizes of the parameters, are tabulated below.

Effect on	Y	P
of a rise in a	+	+
W	+	+
b	−	−
k	+	−
h	+	−

What Determines the Parameters?

To find out what will happen to Y and P, we need to know how the parameters a, etc., are determined. In particular we are interested to know how they can be affected by any policies the home country could adopt.

a: World Demand for Exports, Given W

This could be raised by any of the following changes (in each case *a* would be lowered by the opposite change).

(1) Technical progress could make exports more attractive to customers in the rest of the world.

(2) Other improvements in efficiency, such as improved reliability of products, earlier delivery dates, a better supply of spares and standard of after-sales service, would help exports.

(3) Less inflation than abroad, making exports cheaper relative to rival products, would help.

(4) Cuts in foreign tariffs or relaxation of foreign import controls would increase exports. The home country cannot directly affect these, unless it has colonies whose trade policy it can decide, but it can negotiate with other countries about them, and it may be able to induce relaxation in other countries' restrictions on trade in return for similar concessions over its own.

(5) A lower exchange rate could help exports. If the foreign currency price goes down, exports will be cheaper to customers. If the foreign currency price is kept up, the home currency price will rise, making them more profitable to sell, and making it more worthwhile for firms to incur selling costs in order to push sales. Exporters will have to decide whether they can make better use of a relative cost advantage by cutting their prices or by increasing their selling costs. They will keep the cost advantage only if the home country can avoid cost inflation following devaluation and cancelling out its effects.

W: World Income Levels

There is nothing the home country can do about these directly, though it may be possible via international negotiation to get agreed policies of monetary and fiscal expansion all round. If the home country has a trade surplus, it may be able to encourage expansionary policies in the rest of the world by encouraging foreign lending, so that the trade surplus does not lead to losses of exchange reserves for other countries.

b: Home Demand for Imports per unit of Total Final Demand

This can be reduced by the following policies, which are known as expenditure switching policies, since they induce people to spend the same amount of money in different ways.

(1) Technical progress at home will lead to home-produced goods becoming more attractive relative to imports.

(2) Other improvements in efficiency will reduce imports, as people will not be forced to buy imports because home-produced goods are unavailable or unsatisfactory.

(3) Less inflation at home than abroad will make home-produced goods cheaper relative to imports.

(4) Higher tariffs or more stringent restrictions on imports will reduce them. The home country's ability to use tariffs and trade controls will be limited if it is a member of the GATT (General Agreement on Tariffs and Trade), or if it is a member of some group such as the EEC with internal free trade and a common external tariff.

(5) A lower exchange rate will make imports more expensive than home products, if the foreign currency price is maintained. If the foreign currency price falls, the profit margins of foreign suppliers will be cut and they will be less keen to incur selling costs or to allow their distributors high enough profit margins to make them keen on pushing the products. This advantage depends on the home country being able to avoid cost inflation following devaluation.

k: Home Country Autonomous Expenditure

Alterations in k, or in h, are known as expenditure-changing policies, because they are concerned with how much people spend in the aggregate, rather than how they divide their spending between home-produced goods and imports. Any cut in autonomous spending, whether in the constant term of the consumption function, in investment or in real government spending, will lower Y and raise P.

h: Home Country Induced Spending

Any reduction in induced spending, for example through higher tax rates, will lower Y and increase P.

A NUMERICAL EXAMPLE

This example is not actually based on statistically fitted propensities, but the orders of magnitude were chosen so as to make them fairly realistic for the UK economy in 1977, in £b at current prices.

We assume that

$$a = 0.05$$
$$W = 870$$
$$b = 0.26$$
$$k = 61.08$$
$$h = 0.5$$
$$Y = (1 - b)Z = (1 - 0.26)Z = 0.74Z$$
$$Z = k + hY + X$$
$$= 61.08 + 0.5(0.74)Z + 43.5$$

so

$$Z(1 - 0.37) = 104.58$$

and

$$Z = \frac{104.58}{0.63} = 166.$$

Thus

$$Y = 0.74(166) = 122.84$$

and

$$P = X - M = 43.5 - 0.26(166)$$
$$= 43.5 - 43.16$$
$$= 0.34.$$

We thus have an initial situation with $Y = 122.84$ and a small balance of trade surplus, $P = 0.34$.

Effects of Changes in the Parameters

We will now try the effects of varying each parameter in turn by 10 per cent either way, which seems a reasonable order of magnitude for the kind of change the UK economy is liable to encounter in any single year. In real life several of the parameters will probably change, but for purposes of analysis we will vary them one at a time, each one going back to its original value before the next one is altered. Each new situation will be compared with the original one described above.

(1) *Changes in* a *or* W. As they occur only in conjunction, it does not matter which is altered by 10 per cent; their product also alters by 10 per cent. We therefore consider them together.

A 10 per cent increase in a or W raises X to 47.85. Thus

$$Z = \frac{61.08 + 47.85}{0.63} = 172.90$$

so

$$Y = 0.74(172.90) = 127.95.$$

This is a 4.16 per cent increase on its original level.

$$P = 47.85 - 0.26(172.90)$$
$$= 47.85 - 44.95$$
$$= 2.90.$$

Thus export-led growth means a rise in Y and an improvement in P.

A 10 per cent fall in a or W lowers X to 39.15. Thus

$$Z = \frac{61.08 + 39.15}{0.63} = 159.10$$

and

$$Y = 0.74(159.10) = 117.73.$$

This is a reduction by 4.16 per cent from its original level.

$$P = 39.15 - 0.26(159.10)$$
$$= 39.15 - 41.37$$
$$= -2.22.$$

Thus a slump in exports cuts Y and produces a trade deficit.

(2) *Changes in b, the home country propensity to import.* If b rises to 0.286 (a and W returning to their original levels),

$$Z = \frac{61.08 + 43.5}{1 - 0.5(1 - 0.286)}$$

$$= \frac{104.58}{1 - 0.5(0.714)}$$

$$= \frac{104.58}{1 - 0.357} = \frac{104.58}{0.643}$$

$$= 162.64.$$

So

$$Y = (1 - 0.286)(162.64) = 0.714(162.64)$$

$$= 116.13.$$

This is a reduction of 5.46 per cent on its original level.

$$P = 43.5 - 0.286(162.64) = 43.5 - 46.52$$

$$= -3.02.$$

Thus a higher propensity to import leads to lower Y and a balance of trade deficit.

If b falls to 0.234,

$$Z = \frac{104.58}{1 - 0.5(1 - 0.234)}$$

$$= \frac{104.58}{1 - 0.5(0.766)}$$

$$= \frac{104.58}{1 - 0.383}$$

$$= \frac{104.58}{0.617}$$

$$= 169.50.$$

So

$$Y = (1 - 0.234)(169.50)$$
$$= 0.766(169.50)$$
$$= 129.84.$$

This is an increase of 5.70 per cent.

$$P = 43.5 - 0.234(169.50)$$
$$= 43.5 - 39.66$$
$$= 3.84.$$

Thus a fall in the propensity to import raises Y and produces a trade surplus.

(3) *A change in* k, *autonomous domestic expenditure.* If k rises to 67.19,

$$Z = \frac{67.19 + 43.5}{0.63} = 175.70.$$

So

$$Y = 0.74(175.70) = 130.02.$$

This is an increase of 5.84 per cent.

$$P = 43.5 - 0.26(175.70)$$
$$= 43.5 - 45.68$$
$$= -2.18.$$

A rise in autonomous home spending raises Y and produces a trade deficit.

If k falls to 54.97

$$Z = \frac{54.97 + 43.5}{0.63} = 156.30.$$

So

$$Y = 0.74(156.30) = 115.66.$$

This is a reduction of 5.84 per cent.

$$P = 43.5 - 0.26(156.30)$$

$$= 43.5 - 40.64$$

$$= 2.86.$$

A fall in autonomous home spending produces a fall in Y and a trade surplus.

(4) *A change in* h, *the marginal propensity for induced home country expenditure.* If h rises to 0.55,

$$Z = \frac{61.08 + 43.5}{1 - 0.55(1 - 0.26)}$$

$$= \frac{104.58}{1 - 0.55(0.74)}$$

$$= \frac{104.58}{1 - 0.407}$$

$$= \frac{104.58}{0.593}$$

$$= 176.36.$$

$$Y = 0.74(176.36) = 130.50.$$

Thus is an increase of 6.24 per cent.

$$P = 43.5 - 0.26(176.36)$$

$$= 43.5 - 45.85$$

$$= -2.35.$$

A rise in home-induced spending thus produces a rise in Y and a trade deficit.

If h falls to 0.45,

$$Z = \frac{104.58}{1 - 0.45(0.74)}$$

$$= \frac{104.58}{1 - 0.333}$$

$$= \frac{104.58}{0.667}$$

$$= 156.79.$$

$$Y = 0.74(156.79) = 116.03.$$

This is a reduction of 5.55 per cent.

$$P = 43.5 - 0.26(156.79)$$

$$= 43.5 - 40.77$$

$$= 2.73.$$

Thus a cut in home-induced spending produces a fall in Y and a trade surplus.

26. International Comparisons

We have seen that there are several major objectives of macroeconomic policy. These we take to include

(1) a respectable growth rate for real incomes;
(2) stability of the economy, i.e. the avoidance of sharp fluctuations in the level of real incomes;
(3) control of inflation, i.e. the achievement of a low and stable level of growth of prices and money incomes;
(4) balance of payments equilibrium.

We have seen that in each respect the performance of the UK economy has not been perfect. Nobody is perfect, however, and in this chapter we will seek to compare the performance of the UK with that of a selection of other advanced industrial countries.

For this purpose we have to select which other countries to use. Ten countries have been used, all technically advanced and heavily engaged in international trade. These fall into three groups:

(a) five EEC countries; France, West Germany, Italy, Belgium and the Netherlands;
(b) three non-European countries; the United States, Canada, and Japan;
(c) Two minor European countries; Sweden and Switzerland.

All the comparisons are based so far as possible on trends fitted by least squares through the logarithms of price and output data from 1968 to 1978. When growth has been fairly steady this gives much the same results as just calculating the average percentage changes. When growth has been irregular, the fitted trends are less influenced by the chance of whether the first and last years are above or below normal. All the data are taken from *International Financial Statistics*, published monthly by the International Monetary Fund.

Because of fluctuating exchange rates and differences in national consumption habits, it is not easy to make exact comparisons of the standard of living in various countries. Using GNP per capita, for the average of the years 1976 to 1978, and converting at current exchange rates, shows that if the USA is taken as 100, the other countries' per capita incomes were approximately Switzerland 124, Sweden 109, Germany 98, Canada 97, Belgium 94, the Netherlands 89, France 85, Japan 73, UK 53 and Italy 44. The average for the eleven was 88. The UK was thus well below the average of the group.

COMPARISON OF REAL ECONOMIC GROWTH

Table 26.1 shows the trend growth rates of GNP, population and GNP per head for each country and for their unweighted average. To show how growth has slowed down in most advanced countries since the oil crisis, the trends in real GNP for 1968–73 and for 1973–78 are shown as well as those for the whole period. The slowing down of growth since 1973 can be seen for every country in the table. The average growth trend of GNP for 1968–73 was 4.9 per cent, while for 1973–78 the trend was only 2.1 per cent. There was a 3.4 per cent real growth trend over the decade as a whole.

The UK did worse than the average in both periods; in 1968–73 the UK's trend growth rate was 3.0 per cent, and for 1973–78 it was 1.1 per cent, making an average growth rate of 2.1 per cent over the decade. In 1968–73 only Sweden grew as slowly as the UK; in 1973–78 Sweden and Switzerland did worse; and for the decade as a whole only Sweden did as badly as the UK and only Switzerland did worse. Column (4) of Table 26.1 shows the growth rates of population; here also the UK grew relatively slowly, with a trend rate of population growth of only 0.1 per cent, compared with the average of 0.6 per cent a year. Column (5) then shows trend rates over the decade of GNP per capita. Over the decade the UK had a growth rate of per capita GNP of 2.0 per cent, compared with an average of 2.7 per cent. Again, only Sweden and Switzerland did worse.

TABLE 26.1   *Comparative Growth, 1968–78*

Country	GNP Growth Trend			Population 1968–78 %	GNP per capita 1968–78 %	Industrial production 1968–78 %	Invest-ment/ GNP 1968–78 %
	1968–73 %	1973–78 %	1968–78 %				
	(1)	(2)	(3)	(4)	(5)	(6)	(7)
Japan	9.2	3.9	6.0	1.2	4.8	4.6	33.4
France	5.9	2.9	4.3	0.6	3.7	4.0	23.9
Canada	5.1	3.2	4.3	1.3	3.0	3.9	22.3
Belgium	5.7	2.2	4.0	0.2	3.8	2.8	21.5
Netherlands	5.1	2.4	3.7	0.9	2.8	4.0	22.9
Italy	4.2	2.1	3.2	0.7	2.5	3.4	20.3
Germany	4.8	2.1	3.1	0.3	2.8	2.7	23.3
USA	3.3	2.8	2.9	0.8	2.1	2.6	17.3
UK (GDP)	3.0	1.1	2.1	0.1	2.0	1.0	18.7
Sweden	2.9	0.9	2.1	0.4	1.7	2.3	21.4
Switzerland	4.4	−0.9	1.5	0.4	1.1	1.0	24.8
Average of 11 above	4.9	2.1	3.4	0.6	2.7	2.9	22.7

Source: International Financial Statistics, Country Tables.

Industrial Production

Column (6) shows the growth rate of industrial production for the decade. This is given partly as a check on the GNP figures, since industrial production forms a major part of GNP for each of the countries. The picture for industrial production is in fact consistent with that for GNP. The average growth rate of industrial production for 1968–73 was 5.3 per cent, while for the UK it was 2.1 per cent. For 1973–78 the average growth rate of industrial production was 0.9 per cent, while for the UK it was 0.1 per cent. Over the decade as a whole average industrial production grew at 2.9 per cent, while for the UK its growth rate was 1.0 per cent. The story told by industrial production, as by GNP, is that for most countries growth after 1973 slowed down considerably, and that the UK lagged behind in both halves of the decade.

The other reason for interest in the growth of industrial production is that it is sometimes argued that the UK's slow growth is connected with 'deindustrialization', or a tendency for industrial production to lag behind GNP. From Table 26.1 we can see, however, that this tendency was by no means confined to the UK; over the decade from 1968 to 1978 eight of the eleven countries shown had industrial production growing more slowly than GNP. The exceptions were the Netherlands, Italy and Sweden; deindustrialization proceeded fastest in the UK, Japan and Belgium. As Japan had the fastest growth of the eleven countries, it is not obvious that deindustrialization need be a handicap to growth.

Growth and Investment

The final column of Table 26.1 shows a measure of one of the main sources of economic growth, the average percentage of fixed investment in GNP over the decade for each country. For the eleven countries, the average share of fixed investment was 22.7 per cent; the UK invested only 18.7 per cent of GNP, and only the USA had a lower share of investment.

As a very crude test of the relation between the growth of GNP per capita, investment, and population growth, the growth rate of GNP per capita was regressed on the others. The results show that GNP per capita grew $\frac{1}{4}$ per cent faster for every extra 1 per cent investment share, and $\frac{1}{4}$ per cent slower for every extra 1 per cent population growth. The fit of this relation is not very good, however, only 64 per cent of the observed variance in per capita real growth rates being explained.

Stability

Again, no country has had perfectly stable growth. A country whose GNP showed equal percentage growth rates each year would have a standard deviation of zero if we calculated either
(a) departures from its trend growth path, or
(b) year to year movements.

The UK can be compared with the average of all eleven countries on each of these criteria. Using measure (a), the average is 2.7 per cent, while the UK scores 2.0 per cent. Using measure (b), the average is 2.8 per cent while the UK scores 2.7 per cent. Thus the UK is either more stable than the average, or about the same, according to which measure is preferred.

It is arguable how independent the income variations of various countries can be, given their close trading relations. To check on this, the deviations of each country from its own trend rate of growth over the decade were calculated, and the same was done for the average of all eleven countries' GNP. The deviations for each country were then correlated with the deviations of their average. On this basis, a country whose variations were exactly correlated to the mean of the others would have an R^2 approaching unity, while a country whose deviations were entirely independent would have an R^2 approaching zero. The actual scores for the eleven countries are as follows; France 0.96, Switzerland 0.92, Netherlands and Belgium, 0.91, Japan 0.88, Germany 0.83, Italy 0.72, Canada 0.61, UK 0.54, Sweden 0.45 and USA 0.07. Thus only Sweden and the USA were less closely correlated in their variations with the average of other countries than the UK. In principle, if a country is able to keep its variations independent of the others, it should be possible to use this independence to attain greater stability.

INFLATION

Table 26.2 shows rates of inflation, as measured by indices of consumer goods prices, for the eleven countries from 1968 to 1973, for 1973–78, and for the decade as a whole. In both periods the UK had the highest rate of inflation. For 1968–73 the average inflation rate was 5.3 per cent; the UK's rate of 7.6 per cent was the highest. For

TABLE 26.2   *Comparative Inflation, 1968–78*

Country	1968–73 %	1973–78 %	1968–78 %
	(1)	(2)	(3)
UK	7.6	16.8	12.5
Italy	5.6	16.5	11.6
Japan	6.8	10.8	10.2
France	6.0	10.5	8.6
Sweden	6.3	10.3	8.3
Netherlands	6.7	8.1	7.8
Belgium	4.8	9.3	7.6
Canada	4.3	9.0	7.1
USA	4.9	7.7	6.6
Switzerland	5.6	3.8	5.7
Germany	4.7	4.8	5.2
Average	5.3	9.8	8.3

Source: *International Financial Statistics*, Country Tables.

1973–78 inflation speeded up considerably; the average rate rose to 9.8 per cent, and the UK inflation rate rose to 16.8 per cent. This was again the worst, though Italy came a close second. The only countries where inflation did not speed up after 1973 were Switzerland, where it actually slowed down, and Germany with a negligible change.

For the decade as a whole, the UK's rate of 12.5 per cent was again the worst. There was no obvious reason for this; many other countries were equally dependent on imports of oil and materials. International comparisons provide no evidence of any possible trade-off between the objectives of price stability and faster growth; there is no obvious relation between growth and inflation.

FOREIGN TRADE

Maintaining a satisfactory balance of payments is another major objective of policy. It is impossible for a country's balance of payments to remain permanently in deficit, so we have to use indirect measures of balance of payments problems. Table 26.3 shows two of these.

TABLE 26.3   *Foreign Trade Performance, 1968–78*

Country	Export volume growth rates			Exchange rate 1968–78 %
	1968–73 %	1973–78 %	1968–78 %	
	(1)	(2)	(3)	(4)
Japan	13.2	10.1	11.2	4.5
France	12.6	5.0	8.5	1.5
Netherlands	13.2	2.5	7.7	5.5
Italy	8.3	8.1	7.5	−3.6
Belgium	12.5	3.4	7.3	4.7
Germany	9.1	3.4	6.7	7.2
USA	7.5	2.8	6.6	0.0
UK	6.8	5.0	6.0	−3.0
Switzerland	6.9	4.9	5.5	9.3
Canada	8.3	4.0	5.2	0.0
Sweden	8.1	0.8	4.8	2.0
Average	9.7	4.5	7.0	2.6

Source: *International Financial Statistics*, Country Tables.

Columns (1)–(3) show the growth rates of export volume, for 1968–73, 1973–78 and for the decade as a whole. For 1968–73 average export volume grew at 9.7 per cent a year; the UK at 6.8 per cent was slowest. In 1973–78 the growth of exports slowed down. The average fell to 4.5 per cent, but for this period the UK did slightly better than average with 5.0 per cent growth of exports. For every country the export growth rate in 1973–78 was slower than in the earlier period. Over the decade as a whole the average growth rate of export volume was 7.0 per cent; for the UK the growth rate was 6.0 per cent, but Switzerland, Canada and Sweden did worse.

In each period the growth rate of trade for the average of eleven countries was about twice the growth rate of GNP. All these countries have been sharing the experience of the UK, that their economies have been becoming more open, with trade forming a higher proportion of GNP.

Exchange Rates

Column (4) of Table 26.3 shows another indicator of foreign trade problems, the trends in movements of exchange rates. These are measured as the value of a unit of each country's currency in US dollars, so that depreciation appears as a negative and appreciation of a currency as a positive trend. The value for the USA is thus zero by definition; Canada has had a floating exchange rate, and the zero trend there is simply the best statistical fit. The average of the eleven currencies appreciated at 2.6 per cent a year between 1968 and 1978; the pound sterling depreciated at an average rate of 3.0 per cent. The only other currency among the eleven which depreciated was the Italian Lira. There seems to be a relation between rates of internal inflation and changes in the external value of the currency. The UK and Italy had the highest rates of inflation and depreciated; Switzerland and Germany had the lowest inflation rates and appreciated fastest. The overall fit of this relation is not very good, however, with an R^2 of only 0.51.

CONCLUSIONS

The conclusion of this brief survey of comparative economic performance must be that when viewed against the background of what comparable economies have been able to achieve, the UK does not appear to have done at all well. Whether one measures by GNP, exports, or industrial production, the UK has been growing more slowly than the group of countries which we would like to think of as our peers. Our inflation has been consistently faster, and our exchange rate has depreciated.

27. The Recent History of the UK Economy

Up to now the various aspects of the economy have been dealt with thematically. This chapter will try to pull the threads together, giving an historical approach to the development of the economy. The final section will attempt to bring the story as nearly up to date as printing schedules allow, in this case to the end of 1979. This will also serve as a background for the final chapter, giving the author's views on macroeconomic policy.

THE BACKGROUND

This book has concentrated on the decade since 1968; events during this period have to be seen against the story of the previous decade. In this earlier period, real growth in the UK was slower than in other OECD countries (the Organization for Economic Co-operation and Development provides a convenient label for the non-Communist developed countries). Inflation in the UK was also slightly faster than in the rest of the OECD.

These differences were coupled with the adoption, from 1949 to 1967, of a fixed exchange rate for sterling. This combined with our inflation and our lags in productivity growth to impair our ability to compete in world markets, and this in turn led to chronic balance of payments problems. As a result of these problems, successive governments adopted periodic bouts of restrictive monetary and fiscal policies, given the pejorative name of 'stop-go', which were believed to be responsible for irregular growth of output, and for caution on the part of investors which restricted the growth of productivity.

262

This earlier period culminated in the decision in November 1967 to devalue sterling from $2.80 to $2.40. This did in fact give the UK a four-year period during which exports were the most rapidly increasing part of total final demand. The UK's economic problems were not cured, however.

1968–73   Gentle Deterioration

The period from 1968 to 1973 saw a gentle deterioration in the UK economy. In 1971 and 1972 employment incomes rose faster than productivity, the share of company profits and company investment in national income were squeezed, and unemployment rose. The tendency of wages to rise even in the presence of increased unemployment is thought to have been encouraged by the adoption of wage-related unemployment benefits and improved redundancy payments, which improved the bargaining position of workers. Concern about the rise in unemployment led to the next phase of economic policy.

1971–3   The Dash for Growth

During this period taxes were cut, from 37.1 per cent of GNP in 1970 to 33.7 per cent in 1972; as a result government borrowing rose from −0.6 per cent of GNP in 1970 to 3.8 per cent in 1972. The money supply was allowed to rise by 13.3 per cent in 1971 and 16.5 per cent in 1972. These policies produced excess demand in the economy in 1973, which was accentuated by the fact that 1973 saw an exceptionally large rise in export demand. In retrospect, the stimulus to demand was clearly too large and too rapid.

Several factors contributed to this. The changes in the rules of the monetary system in 1971 made it more difficult than usual to understand what was happening to the money supply, until experience had been gained of how the new system worked. Shortages were encountered in 1973 at a relatively high level of unemployment because of the unprecedentedly rapid rise in total demand. Entry to the EEC in 1973 saw a rapid rise in both exports and imports relative to GNP. This increase in the exposure of the economy to competition involved changes in the composition of output at an abnormally rapid rate, which tended to increase structural unemployment. The other factors tending to raise the natural rate of unemployment were ignored or underestimated.

1973-4   The Oil Crisis

In 1973 there was a world-wide boom, and commodity prices rose rapidly even before the OPEC action on oil prices towards the end of the year. The OPEC (Organization of Petroleum Exporting Countries) then quadrupled oil prices in a few months. Between 1972 and 1974 the UK's terms of trade worsened by over 20 per cent, reducing the real purchasing power of the goods the UK produced over the goods we wanted to consume by over 5 per cent. Some of this loss has since been recovered, as industrial prices have risen in pursuit of commodity prices.

The real cost to the UK of the deterioration of the terms of trade since 1973 has at most been an annual loss equal to about $1\frac{1}{2}$ years' normal growth of the economy. This is about half the size of the additional loss we have inflicted on ourselves through the failure of real output to maintain its normal rate of growth. Real output has in fact grown at an average rate of only just over 1 per cent a year, which has meant a high output gap and has resulted in high unemployment. The other OECD countries also suffered worsened terms of trade, and shared a real slump in 1975, but have managed to recover from this better than the UK.

The initial impact of the reduction in the real purchasing power of our production was taken by large balance of payments deficits in 1974 and 1975, and by a large fall in profits and investment by companies.

Real government spending kept rising until 1977. This can mainly be attributed to wishful thinking; expenditure plans were still geared to assumptions of rising national real income, and in an inflationary period there was habitual underestimation of what projects would actually cost. Real wages, before tax, rose in 1974 and 1975, and while they fell in 1976 and 1977 they were still above their 1973 level. Industrial production fell, and only in 1978 did it regain its 1973 level.

1974-78   The Slump

The main real effect of the slump was a rise in unemployment to 6 per cent; this was due to several causes. The main cause is simply that cuts in profits and investment have made offering new jobs appear unprofitable. The increase in the exposure of the economy to foreign competition has increased transitional and structural unemployment. The unemployment problem has been made worse as a period of increasing numbers of people seeking work has coincided with slack demand for labour.

At a more microeconomic level, security of employment legislation and charges for redundancy payments have made potential employers hesitant about taking on new employees unless they can be sure they will want them permanently, of which it is hard to be confident in a slump. Higher benefits when unemployed relative to earnings may have made some workers keener on holding out for better jobs.

The final, and most decisive, cause of increased unemployment has been the fact that, as wages have continued to rise in spite of both high unemployment and the existence of incomes policies which were supposed to control them, the authorities have felt obliged to maintain relatively restrictive monetary and fiscal policies through fear of allowing inflation to turn into hyperinflation if they allowed the level of real demand to rise.

The rate of inflation in the UK since 1973 has been higher than in other OECD countries. This again has several causes. In 1973 the oil crisis added an unusually large cost-inflationary impulse to a situation of unusually high excess demand. The results of these are not necessarily simply additive. Two UK policies interacted to increase inflation in 1974. The flexible exchange rate policy adopted in 1971 meant that when sterling went down import prices rose faster, adding to cost inflation, while the internal rate of inflation kept making further devaluations necessary. Also, the wage indexation policy in 1974 had included provision for compensation once rises in the cost of living passed a 7 per cent threshold. After this point was reached, the policy provided for automatic wage rises for each 1 per cent rise in consumer prices, on a flat-rate scale that actually over-compensated lower paid workers. In this case the policy of indexing wages seems to have speeded up inflation.

A persistently high level of unemployment has in fact seen the rate of inflation reduced up to 1978, though not to the levels that the government and the public would both like to see, and that has actually been achieved by most other OECD countries. In 1979 inflation speeded up again although unemployment fell very little.

THE SITUATION IN 1979

Because of problems over the availability of data, the end of 1978 has so far been treated as the cut-off date. This section will attempt to bring the picture up to the end of 1979. The main source for this is *Economic Trends* of January 1980, published by the Central Statistical Office. Some of the figures are avowedly provisional, and are liable to subsequent modification. In some cases at the time of going to press data were only available for the first three quarters of 1979. Various other sources were used, including the *Bank of England Quarterly Bulletin* and *International Financial Statistics*. In view of the provisional nature of the data no attempt will be made to identify the source of each fact, though the author has deliberately confined himself to readily available published sources. Official policy makers would have about three months' advantage in data availability.

Real GDP in the first three quarters of 1979 was 1.8 or 1.9 per cent higher than in the corresponding period of 1978, according to figures based on measures of output and incomes. Figures based on expenditure show a 0.5 per cent decline in GDP, but a rise of 2.8 per cent in the index of industrial production for the period makes the 1.9 per cent rise in GDP seem more plausible. This increase was too small to narrow the output gap.

The pattern of growth, in the first three quarters of 1979, shows consumption 4.2 per cent higher than in 1978, government spending 2.3 per cent higher, and fixed investment 4.6 per cent down. Exports were 2 per cent higher, but imports were 10.4 per cent higher; the result was a move into deficit of the balance of payments on current account, of about £2b or 1.8 per cent of GNP in the first three quarters. If the third quarter of 1979 is compared with the third quarter of 1978, sterling rose by about 10 per cent compared with an average of OECD currencies, while the UK inflation rate was about 7 per cent faster than the average. This rise in sterling at a time of current account deficit must have resulted from inward capital movements, presumably based on the prospects of North Sea Oil. It helps explain why the authorities greatly relaxed controls on outward capital movements in late 1979. The rise in sterling put UK exports at a large price disadvantage which helps to explain the trade deficit.

Unemployment in 1979 fell slightly, from 6.1 to 5.6 per cent of the employed labour force. Unemployment among school leavers also fell, from 99,000 to 89,000. Vacancies in the first three quarters rose from 210,000 to 245,000. This improvement in the labour market probably reflects the previous year's rise in output; in 1980 unemployment is expected to rise again.

Inflation speeded up during 1979. Retail prices were 13.3 per cent above 1978, on average. As inflation was speeding up during the year, by December 1979 the rate of increase of retail prices over 12 months before had risen to 17.2 per cent. Wages and salaries per unit of output in the first three quarters were 12.9 per cent above 1978; earnings for the first 11 months were 15 per cent above 1978.

This speeding up of inflation considerably weakens the case for the expectations augmented Phillips curve, as given in Chapter 19, which would lead to an expectation that the inflation rate would fall in 1979. The speeding up of inflation may be related in two possible ways to changes in government policies following the 1979 General Election which brought in a Conservative government. The new government formally ended 'incomes policy'. This may have led to an increase in wage demands, because people felt that the policies had been holding down their wages and tried to recover losses they felt they had suffered.

The other relevant policy change was a slight shift in the burden of taxation from direct to indirect taxes made in the 1979 budget, which cut some direct taxes and raised VAT to 15 per cent. It can be argued that any change in the burden of taxation is liable to be inflationary on balance, because those who gain by the shift try to retain the benefit for themselves, while those who lose try to pass on the burden to their employers via wage increases or to their customers via price increases. If this view is correct, it would be an equal mistake to try shifting the burden back again onto direct taxes.

The trading profits of companies, excluding stock appreciation, were 9.2 per cent higher in money terms in the first three quarters of 1979 than in 1978. This means that the share of profits in total incomes fell, which is consistent with the fall in investment.

Personal disposable incomes in the first three quarters were 5.1 per cent higher in real terms than in 1978, and the share of savings rose, which is consistent with a 4.2 per cent rise in real consumption.

Notes and coin were 11.8 and M1 was 11.5 per cent above 1978 levels, well below the rise in money incomes. Interest rates rose; the Treasury bill rate had an annual average of 12.97 per cent, its highest ever; minimum lending rate rose during the year from $12\frac{1}{2}$ to 17 per cent, and other rates including those on mortgages rose in line.

If all these provisional figures are correct, the outlook for 1980 cannot be encouraging. It cannot be good for growth for consumption to rise while investment falls. The share of profits in total incomes, already far too low to stimulate adequate investment, has fallen still further. Inflation has speeded up to a rate which no government could contemplate allowing to continue, and the balance of payments on current account has moved into deficit. Both these developments must make the authorities very cautious about stimulating any appreciable real growth in effective demand. Thus in 1980 activity is expected to stagnate or fall, and unemployment is expected to rise.

Because the process of publication takes time, these facts will already be out of date when this book appears. The reader is strongly urged to consult sources such as the Blue Book and *Economic Trends* to bring them up to date for himself.

28. Policies for the Future

Policies are inevitably matters of opinion, in which both facts and value judgements are involved. Policies should be related to facts, but any observer's choice of what facts to study, and what interpretation to put on what they discover, is necessarily conditioned by his own preconceptions.

The intention of this chapter is to assist the reader to judge how far my version of the facts about the UK economy, as set out in previous chapters, has been conditioned by my opinions.

My views on policy are put forward in good faith, and so far as I can tell they are consistent with the facts as I perceive them. They are not necessarily implied by these facts, however, and readers are not necessarily expected to agree with them. I would assert however that it is the duty of every serious student of economics to have some opinions on the policy issues raised below; if my opinions are unacceptable, those who dislike them should form some of their own, and think about the reasons why they prefer them.

GROWTH IS POSSIBLE

The first point I would make is that, starting from where the UK economy is in early 1980, real growth is clearly possible. Since 1973 the UK economy has seen a rise by 3 per cent in its available labour force. Though net investment has fallen, it has been quite substantial each year. There have been some mistakes in the choice of investment projects, but productive capacity must have risen by more than the 1 per cent growth rate of output.

There is also plenty of scope for improvements in efficiency, to judge by comparisons of productivity levels in the UK with those achieved in other countries. Finally, the rise of North Sea oil should mean that for a few years at least we should not be too hampered by difficulties with the balance of payments.

This is not to say that unlimited growth is desirable or possible. In the interests of conservation both of limited supplies of resources and of our environment, slower growth may be what we should prefer. There is no reason to suppose, however, that the stagnation of the past seven years has been due to anything except failures of social organization.

I regard the labour supply as being largely outside the scope of economic policy. On the migration side, low productivity and high taxes have ensured that nobody from advanced countries wants to come here except as a tourist, and migration from less developed countries is strictly controlled on non-economic grounds. Improved economic performance might reduce the desire to emigrate, but we would have to improve a lot to make any real difference.

Everybody agrees that our present $5\frac{1}{2}$ per cent unemployment rate is undesirably high. It seems at present however that 5 or 6 per cent unemployment is consistent with attitudes in wage bargaining which ensure that inflation is speeding up again. Levels of monetary demand have been rising faster in the UK than in other advanced countries for decades, and our real growth has been slower. If spending more money could produce growth, it has had plenty of chances to do so.

POLICIES TO REDUCE UNEMPLOYMENT

I do not feel therefore that there is much scope at present for straightforward Keynesian policies to reduce unemployment. Until we are less prone to inflation, Keynesian expansion policies are just a recipe for hyper-inflation. If other policies could change these attitudes so that Keynesian methods of demand stimulation could be used without provoking rapid inflation, then they should be used. We need however to look at some of the other policies which between them might be capable of lowering the present high 'natural rate of unemployment'. Several policies might help, though no one should be regarded as a panacea. They include the following.

(1) *Efficiency and Lame Ducks*

Present policies mean high taxation of industries which ought to be expanding rapidly, to subsidize inefficient businesses which ought to be contracting. The situation in which workers in a firm can adopt restrictive practices and strike for higher wages in the belief that in the last resort, however high they push their employer's costs, they are so large and 'vital to the national interest' that the government will always foot the bill to keep them in business faces people with a severe temptation. Experience has shown that in too many cases they will succumb to this temptation. The government needs to adopt a policy of insisting that loss-making concerns be divided into smaller units, each of which will be shut down if they make persistent losses, if labour is to be used efficiently. The present state of demoralization after a long run of lame duck relief is so profound that it will unfortunately probably take a series of massive closures to convince people that any government really means business over a change of policy; thus I fear that unemployment is likely to have to rise further before it can fall.

(2) *Mobility*

Policies are needed to make labour more mobile. In the case of mobility between occupations, more retraining and other educational facilities are required. Retraining is more likely to be successful if people are first recruited by prospective employers and then trained; this should improve the chance that the trainee will be suitable, and that the training will be in a skill that is actually in demand.

The relevance of education is that unemployment is lower at higher levels of educational achievement. The provision of compulsory education has already passed the point of negative returns, but more aid for those who really want it and cannot afford it, in the shape of 'sixth form' scholarships and mature studentships, would help to provide a more employable labour force.

Another great aid to mobility, between places, would be a reform of the housing market, which at present severely limits the mobility of tenants. The paralysis effect of giving subsidies to sitting tenants, either from the taxpayer or from private landlords, should be replaced by a free market in tenancies and a system by which subsidies, where needed, go to people rather than tenancies. A market in rented housing could also be encouraged by tax concessions for landlords on a par with those available for other forms of investment, and by reform of the present laws governing security of tenure, which are grotesquely biased against landlords who obey them, and deter potential letters of spare parts of houses.

(3) *Taxation and Social Security*

Taxation is currently damaging to effort, mainly at either end of the social scale. The revenue cost of concessions at the upper end would be trivial. The revenue cost of concessions at the lower end would be larger, but the cost would be cut by an integration of the income tax and social security systems. The present tax-free status of social benefits makes it hard to provide decent benefits without making large numbers of the lower paid better off out of work than in jobs. It also provides subsidies for workers who are engaged in searching for well-paid casual work, or who are striking to get higher wages. Integration of social security payments into the PAYE system would allow larger benefits to be paid to those who are permanently unable to get work, out of the money clawed back from those who draw social security for only short parts of the year, at present tax free. There are said to be administrative problems, but if small private firms can be expected to administer VAT and Pay as You Earn, the state agencies could too and should be firmly told that they must. Some steps in this direction have been taken in the 1980 Budget.

(4) *Redundancy*

There are two reforms I would urge in the system of redundancy payments. One, which is pretty uncontroversial, would be to transfer more of the cost from the employer to the state. It is believed that fear of later liability for redundancy payments is at present deterring some firms from expanding employment because they cannot be sure their need for more workers will be permanent. On the principle that it is better to have worked and lost one's job than never to have had the chance to work at all, a shift in the burden of payment would improve the flow of new jobs, some of which would turn out to be permanent.

The other change is more controversial; this would be to have a system by which the basis of redundancy payments would be lowered by a history of industrial disruption or large pay rises. This would give incentives not to bankrupt one's employer, while not impairing the compensation for victims of technical change or import competition.

CAPITAL AND INVESTMENT

I believe that to get more successful investment we need more profits for successful firms, i.e. those that can produce goods and services that people at home and particularly abroad want to buy at prices that make them profitable to produce. The real problem over investment is not just finance, which can be provided by the capital market and by tax allowances, as well as by profits. It is motivation and guidance on what are the right things to invest in. Low profits all round and a system of price controls designed to ensure that no investment ever pays really well produce a situation in which businesses cannot tell what are the right investment projects to choose.

It should be regarded as a test of sensible economic policies that they produce a crop of new businesses. The production of some new millionaires would be accompanied by the creation of a lot of good jobs for other people, and provided that there are favorable opportunities for investment in a fair sized part of the economy, I do not think it matters much how profits change in total. I would cheerfully see a reduction in the tax allowances that induce investment by unsuccessful firms in facilities for producing at high cost low quality products they can't sell. There is no great urgency about increasing the mere quantity of investment; there would be a much better payoff to improving its quality. Once growth picks up again I would expect to see a rise in both profits and investment, as a natural consequence of higher output.

TRADE POLICY

I believe in the theory of comparative advantage. We should aim to get the price of sterling low enough to allow our successful exporting firms to compete in overseas markets. There are plenty of such firms; they have managed to raise exports of goods and services by 80 per cent in the past decade. Where we are not efficient enough to compete with imports we should let them in. The situation in 1977 when the UK had record exchange reserves, and a current account surplus, and was restricting the import of Japanese cars to protect employment in our chaotic motor industry strikes me as a prime example of how not to run an economy.

The UK ought to be using the temporary relief to our balance of payments problems given by the rise of North Sea oil to modernize the economy; an important aspect of this would be to remove restrictions on imports of low-quality manufactures from less developed countries, and put our own resources into something we can do better than them.

I am entirely opposed to suggestions that we should leave the EEC and impose quantitative restrictions on manufactured imports. Leaving the EEC would mean placing its common external tariff between our exporters and the markets they have built up since 1973; these are precisely the parts of the economy we ought to be encouraging. If we cannot compete with other EEC producers inside the EEC, we cannot compete with them in third markets either, and the sooner we get out of losing lines the better. Import restrictions are calculated to protect the least efficient firms in the economy and harm the most successful, either by direct retaliation by our suppliers, or via appreciation of sterling if by any chance there is not direct retaliation to import cuts.

MONETARY POLICY

I do not believe that anybody understands the economy well enough for 'fine tuning' to be practicable. I would therefore prefer to see the monetary authorities maintaining a smooth and gradual increase in the money supply. An aspect of monetary policy I would like to see stressed is that the authorities should regard it as a criterion of proper monetary management that the real interest rate, i.e. the money interest rate minus the rate of inflation, should be kept positive. In recent years real interest rates have typically been negative; this is unfair on savers, and tends to encourage inefficient investment, and put profits into the pockets of people who hold unproductive stocks on borrowed money.

GOVERNMENT EXPENDITURE

We should aim at the highest standards of real government expenditure and transfer payments that the electorate are willing to pay for. At present ordinary people in the UK pay most of the taxes; this is inevitable, since they get most of the earned income, and even a lot of profits accrue to them indirectly through insurance companies and pension funds. At present ordinary people value private goods more highly than public, and demand pay rises to compensate them for higher taxes.

Government spending, by this test, is too high. When the national income rises again we ought to hold down government spending until it would be possible to raise it again without provoking further inflation.

A recovery would in any case tend to lower the level of labour incomes relative to the total; as the government's real expenditures are relatively labour-intensive this would lower government spending relative to GNP.

PRICES AND INCOMES POLICIES

I do not believe that these have been or are likely to be very effective. Earnings data show that incomes have typically risen by more than would have been consistent with full compliance with the policies in force. This is not to say that there is not scope for consultation between the government and representatives of business and organized labour. I believe however that this should take the form mainly of clear explanations of what the monetary and fiscal authorities are intending to do, so that other people can appreciate the consequences of their own actions, for market prospects and job security.

At present this should take the form of adopting strictly limited targets for the money supply and government spending, and pointing out that higher wages and prices are liable to mean less business and more unemployment. If this was clear, the unions could choose: would their members prefer higher money wages, more imports, lower output and more unemployment or short time working, or would they prefer moderation in wage demands, more exports, more output, fuller employment and more opportunities for overtime or for promotion?

To take this position is not against the real interests of the working population, though it may displease some of their representatives. The world as a whole does not owe us a living, nor does it think that it does so. The government would merely be making clear to everybody what our national position really is; in the long run it cannot harm people to tell them the truth.

As a country we have a choice between responsible behaviour, higher productivity and more employment, or disruption, inflation, lower productivity and more unemployment. The government should do its best to dispel illusions that somehow political *force majeure* can miraculously allow us to enjoy the fruits of productive activity without accepting its disciplines. I do not think that this is unfair to the labour force; would people prefer to get 80 per cent of the national income of a country with a 1 per cent growth rate and a 9 per cent output gap, or 75 per cent of the national income of a country with a 4 per cent growth rate and rising employment?

POSSIBLE GROWTH RATES

If asked how soon I believe the policies advocated here could restore a decent rate of growth, the answer is quite soon. The UK has successful firms, who have managed to sell an extra 9 per cent of GNP in extra exports of goods and services in world markets during the past decade. If we encourage them to go on expanding, we need not worry too much if other sectors decline. Unemployment might rise for a while, but not necessarily by any more than it will anyway if the policies of stagnation and a vain effort to prop up employment in inefficient, loss-making sectors is continued. In employment as in other fields the best form of defence may be attack.

A successful expanding productive sector should be able to expand for quite a while by taking in the unemployed, and absorbing labour from the over-manned, low-productivity sectors of lame duck firms, private and public. Given that we start from a 9 per cent output gap, if the successful sector could expand at 5 per cent a year it could continue for several years before running up against severe resource constraints. It is even possible that after a few years of policies that promote rather than hinder efficiency, the 3 per cent growth path could be improved upon without renewed demand inflation.

CONCLUSIONS

The most urgent need of the UK economy as I see it is for a radical change in national attitudes to competition and inflation. If we insist on resisting changes that would make us more efficient and competitive, and on reacting in a cost inflationary manner to all economic changes, we will continue to be forced to adopt demand restricting policies, and the economy will continue to stagnate.

It might be urged that the inhabitants of the UK are simply naturally so much more idle, greedy and unintelligent than the inhabitants of Germany or Japan that slower growth and faster inflation are our inevitable fate. Humility may be a virtue, but I feel this is overdoing it. If we would only adopt more sensible attitudes and policies there is no reason why we should not catch up the ground we have lost over recent decades.

Concern about world resources and the environment will almost certainly lead us eventually to choose slower growth rates than the advanced countries of the world enjoyed before 1973. I think however that we should ensure that this is a matter of deliberate choice, and not simply allow ourselves to drift into stagnation and unemployment because of blind persistence in attitudes and policies which have long failed us.

Further Reading

The following will be found to give useful additional information and alternative views on many of the topics treated in this book:

F. S. BROOMAN *Macro-economics*. Allen & Unwin (an Open University text).
A relatively theoretical treatment.

R. G. LIPSEY *An Introduction to Positive Economics*. Weidenfeld & Nicolson.
Also more theoretical, and covers microeconomics as well.

D. FISHER *Monetary Policy*. Macmillan.
A useful short guide to the monetary sector.

J. S. FLEMMING *Inflation*. Oxford University Press.
A more specialized book, probably rather difficult for those without previous knowledge of economics, but very interesting on the inflation section.

A. G. FORD *Income, Spending and the Price Level*. Fontana.
This takes a relatively theoretical approach.

D. MORRIS (ed.) *The Economic System in the UK*. Oxford University Press.
Includes interesting discussions of many areas of economic policy.

A. R. PREST and D. J. COPPOCK (eds.) *The UK Economy: a Manual of Applied Economics*. Weidenfeld & Nicolson.
A very useful survey.

K. A. YEOMANS *Introducing Statistics; Statistics for Social Scientists, Vol I*. Penguin.
This includes sections on presentation of data, index numbers, regression and time series; a very helpful introduction to the statistical methods used here.

Index